Remembering Elvis
30 YEARS LATER

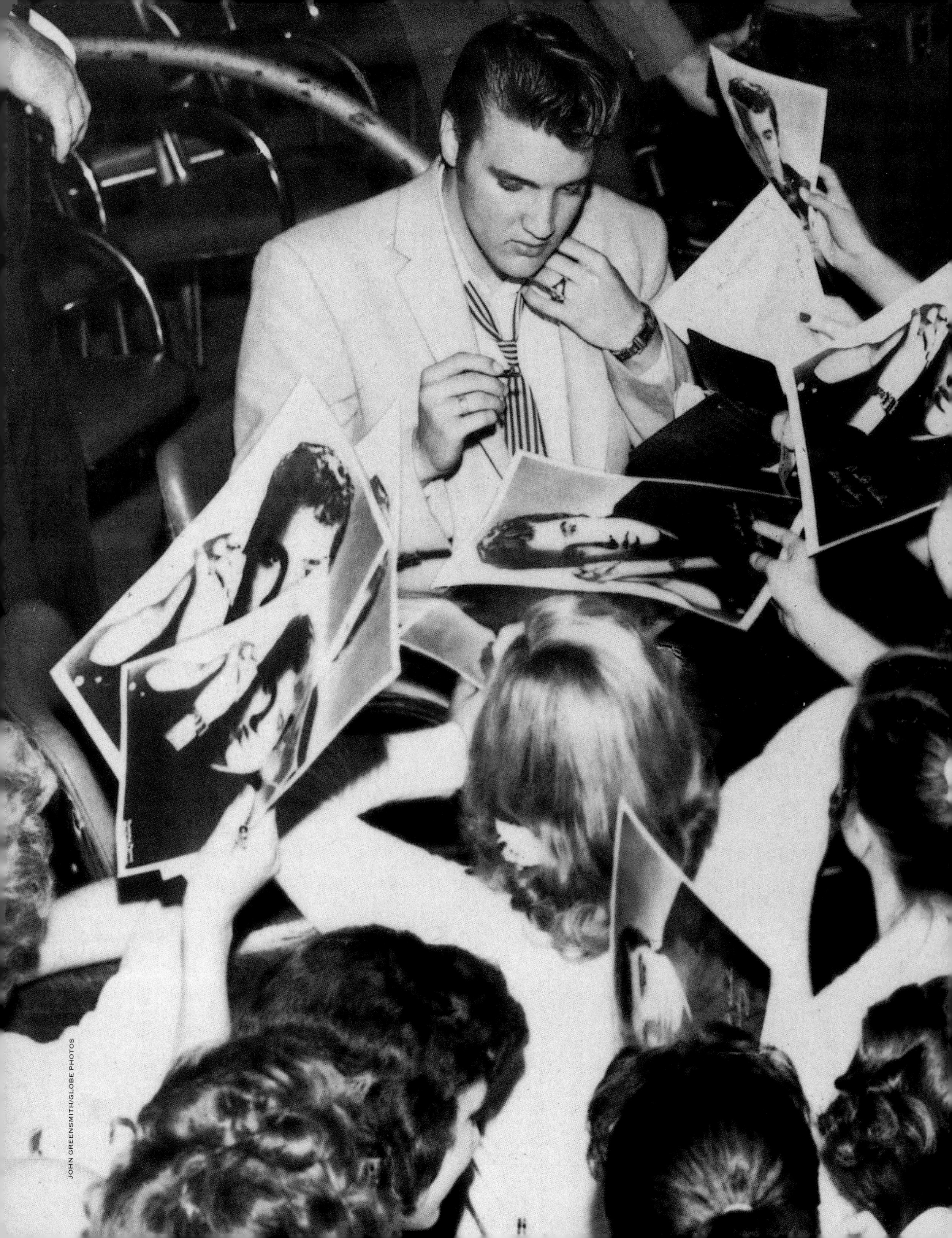

JOHN GREENSMITH/GLOBE PHOTOS

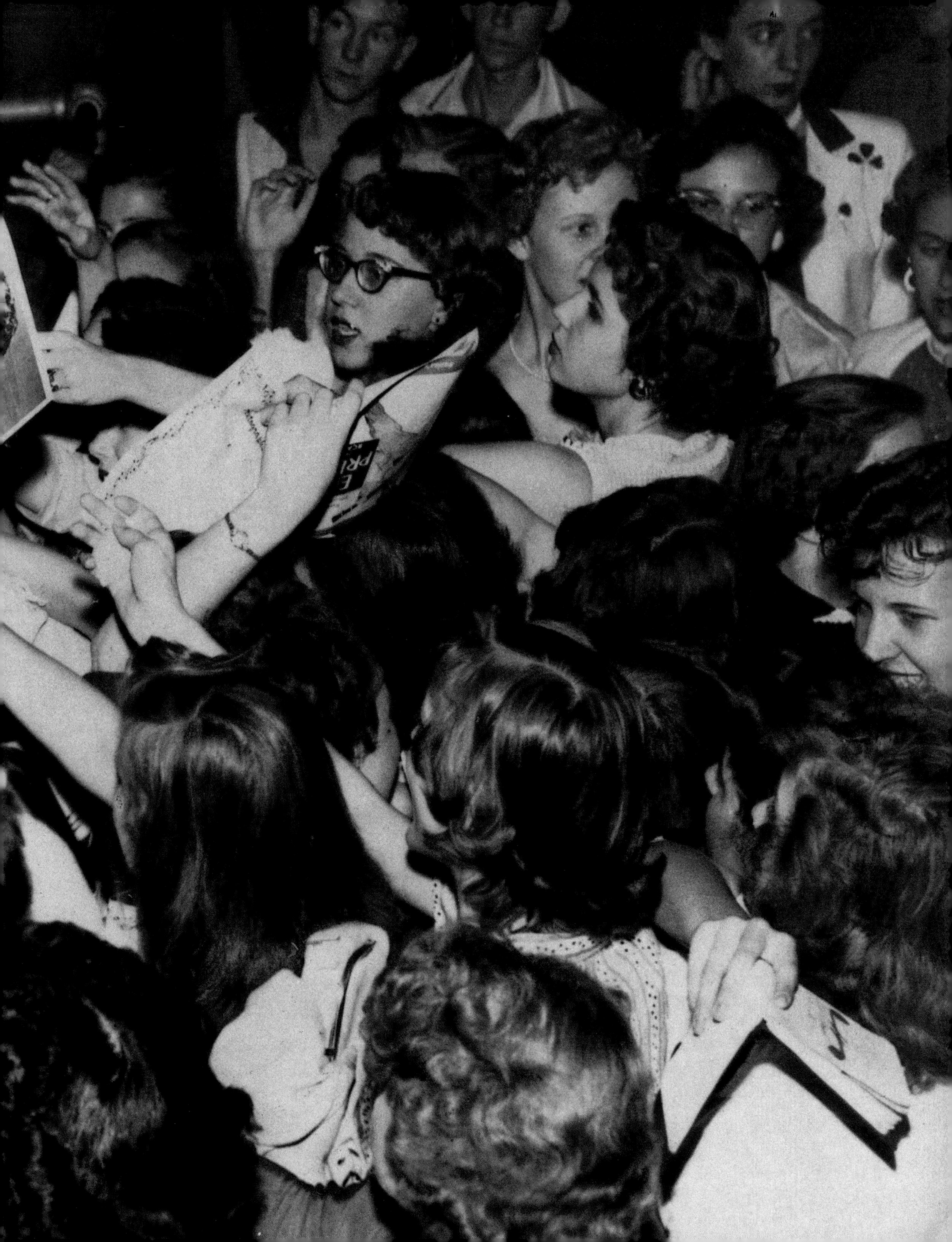

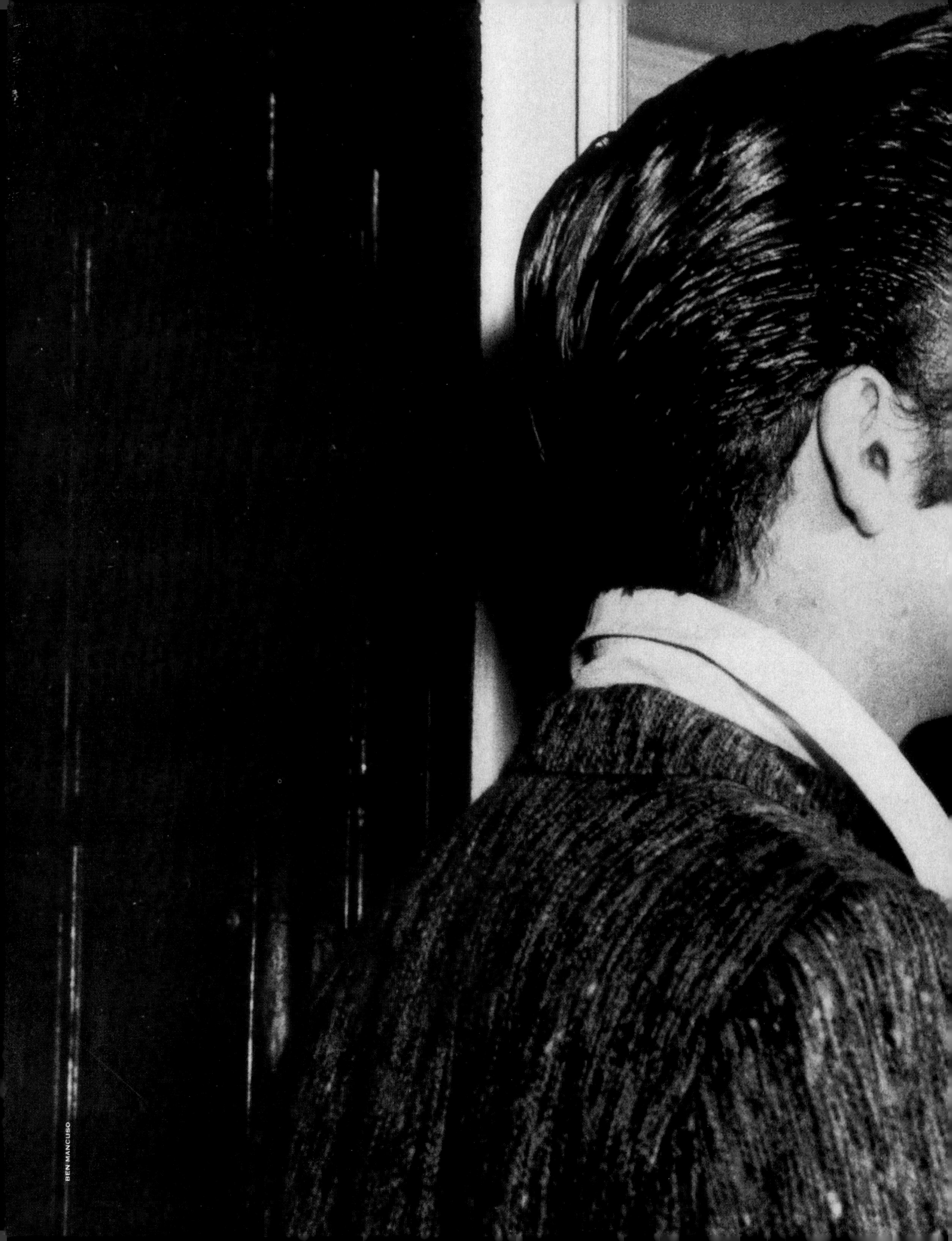
BEN MANCUSO

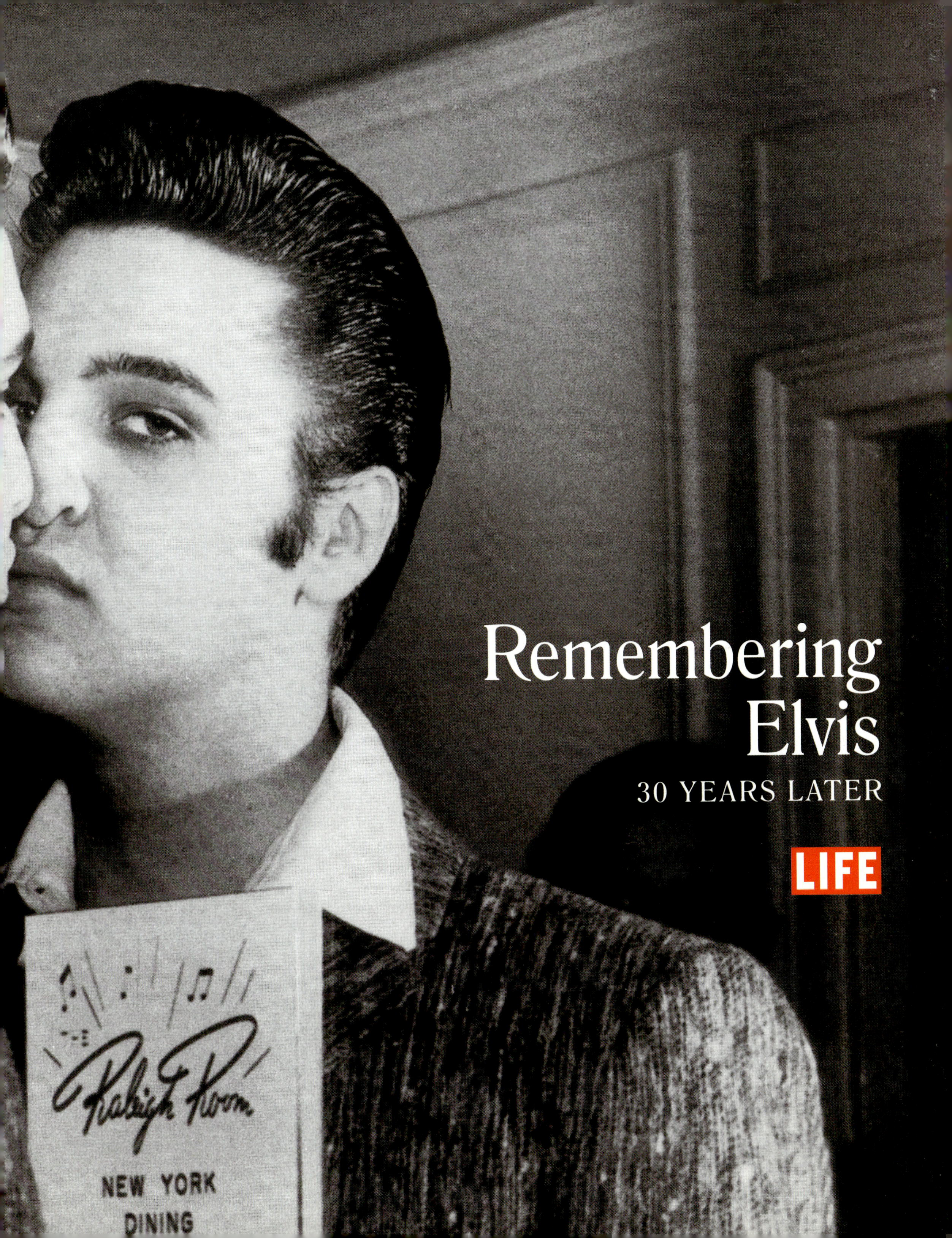

Remembering Elvis

30 YEARS LATER

LIFE

LIFE Books

EDITOR Robert Sullivan
DIRECTOR OF PHOTOGRAPHY Barbara Baker Burrows
CREATIVE DIRECTOR Mimi Park
DEPUTY PICTURE EDITOR Christina Lieberman
WRITER-REPORTER Hildegard Anderson
COPY Lesley Gaspar (Chief), Parlan McGaw
PRODUCTION MANAGER Michael Roseman
CONSULTING PICTURE EDITORS Mimi Murphy (Rome), Tala Skari (Paris)

PRESIDENT Andrew Blau
BUSINESS MANAGER Roger Adler
BUSINESS DEVELOPMENT MANAGER Jeff Burak
BUSINESS ANALYST Ka-On Lee

EDITORIAL OPERATIONS Richard K. Prue, David Sloan (Directors), Richard Shaffer (Group Manager), Burt Carnesi, Brian Fellows, Raphael Joa, Angel Mass, Stanley E. Moyse (Managers), Soheila Asayesh, Keith Aurelio, Trang Ba Chuong, Ellen Bohan, Charlotte Coco, Osmar Escalona, Kevin Hart, Norma Jones, Mert Kerimoglu, Rosalie Khan, Marco Lau, Po Fung Ng, Rudi Papiri, Barry Pribula, Carina A. Rosario, Albert Rufino, Christopher Scala, Vaune Trachtman, Paul Tupay, Lionel Vargas, David Weiner

STAFF FOR THE ORIGINAL 1995 EDITION
EDITOR Jay Lovinger
WRITER Charles Hirshberg
DESIGNERS Tom Bentkowski and Mimi Park
PHOTO EDITOR Adrienne Aurichio
REPORTERS Seth Goddard, Stephanie H. O'Brien
COPY Robert Andreas (Chief), Nikki Amdur, Albert Rufino

TIME INC. HOME ENTERTAINMENT
PUBLISHER Richard Fraiman
GENERAL MANAGER Steven Sandonato
EXECUTIVE DIRECTOR, MARKETING SERVICES Carol Pittard
DIRECTOR, RETAIL & SPECIAL SALES Tom Mifsud
DIRECTOR, NEW PRODUCT DEVELOPMENT Peter Harper
ASSISTANT DIRECTOR, BRAND MARKETING Laura Adam
ASSISTANT GENERAL COUNSEL Dasha Smith Dwin
BOOK PRODUCTION MANAGER Jonathan Polsky
DESIGN & PREPRESS MANAGER Anne-Michelle Gallero
MARKETING MANAGER Joy Butts

Special thanks to Bozena Bannett, Alexandra Bliss, Glenn Buonocore, Suzanne Janso, Robert Marasco, Brooke McGuire, Mary Sarro-Waite, Ilene Schreider, Adriana Tierno, Alex Voznesenskiy

Published by LIFE Books
Time Inc., 1271 Avenue of the Americas, New York, NY 10020

ISBN 10: 1-933821-86-8
ISBN 13: 978-1-933821-86-3
Library of Congress Control Number: 2007903320

A NOTE ON SOURCES

The following friends and associates of Elvis Presley assisted in the preparation of this book: Chet Atkins, Anita and Helen Carter, June and Johnny Cash, Barbara Eden, D.J. Fontana, Mary Jenkins, Tina Louise, Scotty Moore, Dr. George Nichopoulos, Sam Phillips, Linda Thompson, Red West. Three excellent books also proved indispensable: Rose Clayton and Dick Heard's *Elvis Up Close*; Elaine Dundy's *Elvis and Gladys*; and Peter Guralnick's *Last Train to Memphis*. Also consulted: *Elvis and Me*, by Priscilla Beaulieu Presley with Sandra Harmon; and *Elvis: What Happened?* by Red West, Sonny West and Dave Hebler with Steve Dunleavy.

PICTURE SOURCES are listed by page.

Cover: front, RCA Records label/Neal Peters Collection; back, Charles Trainor.

12: AP/Wide World Photos.

14: bottom, Colin Escott Collection.

16: Michael Ochs Archives.

28: left, Michael Ochs Archives; right, Archive Photos.

42: left, Archive Photos; right, Michael Ochs Archives.

51: top, Paul Lichter's Elvis Archives; bottom, Bettmann/UPI.

93: M-G-M.

94-95: Everett Collection (26); The Kobal Collection (2); Motion Picture & TV Photo Archive (3).

96: Paramount Pictures.

98-99: Archive Photos (1); Bettmann/UPI (2); Everett Collection (8); M-G-M (1); Motion Picture & TV Photo Archive (1); Paramount Pictures (1); Photofest (10).

104: Bettmann/UPI.

112: left, Photofest; right, Michael Ochs Archives.

113: clockwise from top left, Photoreporters; Fotos International/Archive Photos; Ron Galella; Everett Collection; Dagmar/Shooting Star; Motion Picture & TV Photo Archive; Globe Photos; Ron Galella; center, Globe Photos.

114: Phil Roach/Photoreporters.

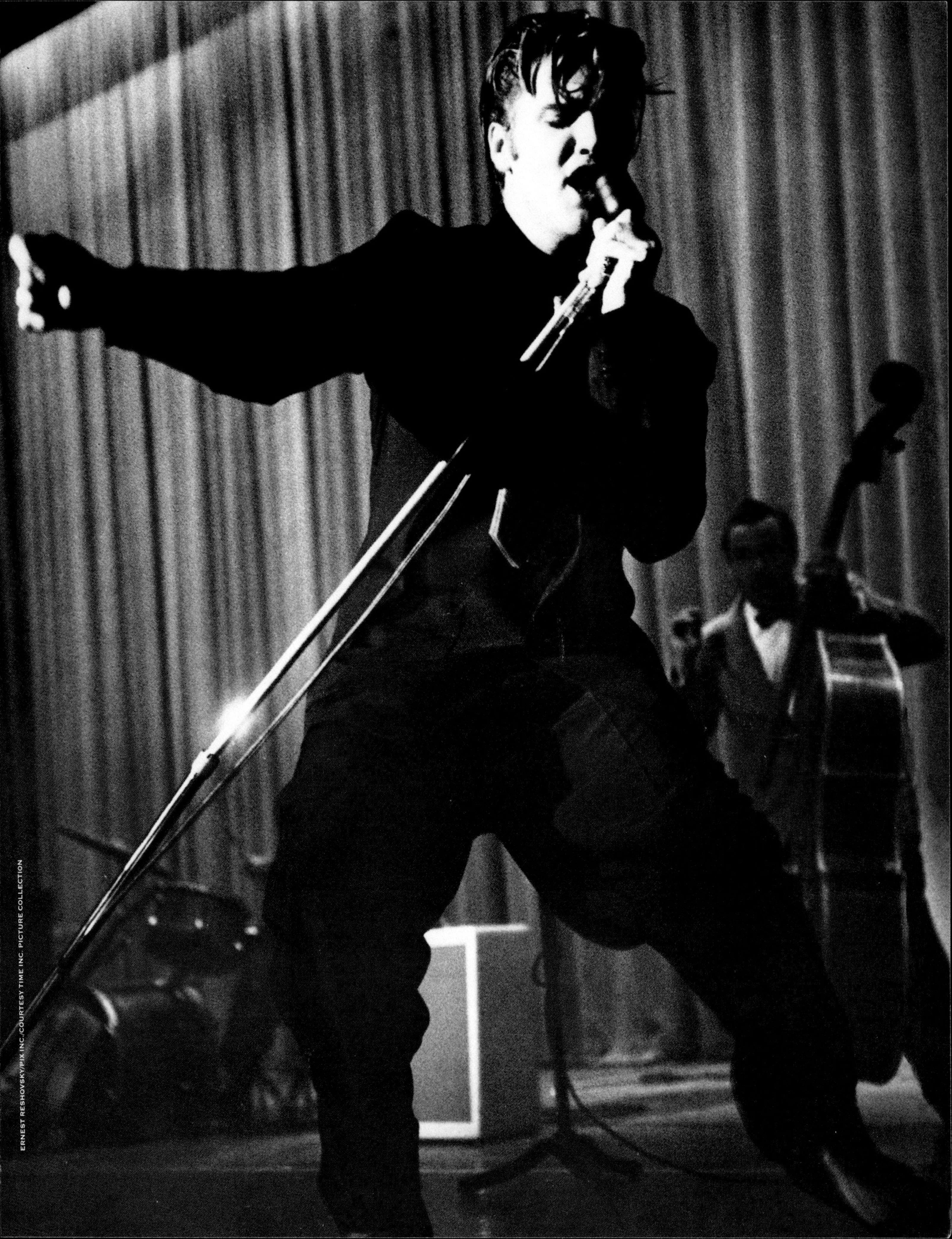

ERNEST RESHOVSKY/PIX INC./COURTESY TIME INC. PICTURE COLLECTION

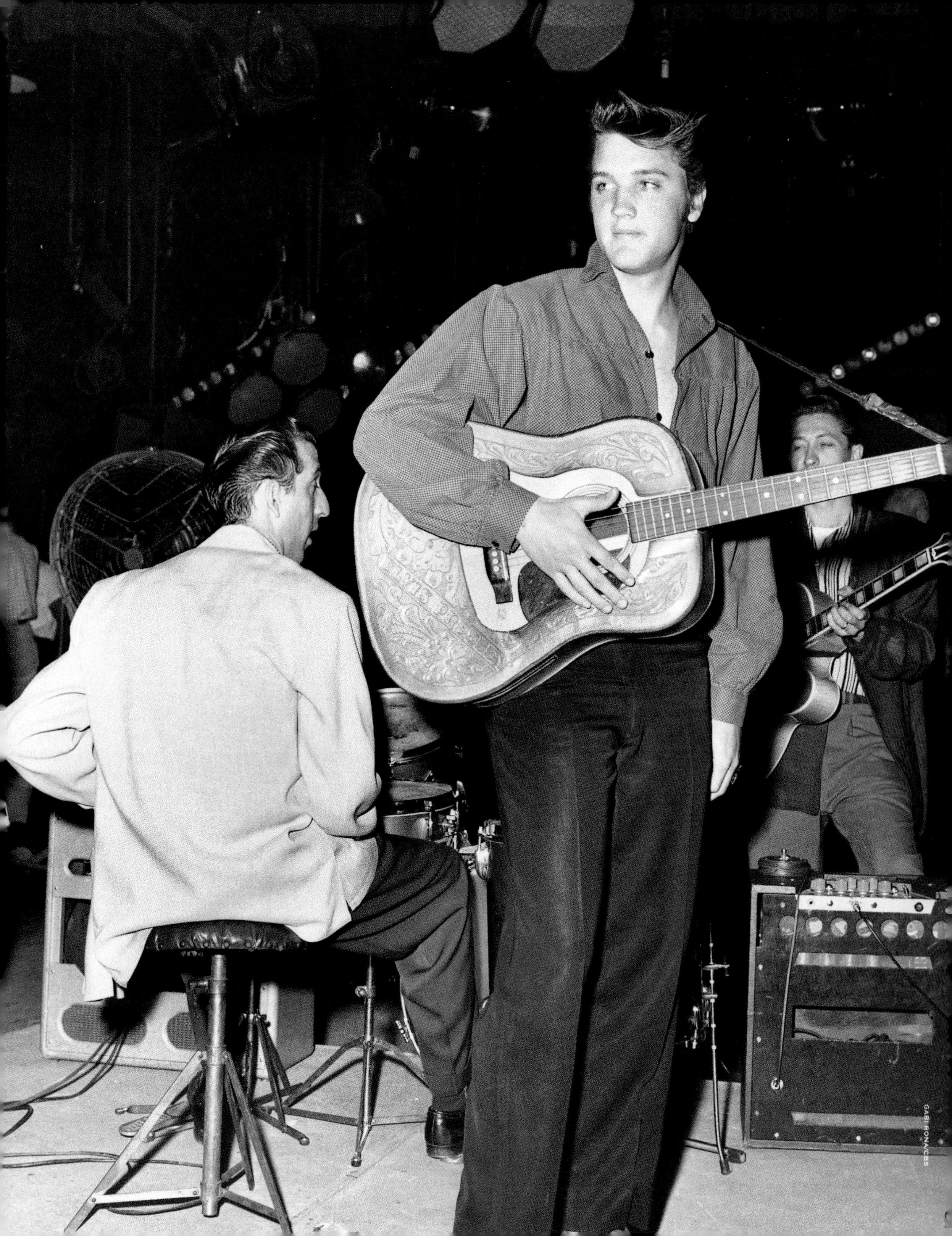

GABI RONA/CBS

INTRODUCTION

When the LIFE book *Elvis: A Celebration in Pictures* was published in 1995, the writer Charles Hirshberg kicked off his introduction with these words: "Let us begin with a confession: This is not the first book ever published on the subject of Elvis Presley. There are, in fact, so many that anyone who ventures to write a new one ought to have a damn good reason. Fortunately, the reason for this one is pretty obvious: LIFE magazine and Elvis Presley go together like ice cream and pie. Both belong to the American landscape almost as much as Mount Rushmore. Both belong to the same generation, too: Elvis was born in January of 1935 and LIFE in November of the following year. And most important, Elvis was one of the most photogenic individuals who ever lived."

So, let us begin *Remembering Elvis: 30 Years Later* with another confession: This is not only not the first book ever published on the subject of Elvis Presley, it isn't even an entirely new book. But it is a timely book, since other salient facts as stated by Hirshberg remain unchanged. LIFE and Elvis still make a great team in 2007; pictures of Elvis remain irresistible. And since the country's love affair with Elvis is undimmed 30 years after his death, it is a good moment to hail the King once more.

We at LIFE quickly decided that there was really no way to trump our original Elvis volume, which has been called by some a classic photographic telling of an epic American story. What we could do was freshen it—update it, expand it, make it a bigger and better book and, in this way, a more complete argument for Elvis's immortality as a cultural icon. In the intervening years since 1995, the man's image has remained indelible and his home has been named a National Landmark. How does Elvis live on in America? Let's go to today's Graceland and find out. Also: New (old) pictures of just about everything, not just celebrities, are always being found. Could there, perhaps, be never-seen or rarely seen Elvis gems out there? Our photo editors went a-huntin' and came back with that answer, too.

In 1995, Charles Hirshberg wrote in his introduction about the 18 years that had then passed since Elvis's untimely death: "America has changed a bit . . . At this writing, Elvis would have been 60 and, had he lived, he, too, would have been surprised to see moms and dads attending Rolling Stones concerts with their children—to say nothing of teenagers with nose rings snapping their fingers to the strains of Tony Bennett."

My goodness, that might have been written yesterday, except that Elvis would now be 72, it's grandmas and grandpas at the Stones' shows and today's Tony Bennett records duets with John Legend and Juanes as well as his old pal Elvis (Costello, that is).

As for the original Elvis, the one and only and forever King of Rock and Roll, we hope that the following pages make one thing abundantly clear:

He has never left the building, and he never will.

IT WAS A TRAGIC AND GLORIOUS DAY WHEN THE TWINS

ARRIVED. TRAGIC BECAUSE THE FIRST, JESSE GARON, WAS

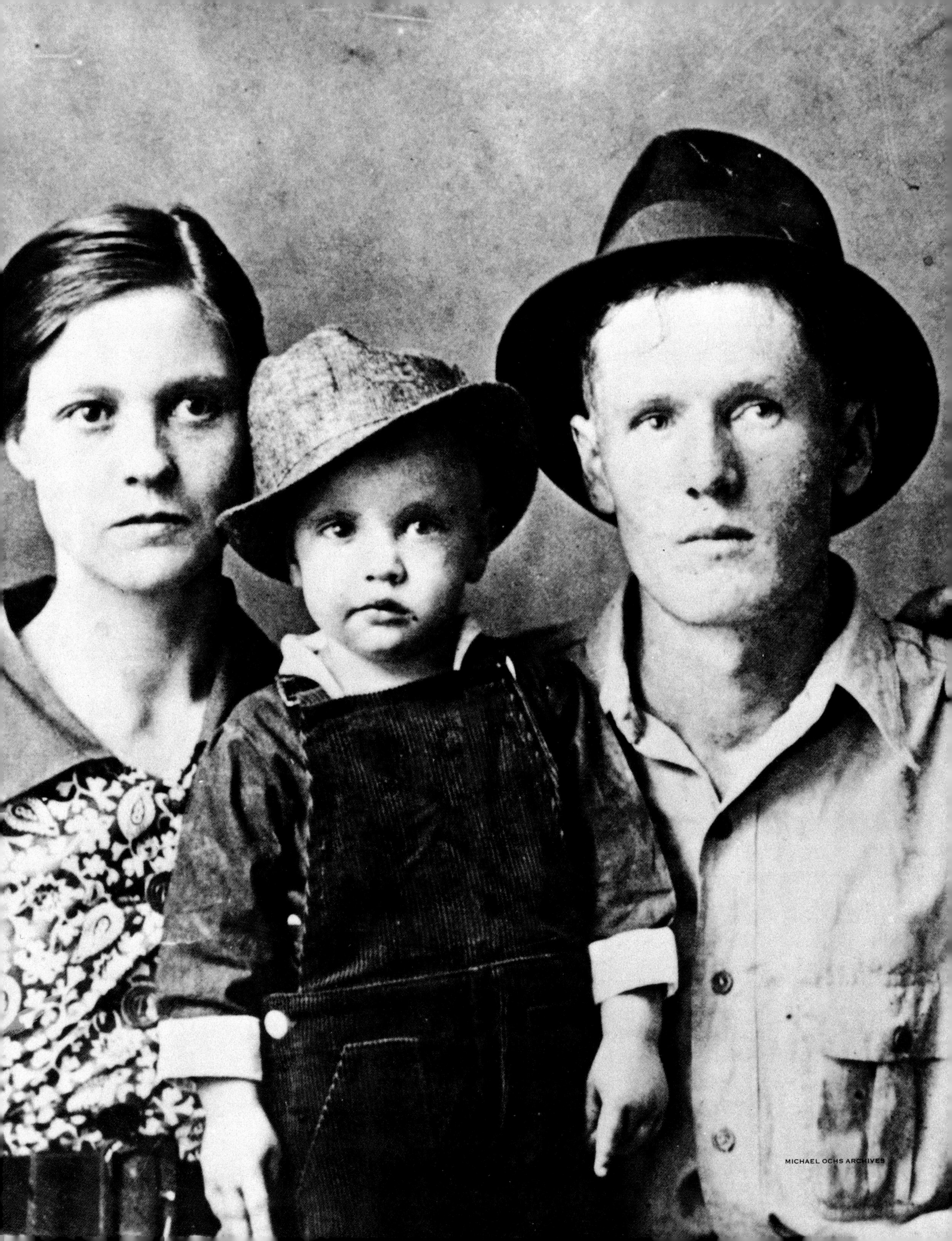

MICHAEL OCHS ARCHIVES

E

Elvis's first performing triumph came at the age of 10, two years prior to this portrait. The occasion was Children's Day at Tupelo's Mississippi-Alabama Fair and Dairy Show. Standing on a chair to reach the mike, he sang "Old Shep," a maudlin ballad about a boy and his faithful dog: "If dogs have a heaven, there's one thing I know/Old Shep has a wonderful ho-o-o-me." Eleven years later, he would record the song for RCA.

Previous Page: Catastrophe awaited Elvis, two, and his parents, Gladys and Vernon. Not long after this picture was taken, Vernon was convicted of forgery (the altered check was worth less than $5); he spent eight months at Mississippi's infamous penitentiary, Parchman Farm. Gladys and Elvis were evicted from their home shortly after Vernon was taken away.

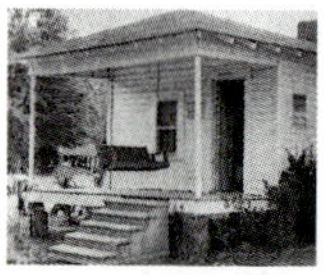

JANUARY 1935

He is born in a two-room shotgun shack in East Tupelo, Miss. Though Elvis's great-uncle Noah Presley is elected mayor of the town shortly after Elvis's birth, the family is so poor that the doctor who delivers Elvis eventually collects his fee from a welfare agency.

JANUARY 1946

For his 11th birthday, Elvis receives the most important gift of his life—a guitar. Soon he is bringing it with him to school almost every day, singing for his friends at lunchtime, talking dreamily about the *Grand Ole Opry*. On one occasion, bullies swipe it and cut the strings.

SEPTEMBER 1949

Unable to hold a steady job, Vernon Presley decides to move the family to Memphis. The city is steeped in music: There is blues on Beale Street, country on the radio and gospel everywhere—especially at the Poplar Street Mission, across the street from the Lauderdale Courts housing project, where the Presleys live. Elvis makes friends with Johnny and Dorsey Burnett, two future rockabilly stars, and the three spend many evenings jamming in the project's laundry room.

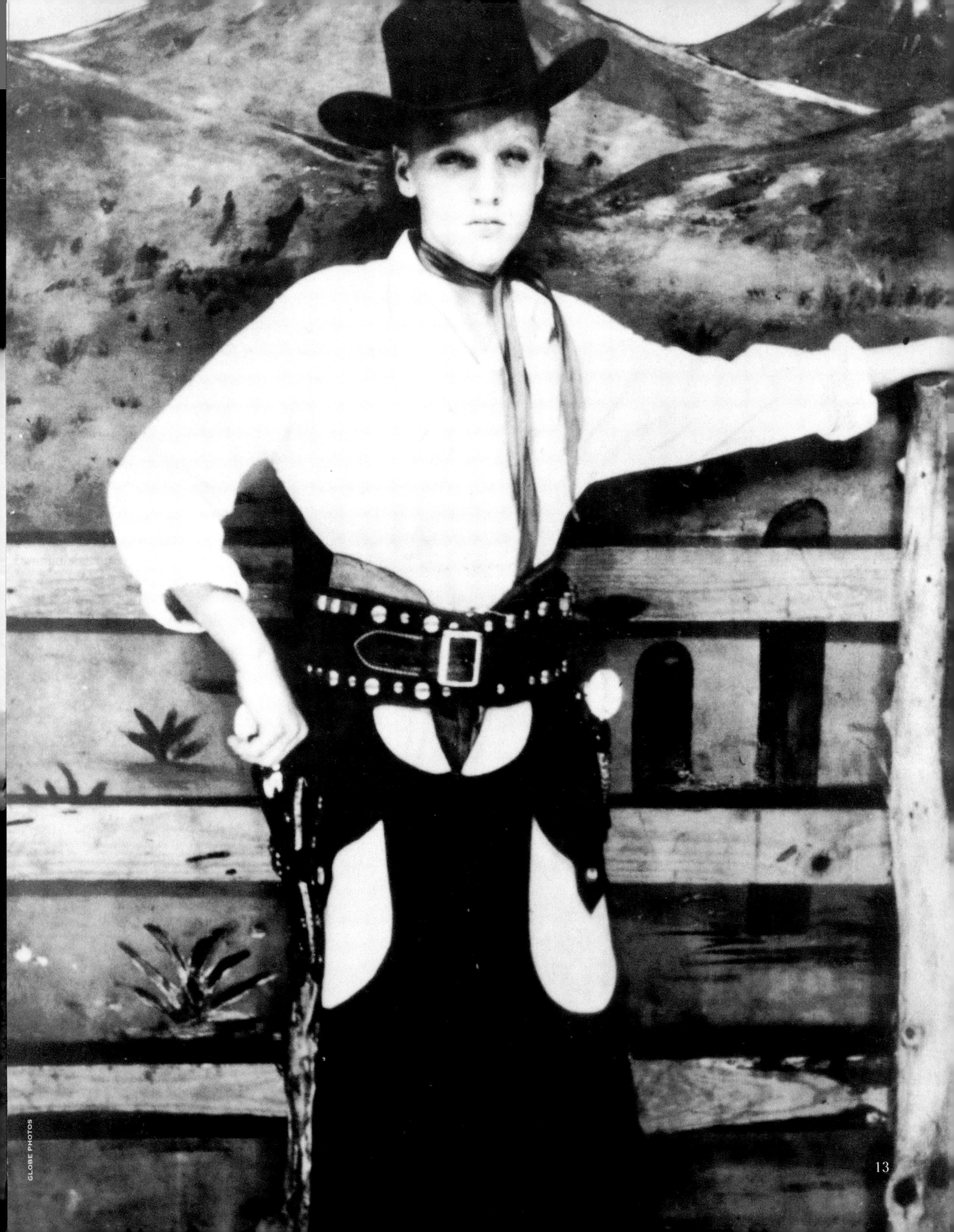

GLOBE PHOTOS

A COUNTRY BOY ROCKED CLEVELAND: ELVIS AT BROOKLYN HIGH SCHOOL IN THE FALL OF '55.

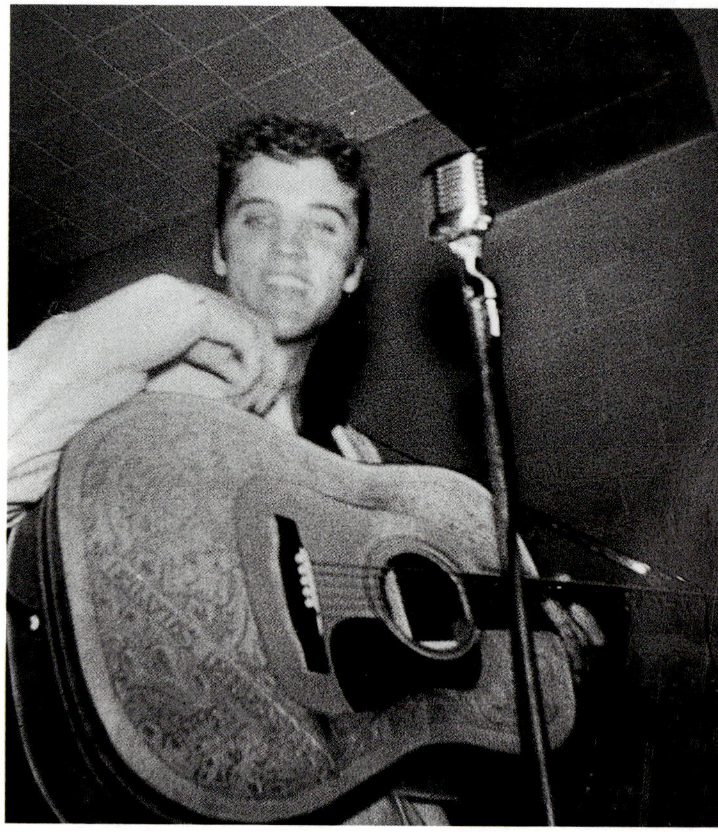

BILL RANDLE COLLECTION

OCTOBER 1954

Elvis's boyhood dream of appearing on the *Grand Ole Opry* comes true. Naturally, he is nervous—the more so since *Opry* star Bill Monroe is rumored to be less than flattered by Presley's version of "Blue Moon of Kentucky." ("I'd heard he was going to break my jaw," Sam Phillips would later say.) But Monroe is polite and stoic. Unfortunately, so is the audience.

OCTOBER 1954

Elvis receives a far more enthusiastic reception at the *Louisiana Hayride,* Shreveport, La.'s answer to Nashville's *Opry*. Says country star Porter Wagoner: "Elvis would throw his guitar around over his shoulder, and then Bill Black would try and do that with his big stand-up bass. People would tear the house down!" In a month, Elvis is headlining the show.

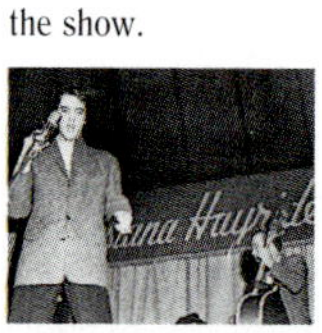

JANUARY 1955

D.J. Fontana, former house drummer for the *Louisiana Hayride,* officially joins Elvis's band. Fontana has experience playing for exotic dancers outside of Shreveport, where he would pound his tom-toms in time to their gyrations. He applies the same technique whenever he sees Elvis "scooting across the stage," and Elvis loves it. This, Fontana speculates, "is why I got the job."

NINETEEN FIFTY-FOUR WAS ELVIS'S LAST YEAR OF INNOCENCE. HE BEGAN IT AS A TRUCK DRIVER AND ENDED IT AS AN UP-AND-COMING "HILLBILLY" SINGER. HE CONTINUED TO TAKE HIS HOMETOWN SWEETHEART, DIXIE LOCKE, FOR MILK SHAKES, AND TO LISTEN TO RECORDS FROM CHARLIE'S RECORD SHOP ON NORTH MAIN STREET. HE WAS SOPHISTICATED ABOUT ONLY ONE THING—MUSIC. AT RIGHT, HE ADMIRED AN OBSCURE R&B RECORD ON THE KING LABEL.

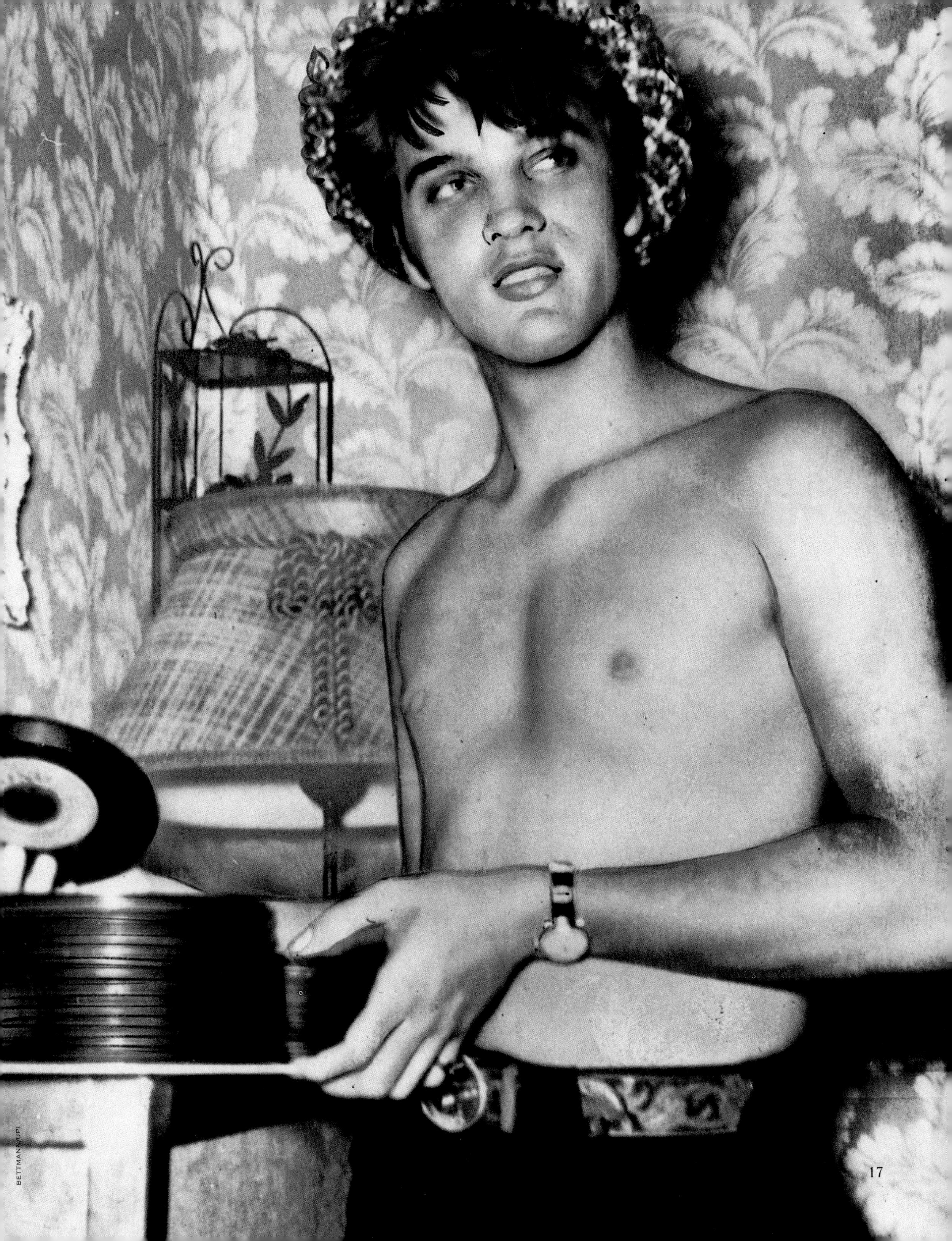

BETTMANN/UPI

HE WAS NEVER SO TERRIFIED AS THE DAY HE WALKED ONSTAGE AT THE OVERTON PARK SHELL IN MEMPHIS, JULY 30, 1954. THE PEOPLE HAD COME TO HEAR SLIM WHITMAN CROON "INDIAN LOVE CALL." BUT FIRST THEY GOT ELVIS. AS SOON AS HE BEGAN TO SING, THEY BEGAN TO HOOT. THEY'RE MAKING FUN OF ME, HE THOUGHT. DEVASTATED, HE FINISHED "BLUE MOON OF KENTUCKY" AND SLUNK OFF. BUT BACKSTAGE EVERYONE WAS ELATED, PUSHING HIM OUT FOR AN ENCORE. *THE GIRLS LOVE YOU,* THEY TOLD HIM. *IT'S THE WAY YOU SHAKE!*

MAKING OF A STAR

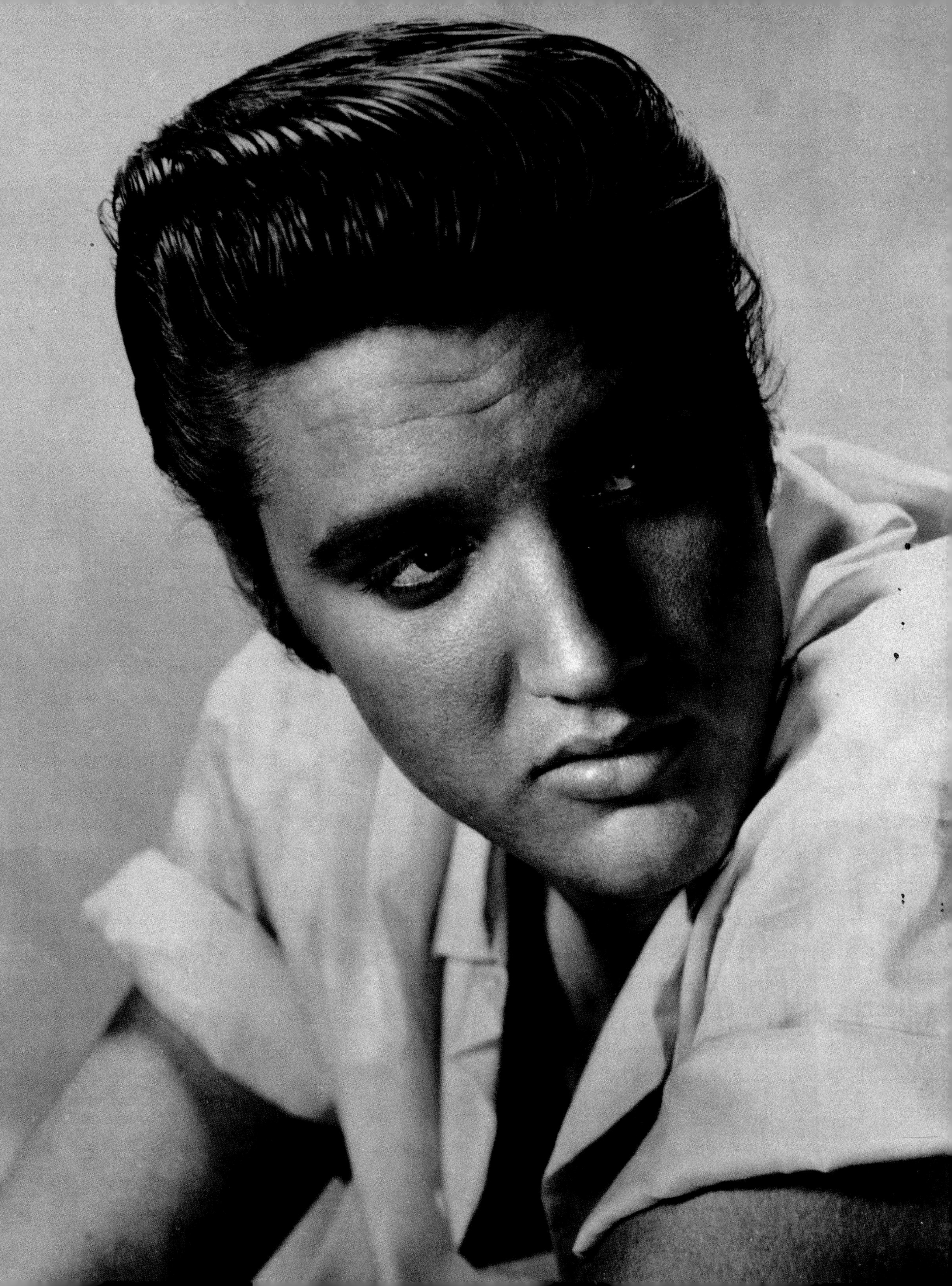

MOTION PICTURE & TV PHOTO ARCHIVE

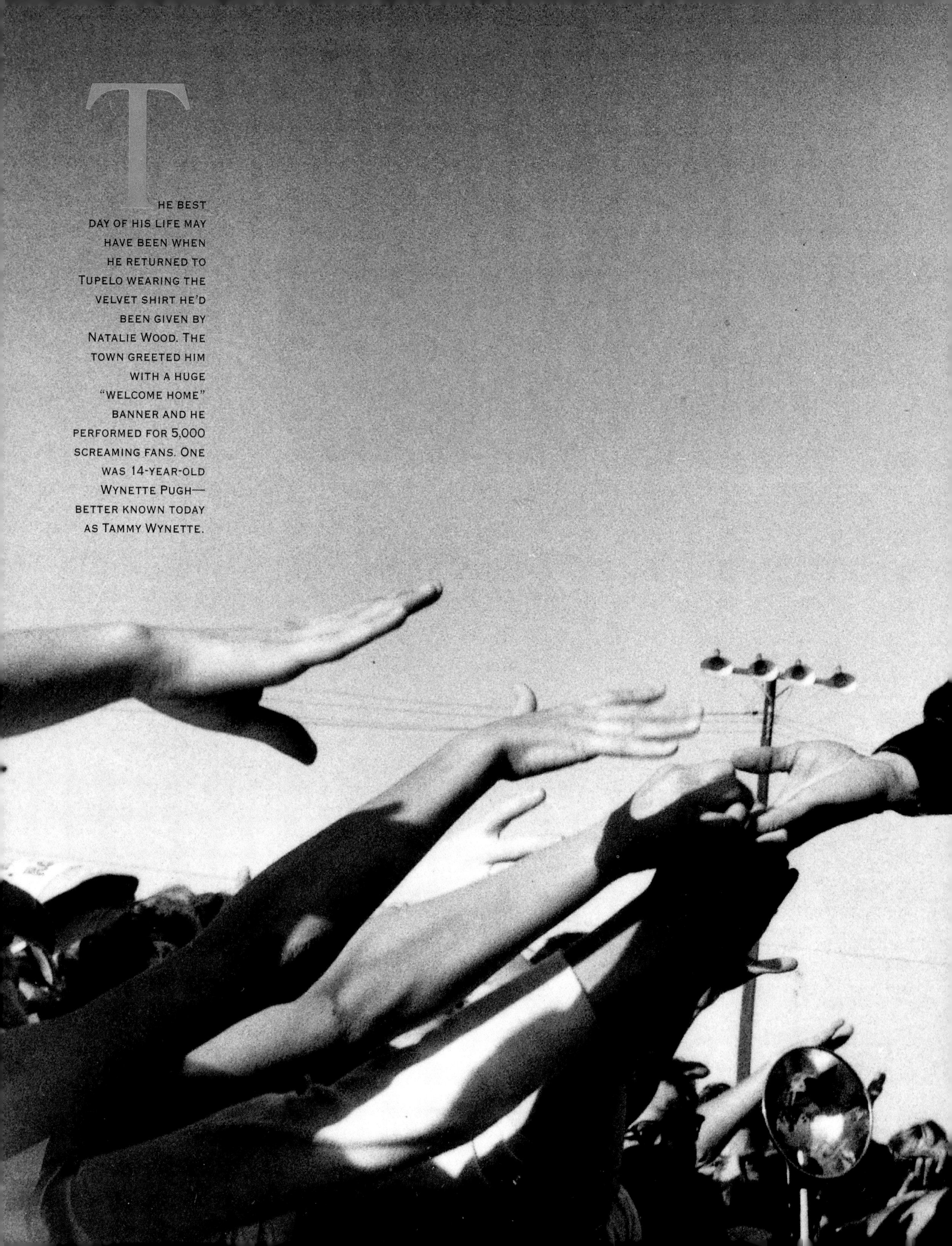

THE BEST DAY OF HIS LIFE MAY HAVE BEEN WHEN HE RETURNED TO TUPELO WEARING THE VELVET SHIRT HE'D BEEN GIVEN BY NATALIE WOOD. THE TOWN GREETED HIM WITH A HUGE "WELCOME HOME" BANNER AND HE PERFORMED FOR 5,000 SCREAMING FANS. ONE WAS 14-YEAR-OLD WYNETTE PUGH—BETTER KNOWN TODAY AS TAMMY WYNETTE.

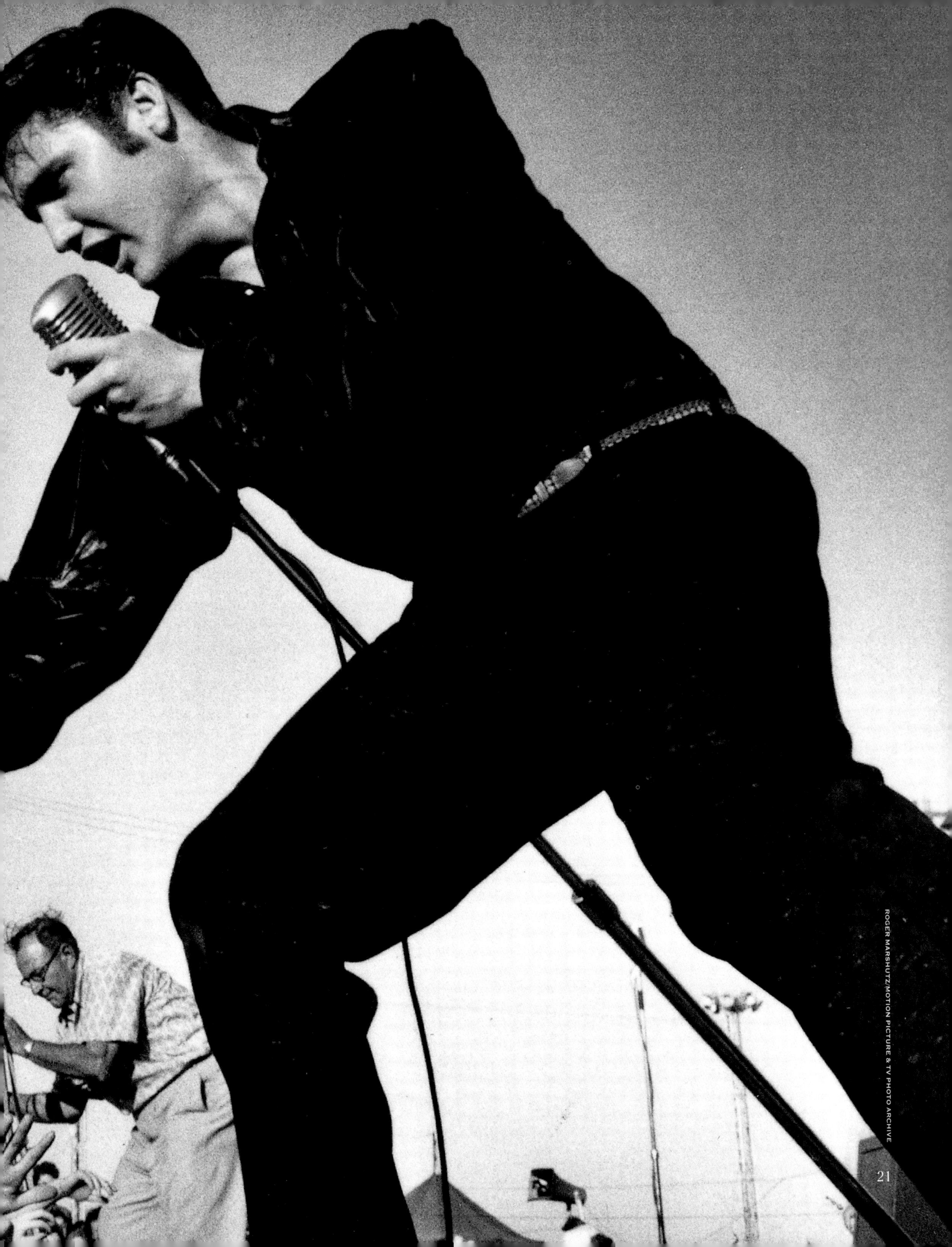

ROGER MARSHUTZ/MOTION PICTURE & TV PHOTO ARCHIVE

IT WAS A TIME WHEN HAIR WAS SHORT, SUITS WERE MADE OF GRAY FLANNEL AND SEX WAS RARELY ON PUBLIC DISPLAY. A LOT OF PEOPLE LIKED IT THAT WAY—AND HATED ELVIS. "THE SPIRIT OF PRESLEYISM HAS TAKEN DOWN ALL MORALS," PREACHED REV. CARL E. ELGENA OF DES MOINES. PSYCHIATRIST RICHARD HOFFMAN LAMENTED FROM HIS PARK AVENUE OFFICE: "INSTEAD OF HONORING NAMES LIKE CARLYLE, THE AVERAGE CHILD IN NEW YORK KNOWS ALL ABOUT PRESLEY." AT FIRST, ELVIS TRIED TO EXPLAIN. "I WATCH MY AUDIENCES AND I LISTEN TO THEM," HE SAID. "I KNOW THAT WE'RE ALL GETTING SOMETHING OUT OF OUR SYSTEM, BUT NONE OF US KNOWS WHAT IT IS." EVENTUALLY, HE GAVE UP TRYING TO PUT IT INTO WORDS.

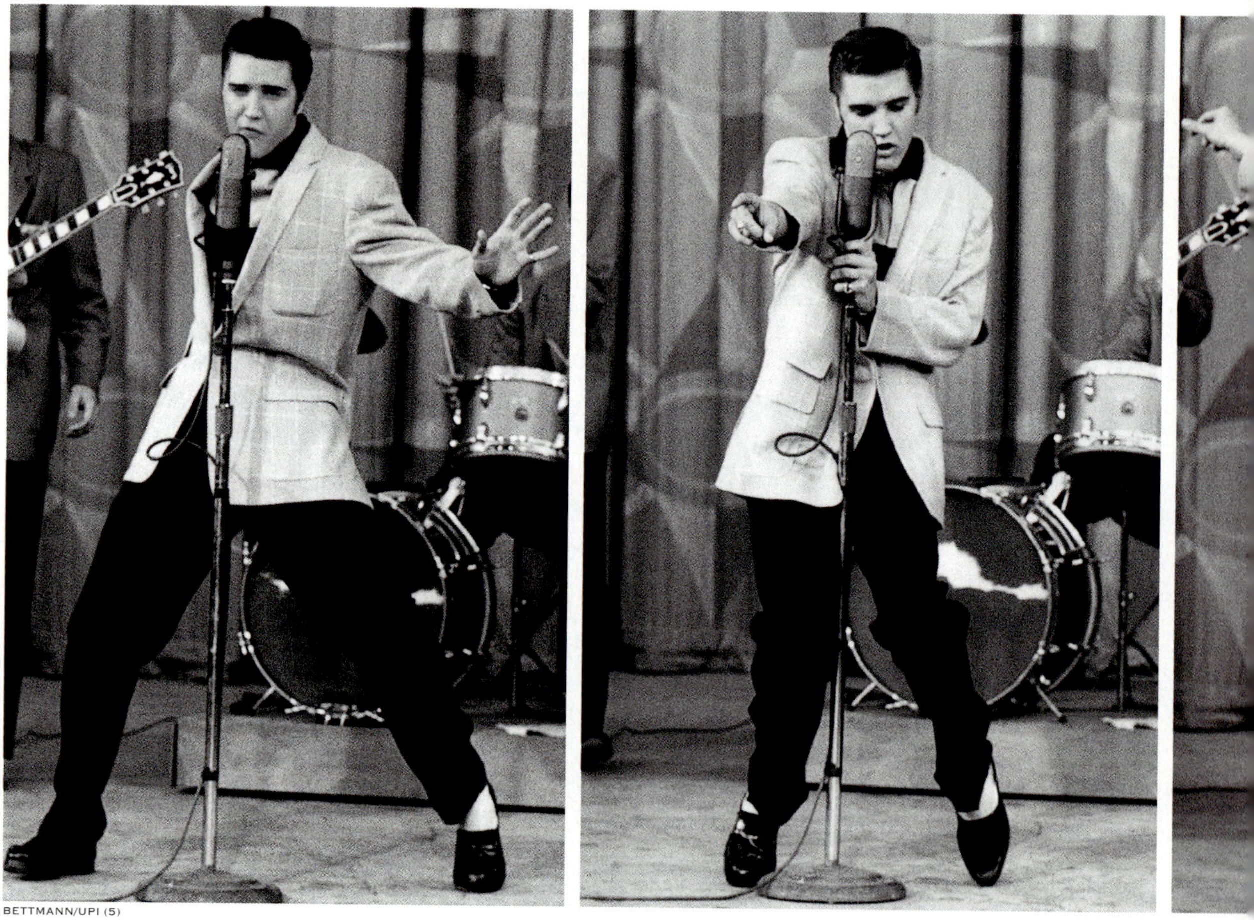

BETTMANN/UPI (5)

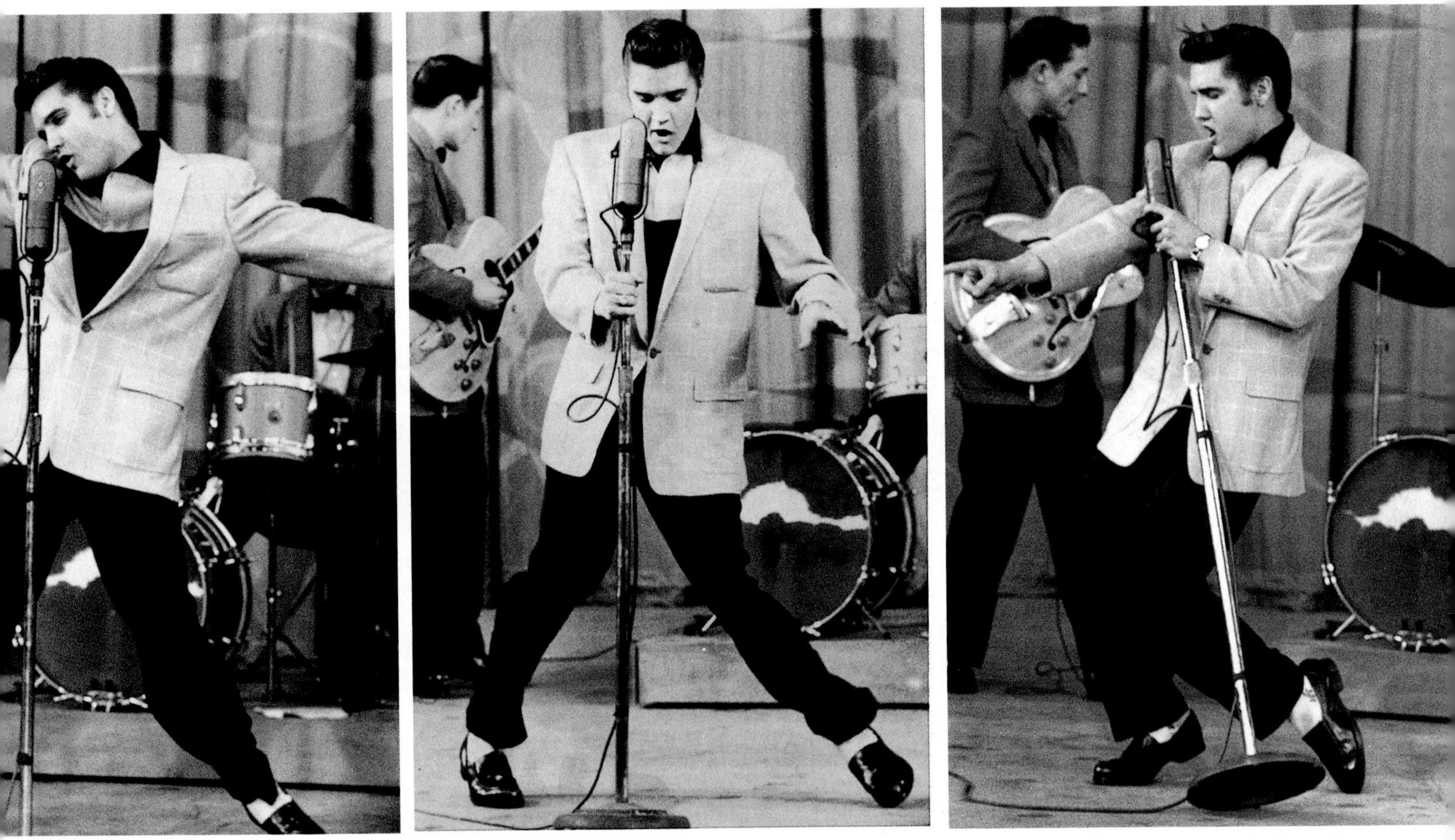

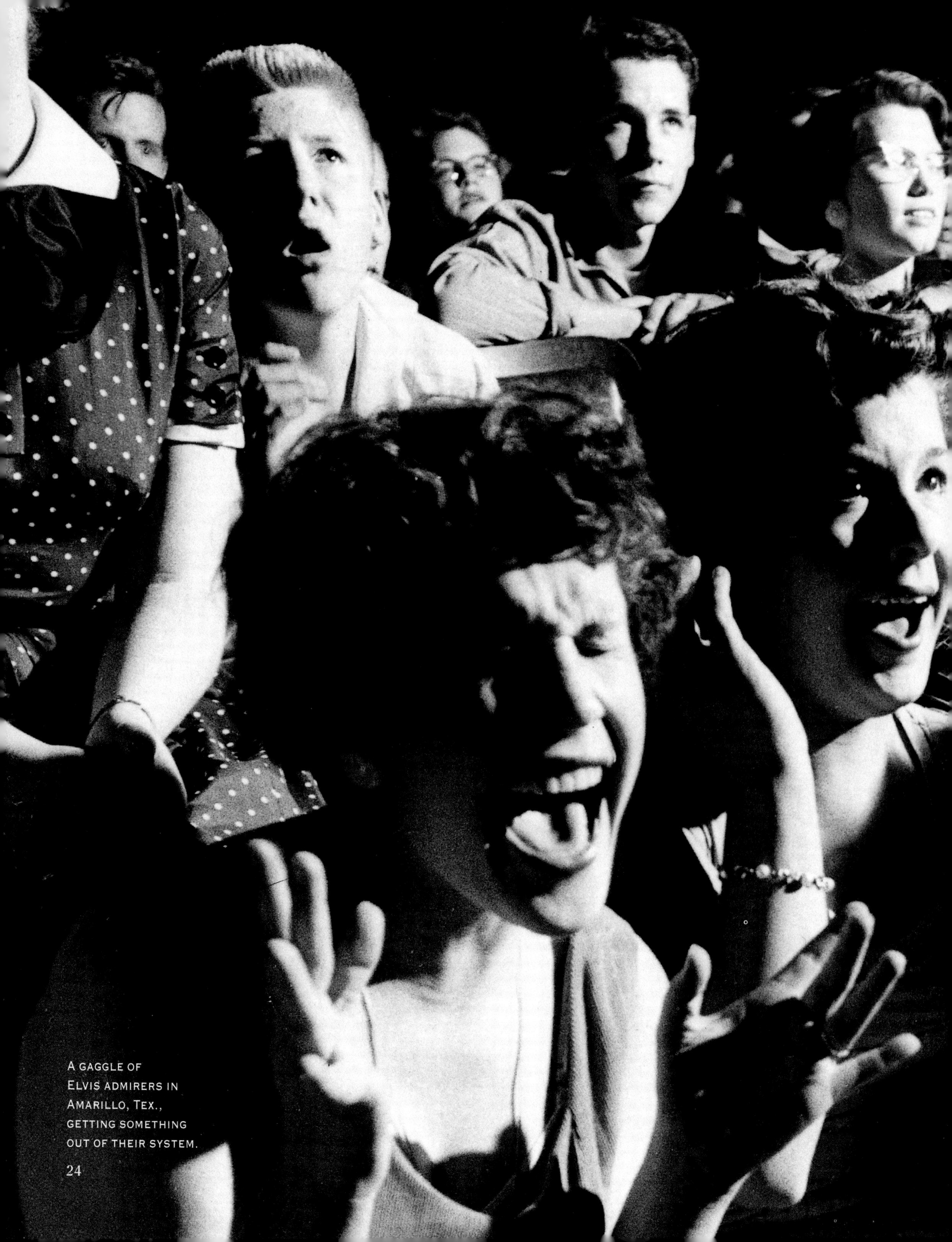

A gaggle of Elvis admirers in Amarillo, Tex., getting something out of their system.

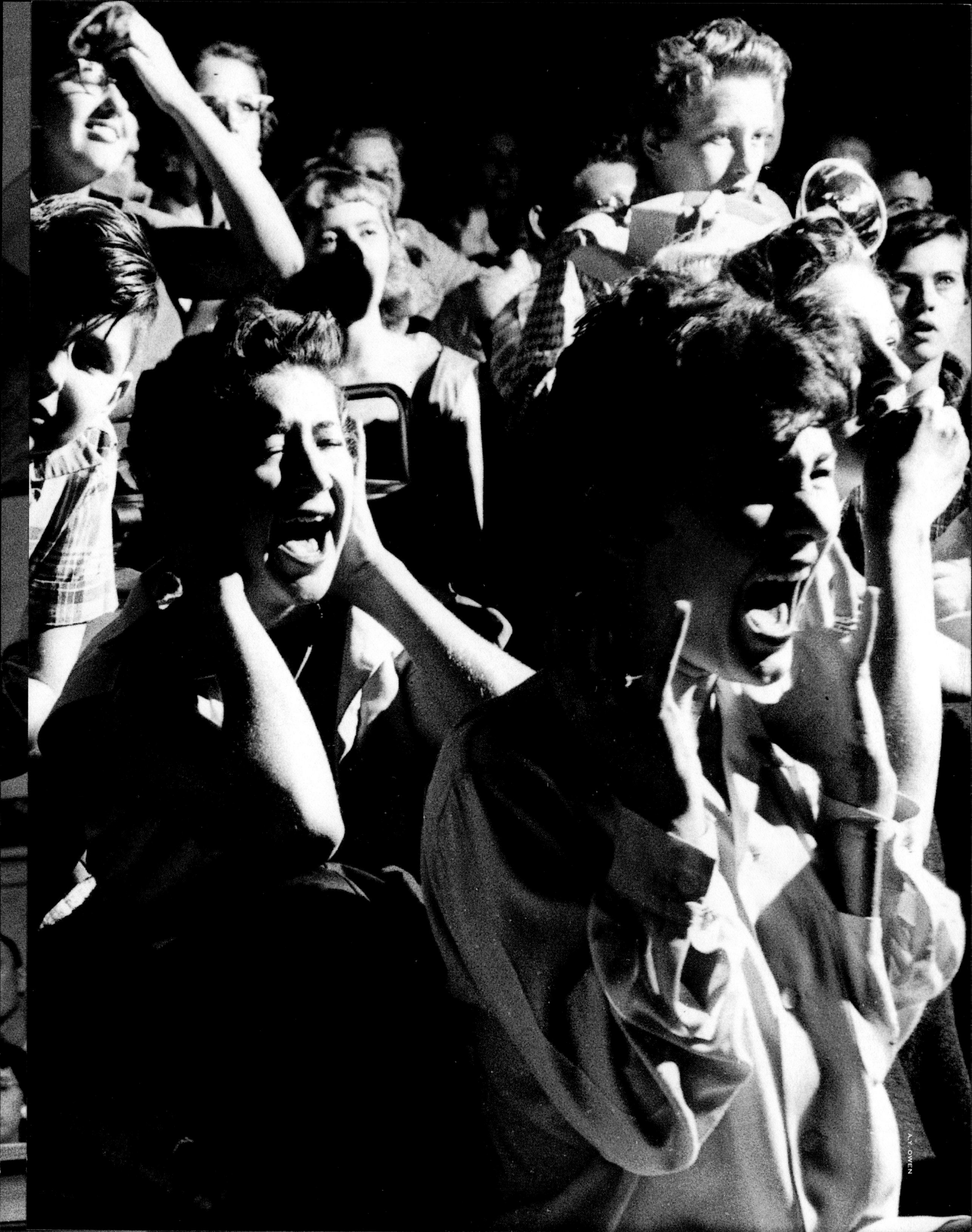

A.Y. OWEN

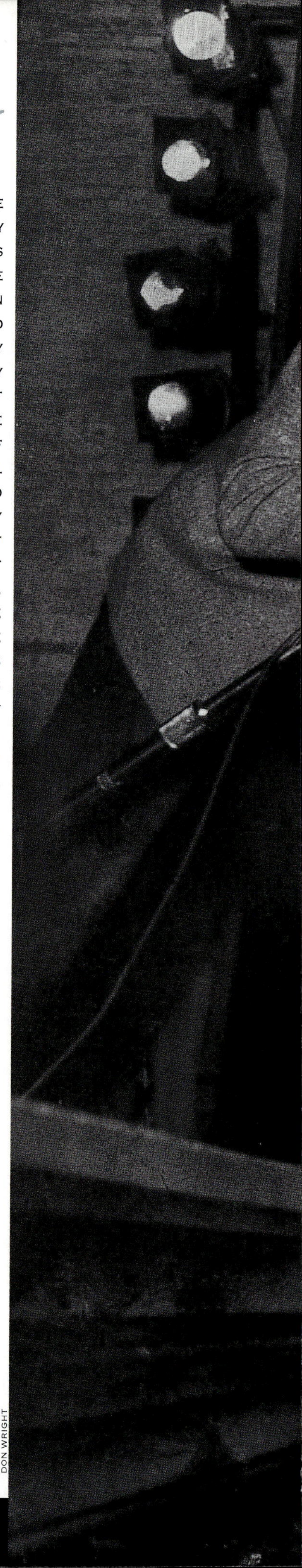

WHILE REVEREND GRAY PRAYED FOR ELVIS'S SOUL, JACKSONVILLE JUDGE MARION GOODING THREATENED TO ARREST HIS BODY ON OBSCENITY CHARGES. "DON'T UNDERESTIMATE THE INTELLIGENCE OF TEENAGERS IN SEXUAL MATTERS," WARNED HIS HONOR. "THEY CAN READ ALL THAT STUFF." ELVIS MET WITH GOODING, PROMISED TO BEHAVE AND THEN DROVE THE JACKSONVILLE GIRLS WILD BY WAGGING HIS FINGER SUGGESTIVELY WHILE SINGING. "DRIVE CAREFUL ON YOUR WAY HOME," HE TEASED THE CROWD. "AND DON'T LET ANYBODY PASS YOU."

OCTOBER 1955

The Elvis Presley Jamboree, managed by Colonel Parker, kicks off in Texas. The bill includes future stars Floyd Cramer and Johnny Cash.

NOVEMBER 1955

Burdened by debts, Sam Phillips sells Elvis's Sun contract to RCA Victor for the unheard-of sum of $35,000, plus $5,000 for back royalties. It's a career-risking bet by RCA executive Steve Sholes.

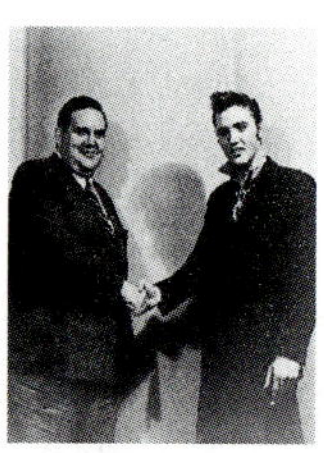

JANUARY 1956

Elvis makes his national television debut on *Stage Show,* produced by Jackie Gleason and hosted by the Dorsey brothers. Gleason's opinion: "He can't last. I tell you flatly, he can't last."

APRIL 1956

The first national magazine to do a story on Elvis is LIFE—which describes him as a "howling hillbilly."

JULY 1956

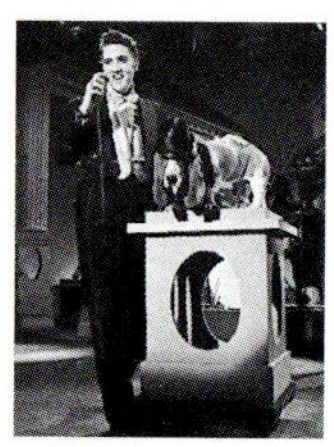

Dressed in tails, he appears on Steve Allen's *Tonight* show and sings "Hound Dog" to a top-hatted basset hound named Sherlock.

DON WRIGHT

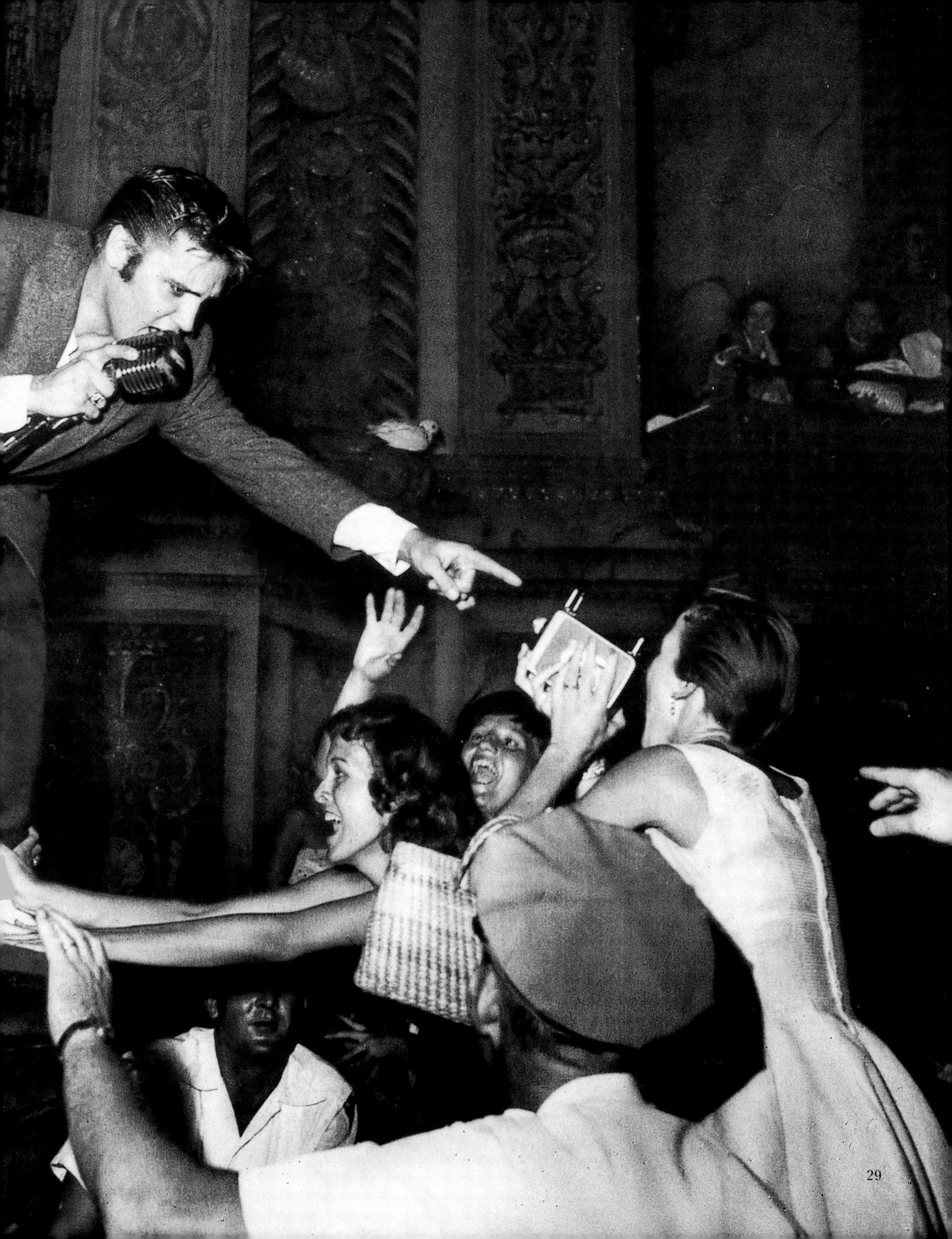

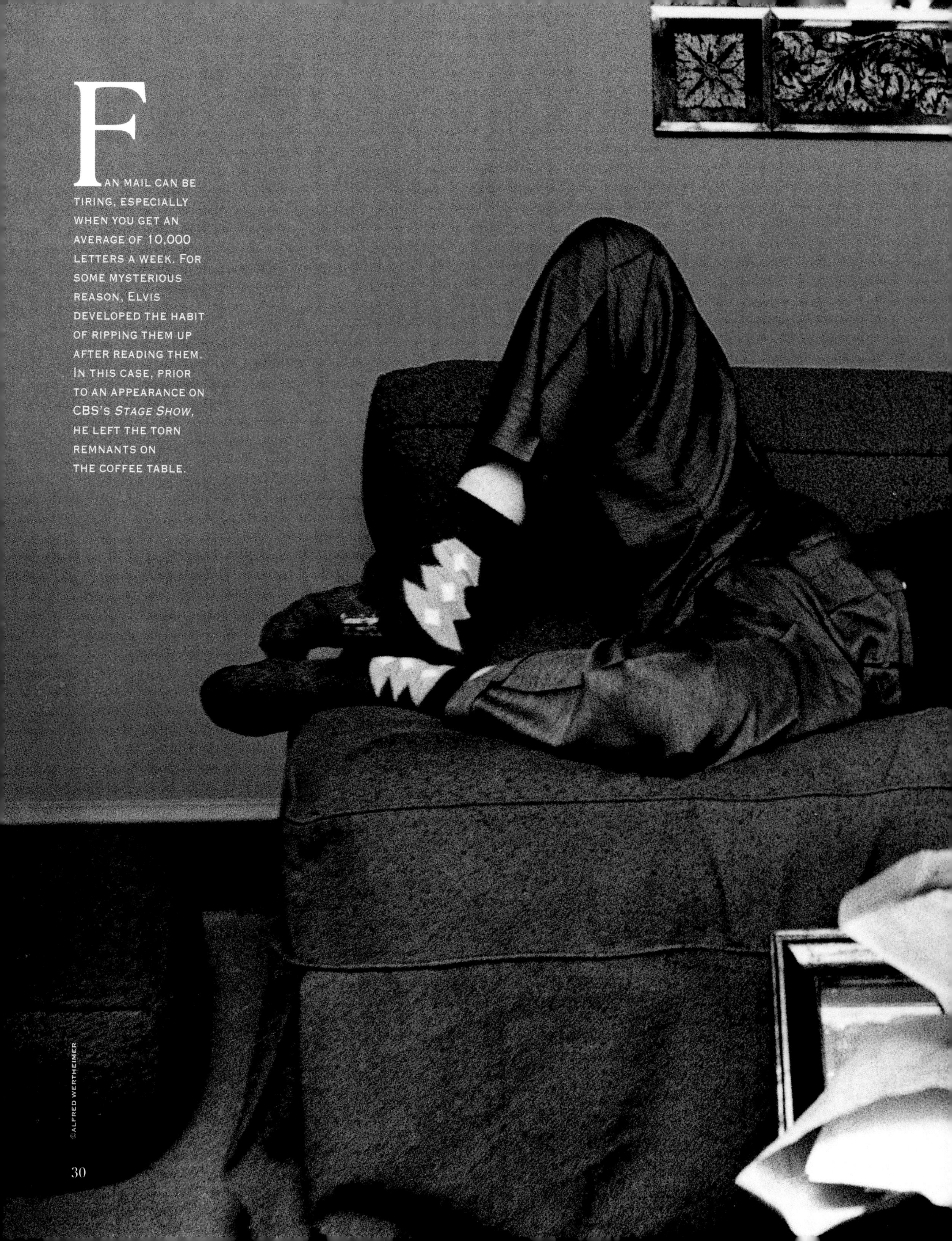

FAN MAIL CAN BE TIRING, ESPECIALLY WHEN YOU GET AN AVERAGE OF 10,000 LETTERS A WEEK. FOR SOME MYSTERIOUS REASON, ELVIS DEVELOPED THE HABIT OF RIPPING THEM UP AFTER READING THEM. IN THIS CASE, PRIOR TO AN APPEARANCE ON CBS'S *STAGE SHOW*, HE LEFT THE TORN REMNANTS ON THE COFFEE TABLE.

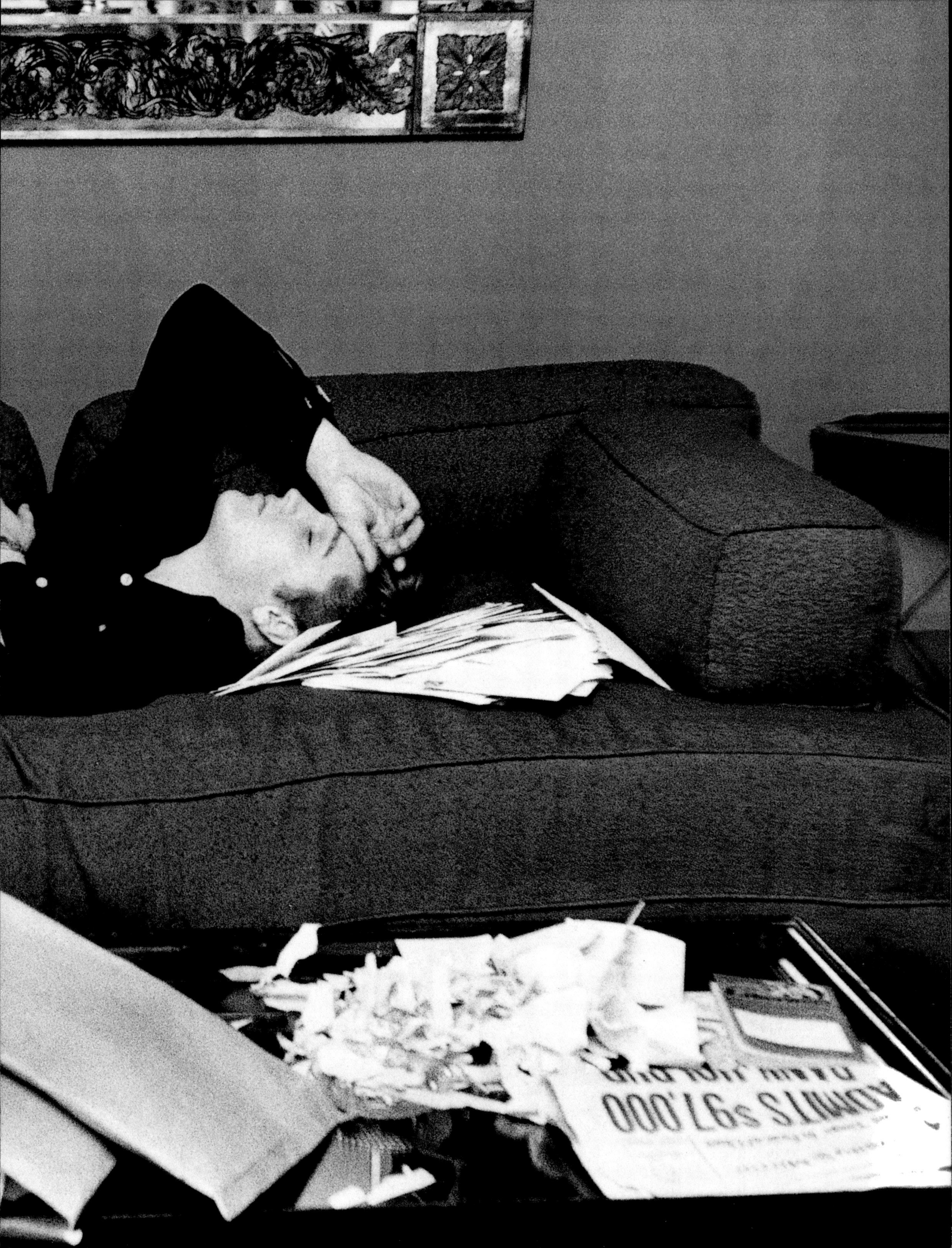
ADMITS $97,000

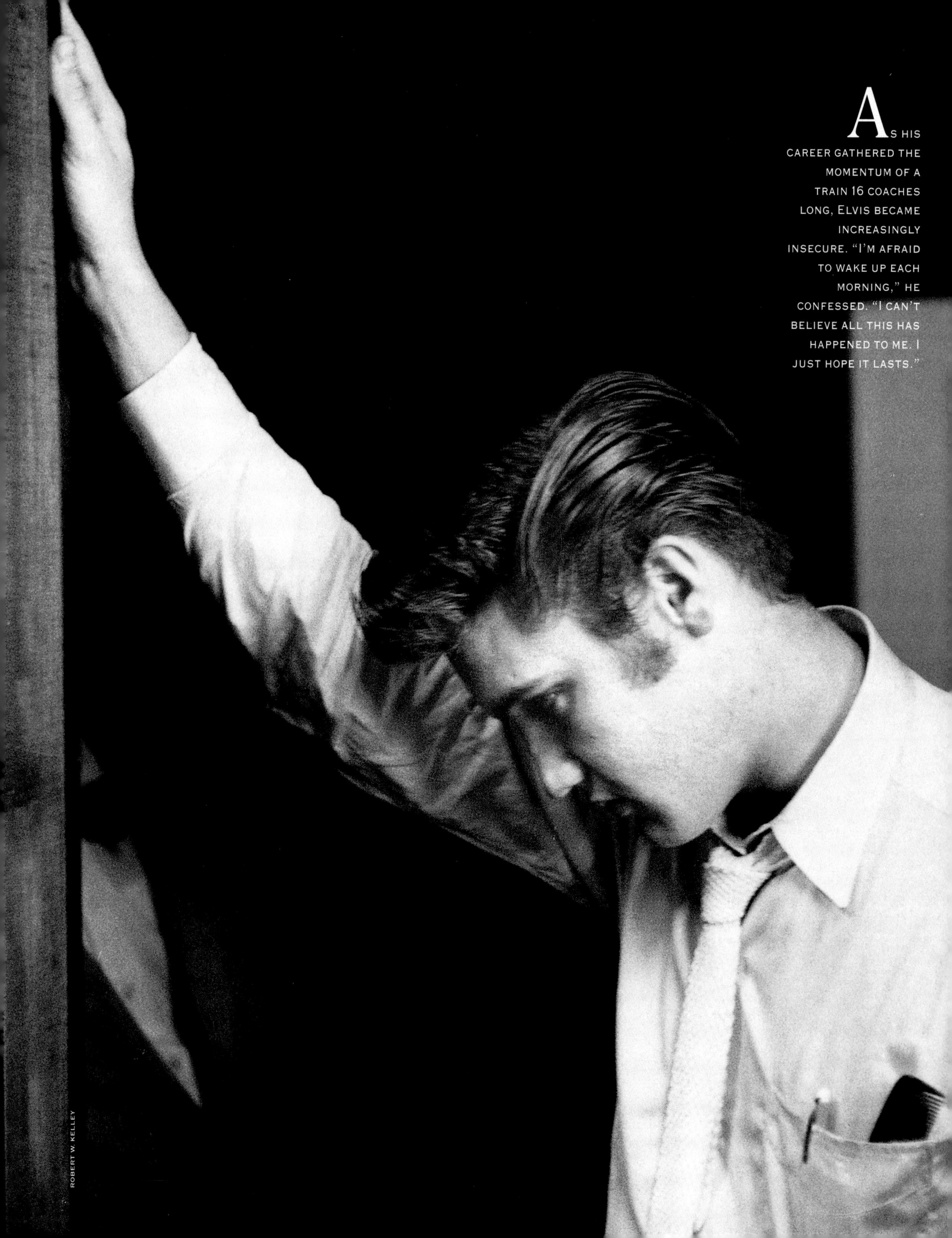

As his career gathered the momentum of a train 16 coaches long, Elvis became increasingly insecure. "I'm afraid to wake up each morning," he confessed. "I can't believe all this has happened to me. I just hope it lasts."

ROBERT W. KELLEY

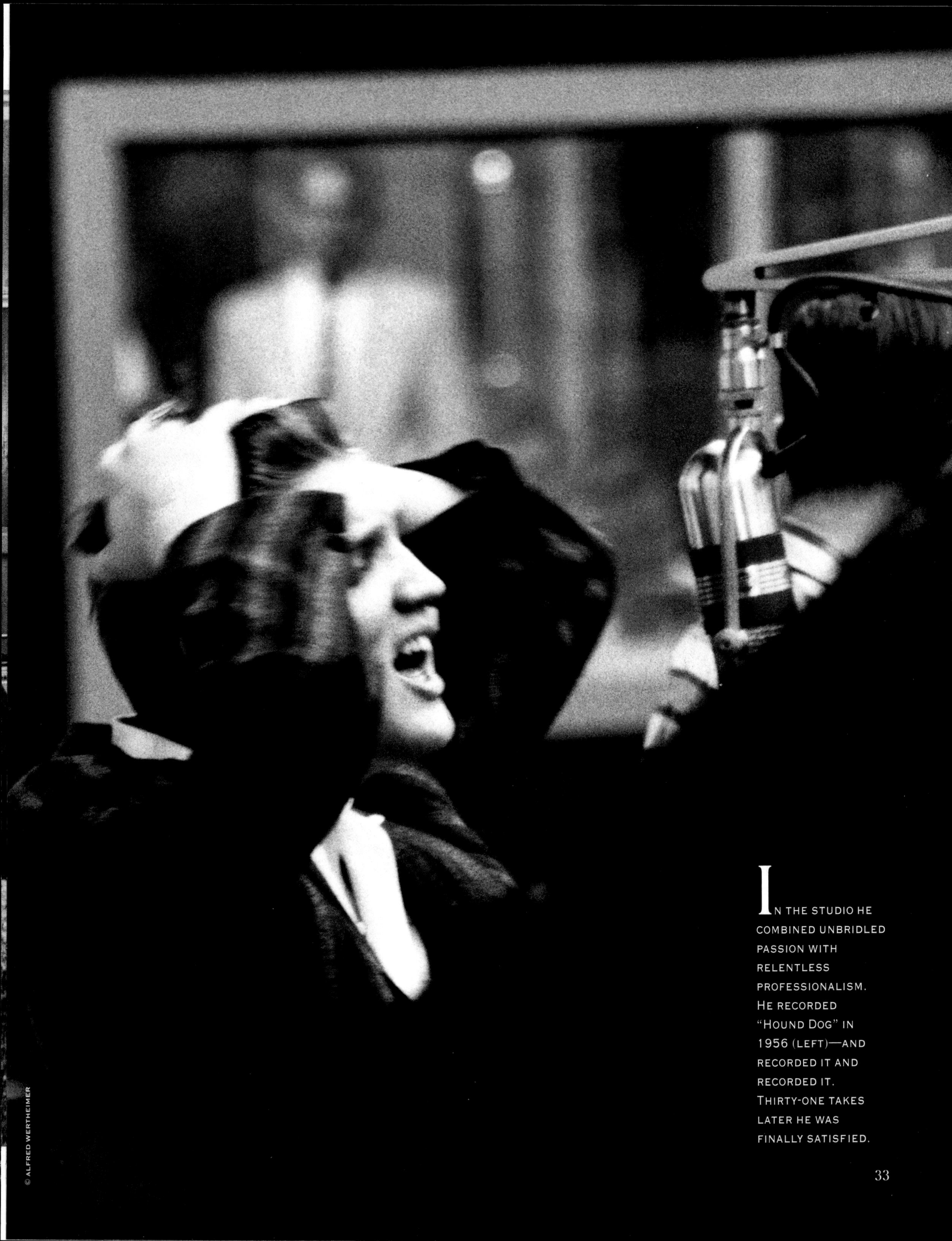

In the studio he combined unbridled passion with relentless professionalism. He recorded "Hound Dog" in 1956 (left)—and recorded it and recorded it. Thirty-one takes later he was finally satisfied.

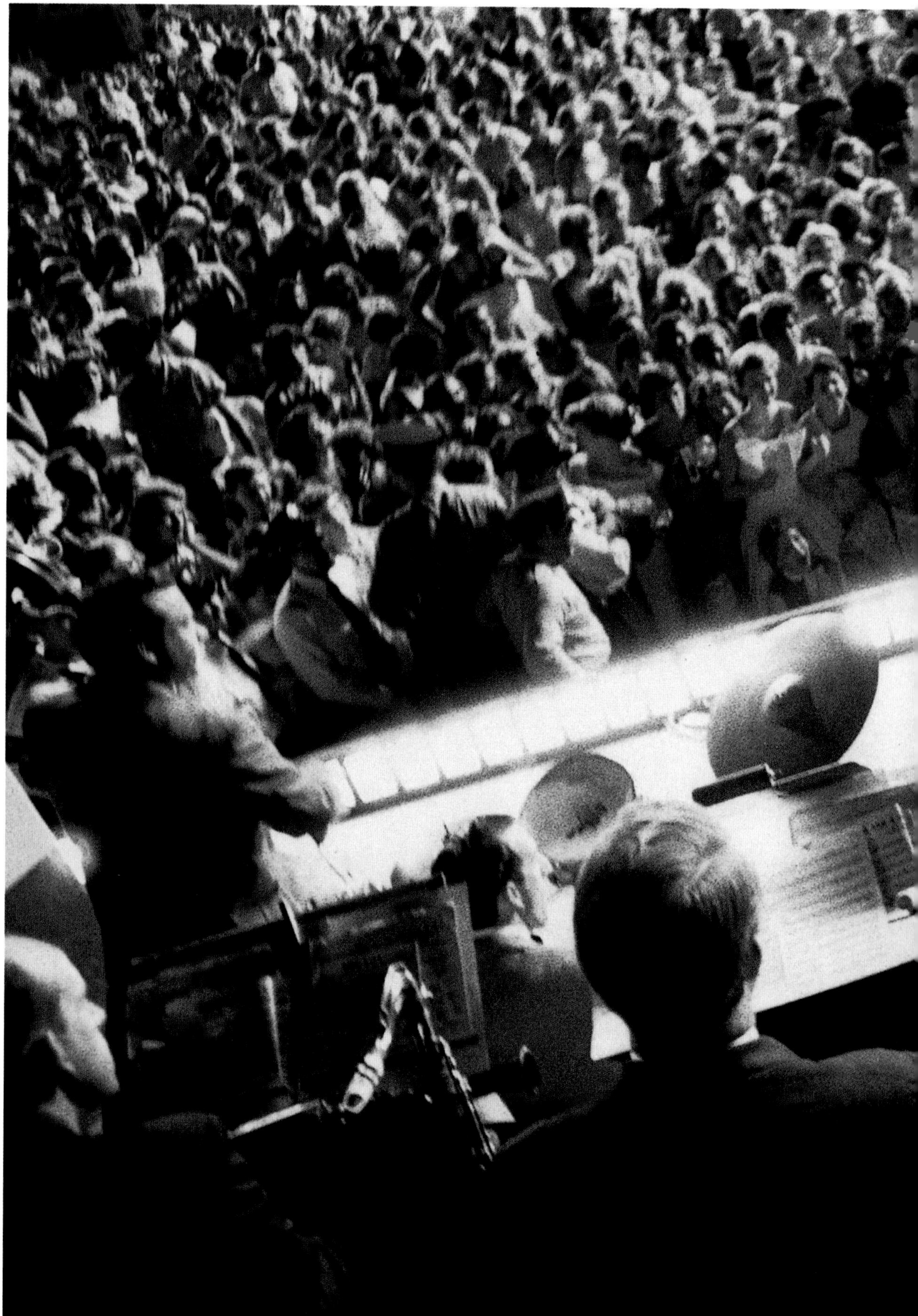

In Memphis, Independence Day 1956 was also Elvis Presley Day by proclamation. Seven thousand fans came to hear him at a benefit. Angered by demeaning treatment he had been subjected to on the *Tonight* show, many rushed the stage to welcome him home. "Those people in New York are not gonna change me none," he promised. "I'm gonna show you the real Elvis tonight."

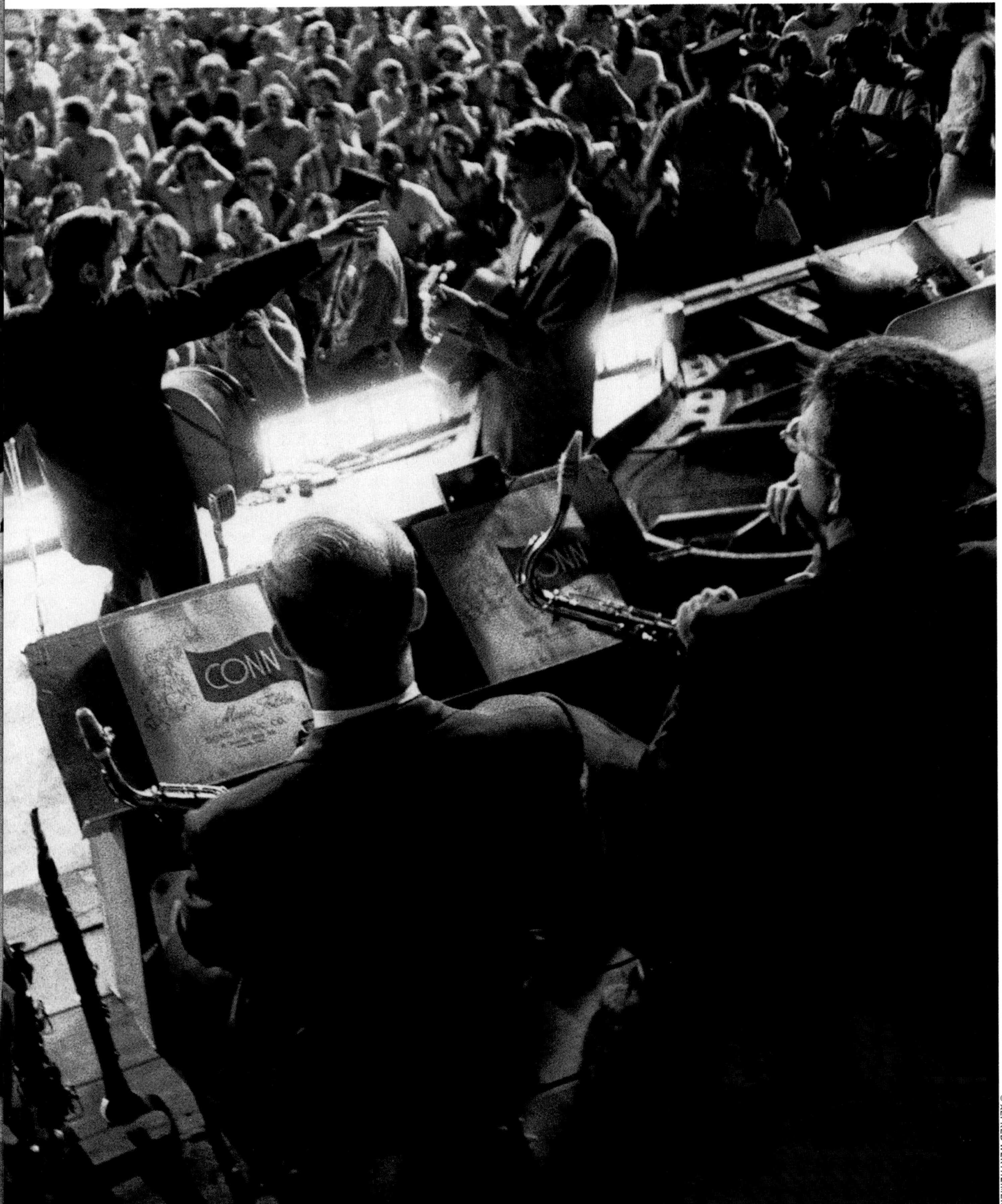

© ALFRED WERTHEIMER

There was always a buzz of expectation in the crowds that assembled before Elvis's shows. Colonel Parker made sure of it by keeping box offices closed as long as possible, so fans had nothing to do but mill around and grow increasingly impatient and excited. But these crowds were outdone by the frenzied mobs that surrounded Elvis backstage after the shows ended. Country singer Helen Carter, who toured with him along with her mother and sisters, recalled one night when "the crowd pushed one little girl clean back into our dressing room. We said, 'Now, honey, we'll let you out the back so you can go to your car.' But she cried, 'I can't! My mama's in there trying to kiss him!'"

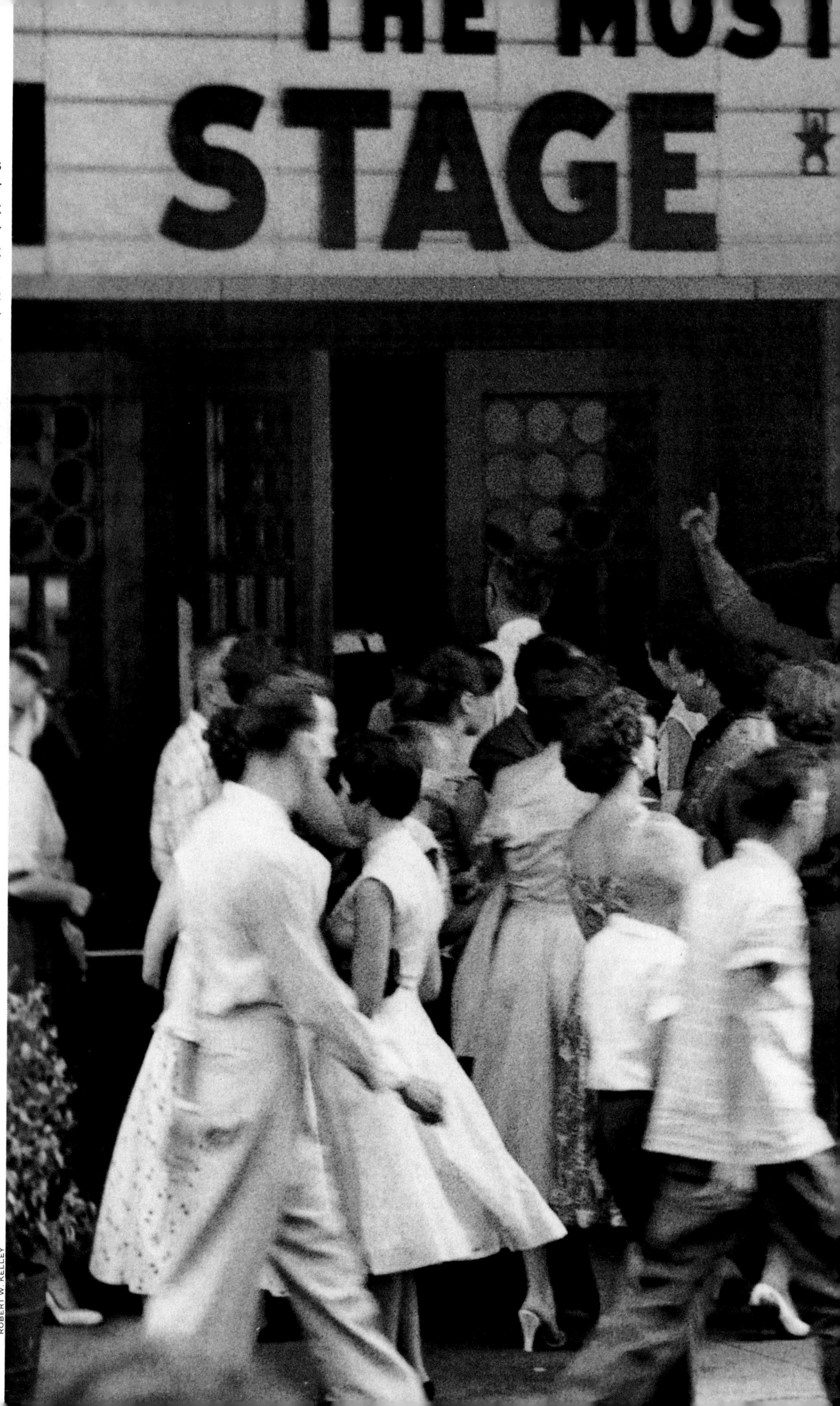

ROBERT W. KELLEY

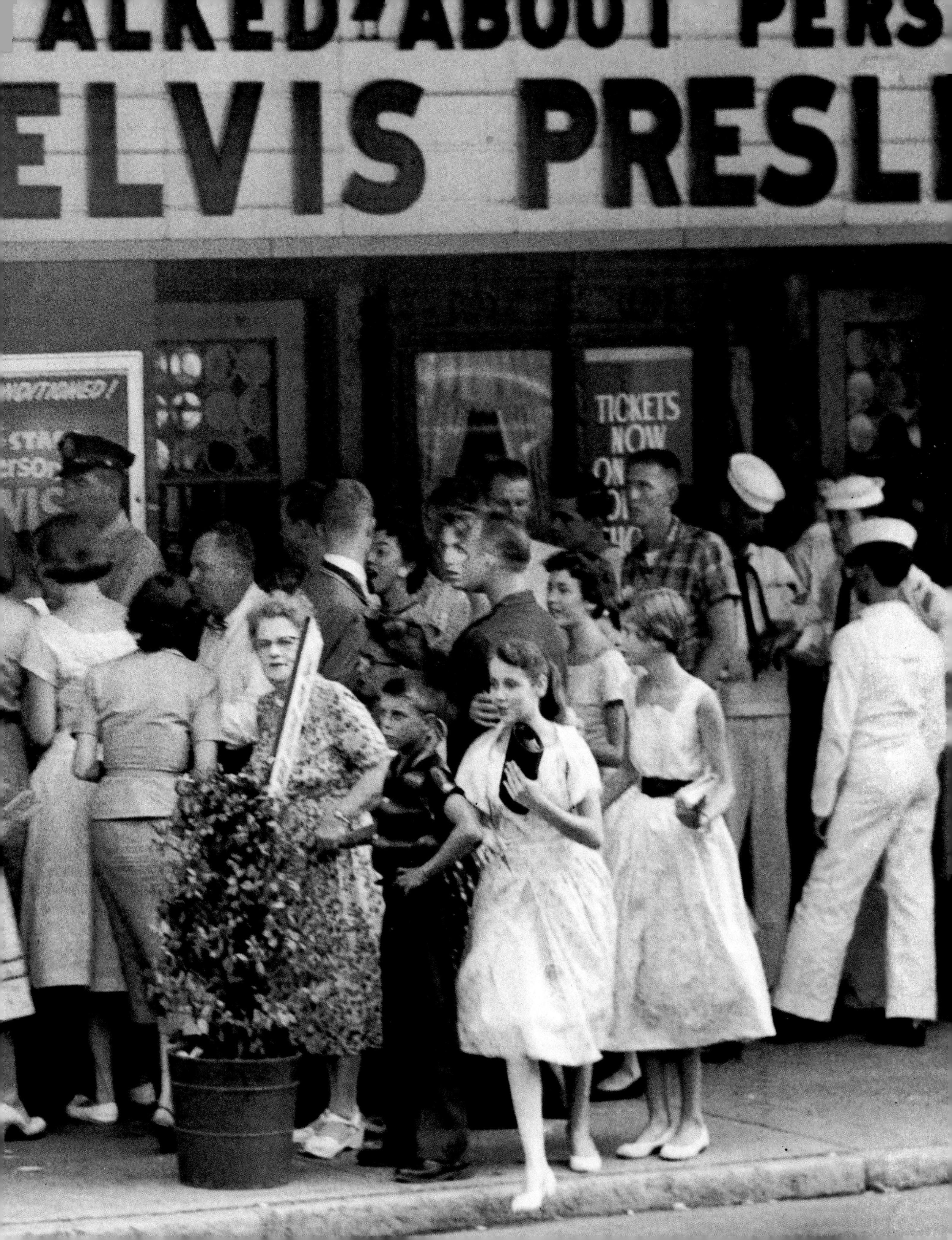
ALKED-ABOUT PERS
ELVIS PRESL
TICKETS NOW

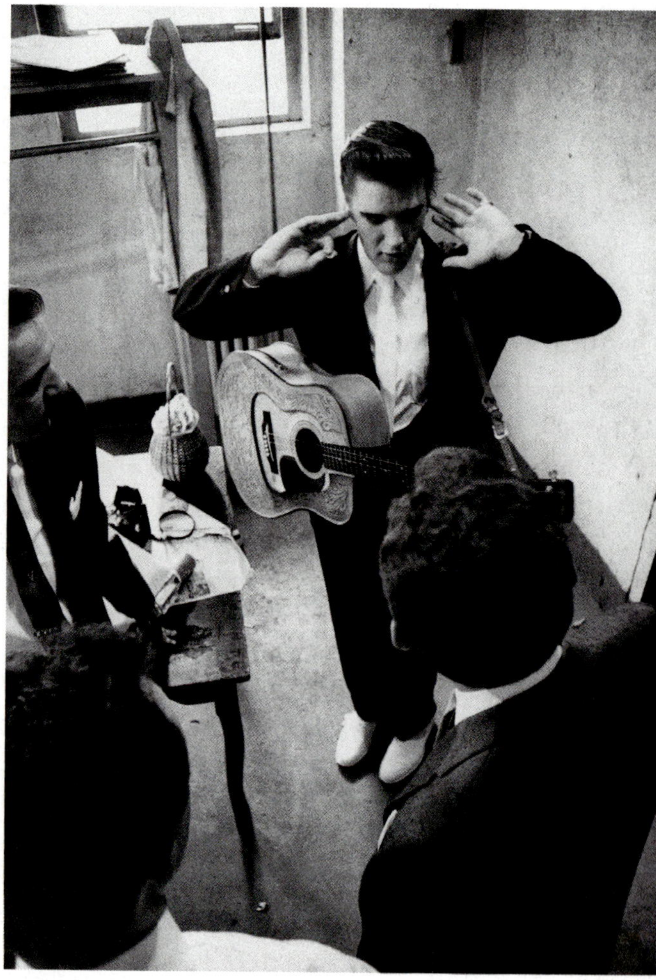

© ALFRED WERTHEIMER

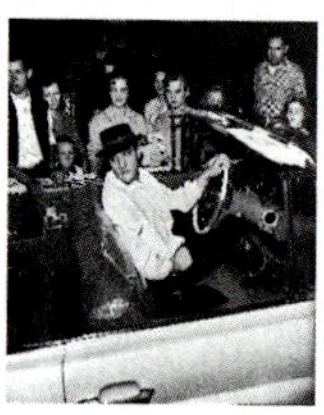

Elvis purchases a custom pink Cadillac Fleetwood for Mama Gladys. (It's still on display at Graceland.)

SEPTEMBER 1956

He finally appears on *The Ed Sullivan Show*. But in one of TV's most notorious—and frustrating—acts of censorship, his spectacular gyrations are shown only from the waist up.

SEPTEMBER 1956

Elvis drops by Sun Studios and spends an evening jamming with Carl Perkins and Jerry Lee Lewis. Elvis is particularly impressed with Lewis: "The way he plays piano just gets inside me." Johnny Cash shows up later and is photographed with the trio, giving rise to the myth of a Million Dollar Quartet.

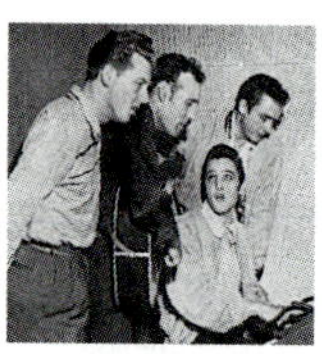

DECEMBER 1956

NOTHING COMPARED TO THE NOISE OF THOSE SCREAMING GIRLS," RECALLS FORMER LIFE CORRESPONDENT (AND LATER MANAGING EDITOR) RICHARD STOLLEY, WHO COVERED ELVIS'S FLORIDA TOUR IN 1956 (OPPOSITE). "IT WAS UNEARTHLY; IT HURT YOUR EARS." THEIR SHRIEKING WAS LESS AGONIZING TO ELVIS, BUT BEFORE ONE CONCERT IN RICHMOND, VA., THEY STOOD OUTSIDE THE WINDOW AND SCREECHED SO LOUDLY HE COULD HARDLY HEAR EITHER HIMSELF OR THE JORDANAIRES, HIS BACKUP VOCAL GROUP.

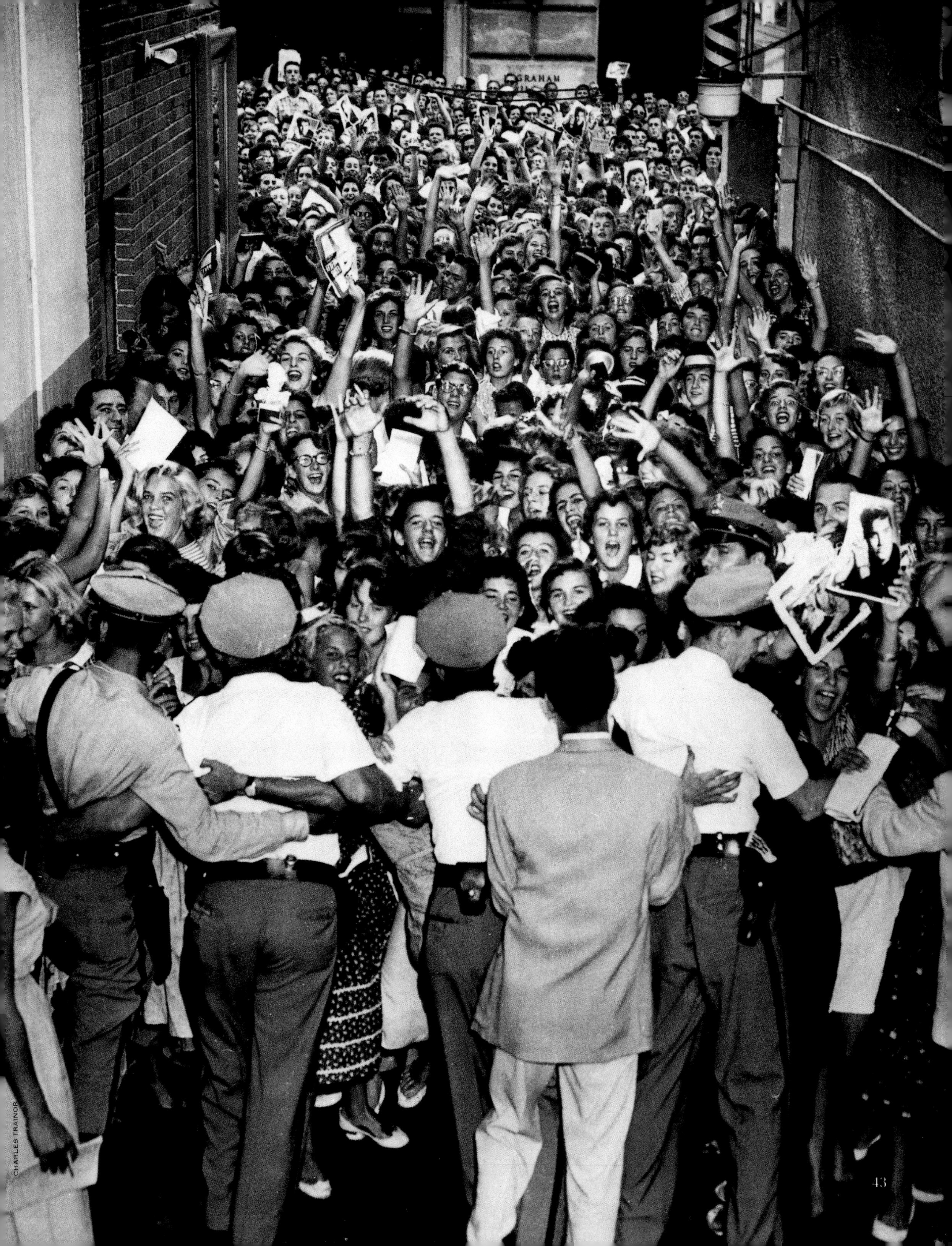

CHARLES TRAINOR

Since reporters had never encountered anything like Elvis before, most didn't quite know what to ask him. Was it true that he once shot his mother?, they wanted to know. Was it true his movements on stage were the result of marijuana use? Was it true he received a cut from the sale of "I hate Elvis" buttons? He answered all such questions with unfailing southern politeness—"No, sir," "No, ma'am" and "Well, I believe that one takes the cake."

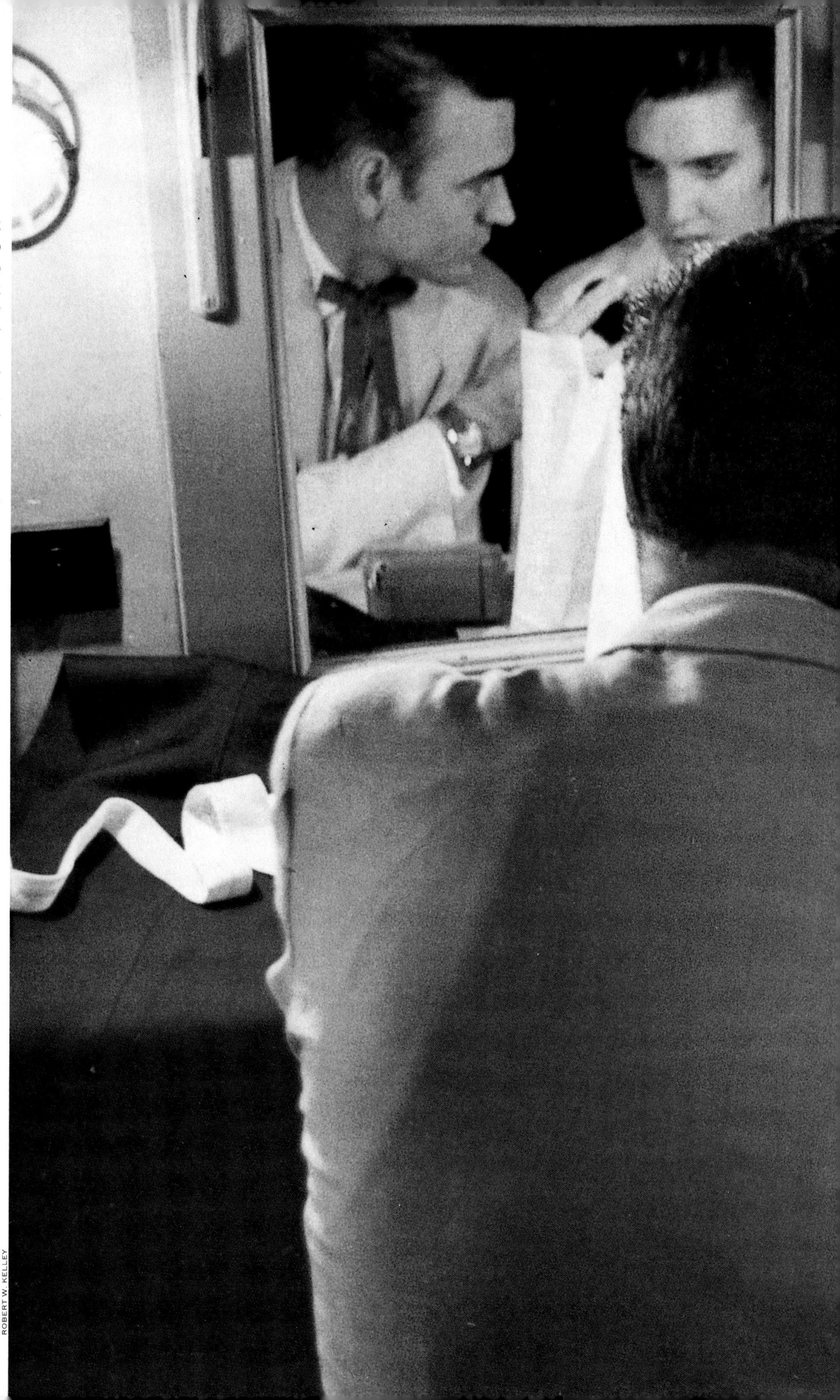

ROBERT W. KELLEY

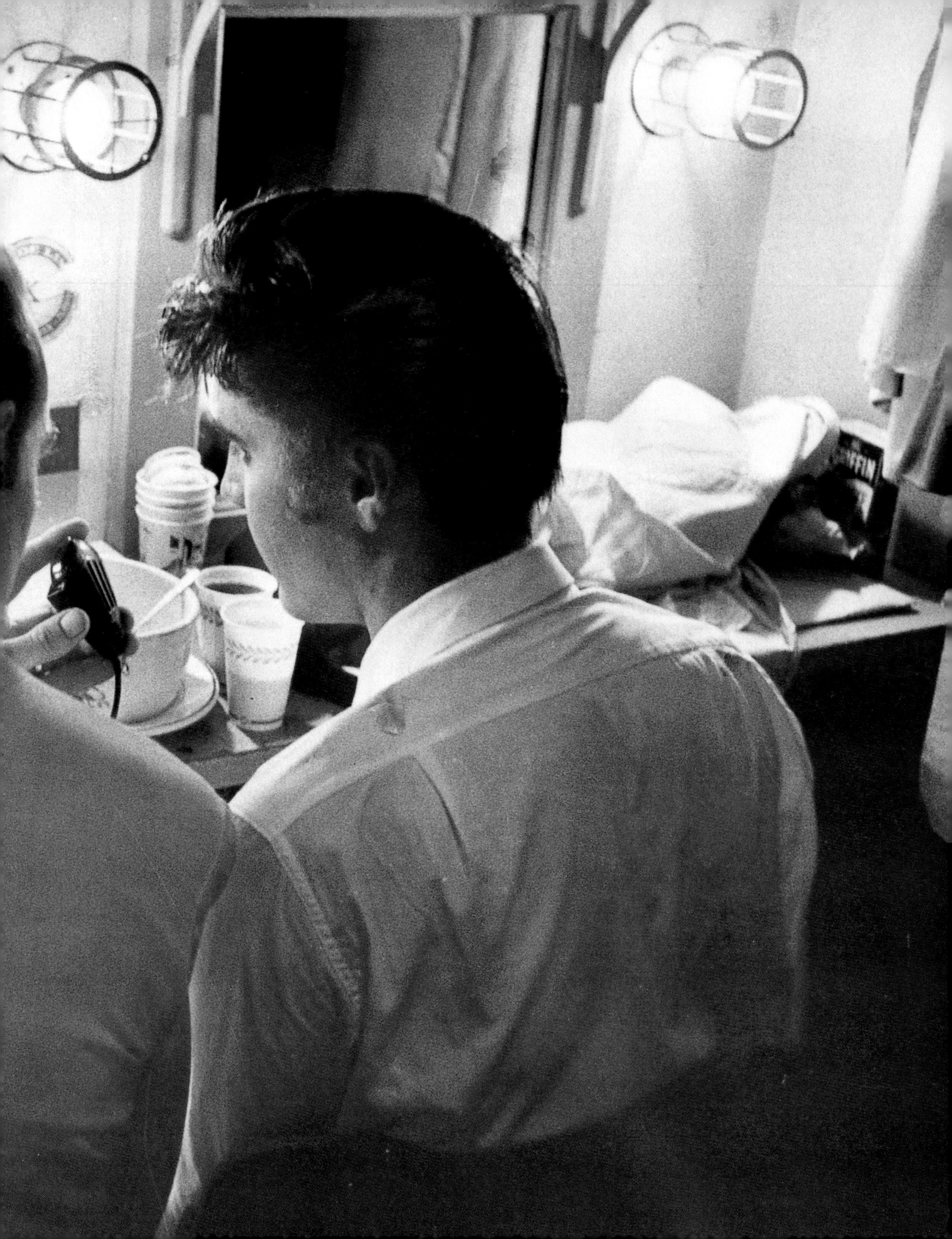

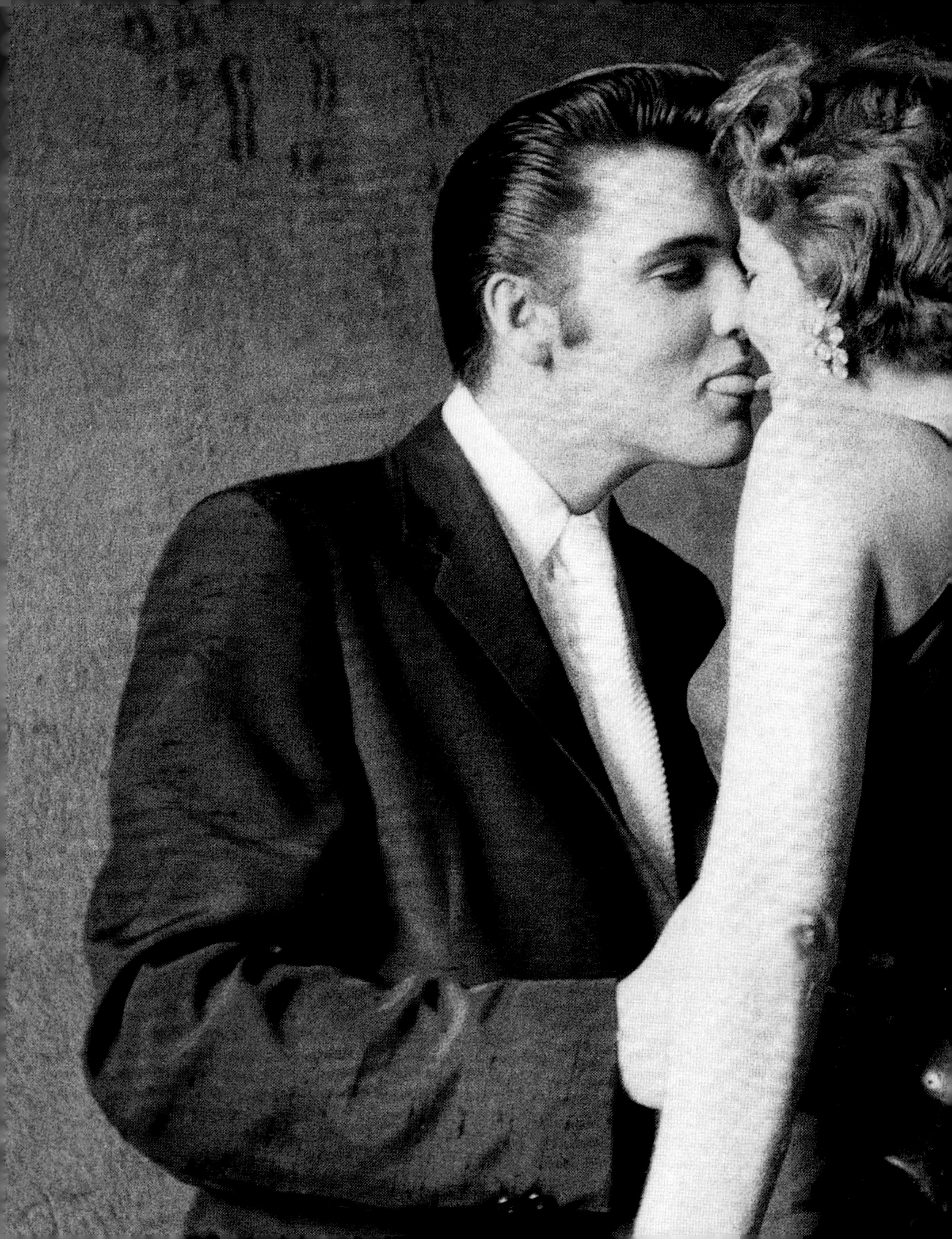

ELVIS SEEMS TO COME ALIVE ONLY WHEN A GIRL IS AROUND," REPORTER KAYS GARY NOTED. IN A STAIRWELL AT THE RICHMOND CONCERT, HE CAME ALIVE WITH ONE HE HAD KNOWN FOR A VERY SHORT TIME. GARY ONCE SAW HIM IN A RESTAURANT, FLIRTING WITH WOMAN AFTER WOMAN. "HE STOOD CHEST-TO-CHEST WITH ONE, RUNNING HIS FINGERS LIGHTLY AROUND THE BLOUSE RUFFLES. AND SHE STOOD STILL AND SAID NOTHING WHILE HE TALKED TO HER IN A LOW VOICE." WHEN HE MET A WOMAN HE LIKED, IT WAS NOT UNCOMMON FOR HIM TO REACH OUT AND TOUCH HER SKIRT OR CRANE HIS NECK TO NIBBLE HER FINGER. SAID CLOSE FRIEND AND BODYGUARD RED WEST: "THAT BOY SURE HAD A CONSTITUTION IN THOSE EARLY DAYS."

I'll regret this day as long as I live," he said on October 19, 1956. The trouble began when he drove his white Continental Mark II into a Memphis service station run by one Edd Hopper. A crowd formed around the car, and Hopper, outraged that other paying customers couldn't reach his pumps, ordered him to move. "I'm fixin' to," Elvis said, but he was hemmed in and had nowhere to go. So Hopper reached in and swatted him on the back of the head. Elvis bolted from his car and socked Hopper in the eye. ("That eye looked like a traveling bag," one witness remarked.) The next day in court, Elvis was exonerated and Hopper (near right, in sunglasses) fined $26. But Elvis had made an ominous discovery: he was no longer free to act like a normal person in public. "It's getting where I can't even leave the house," he sighed.

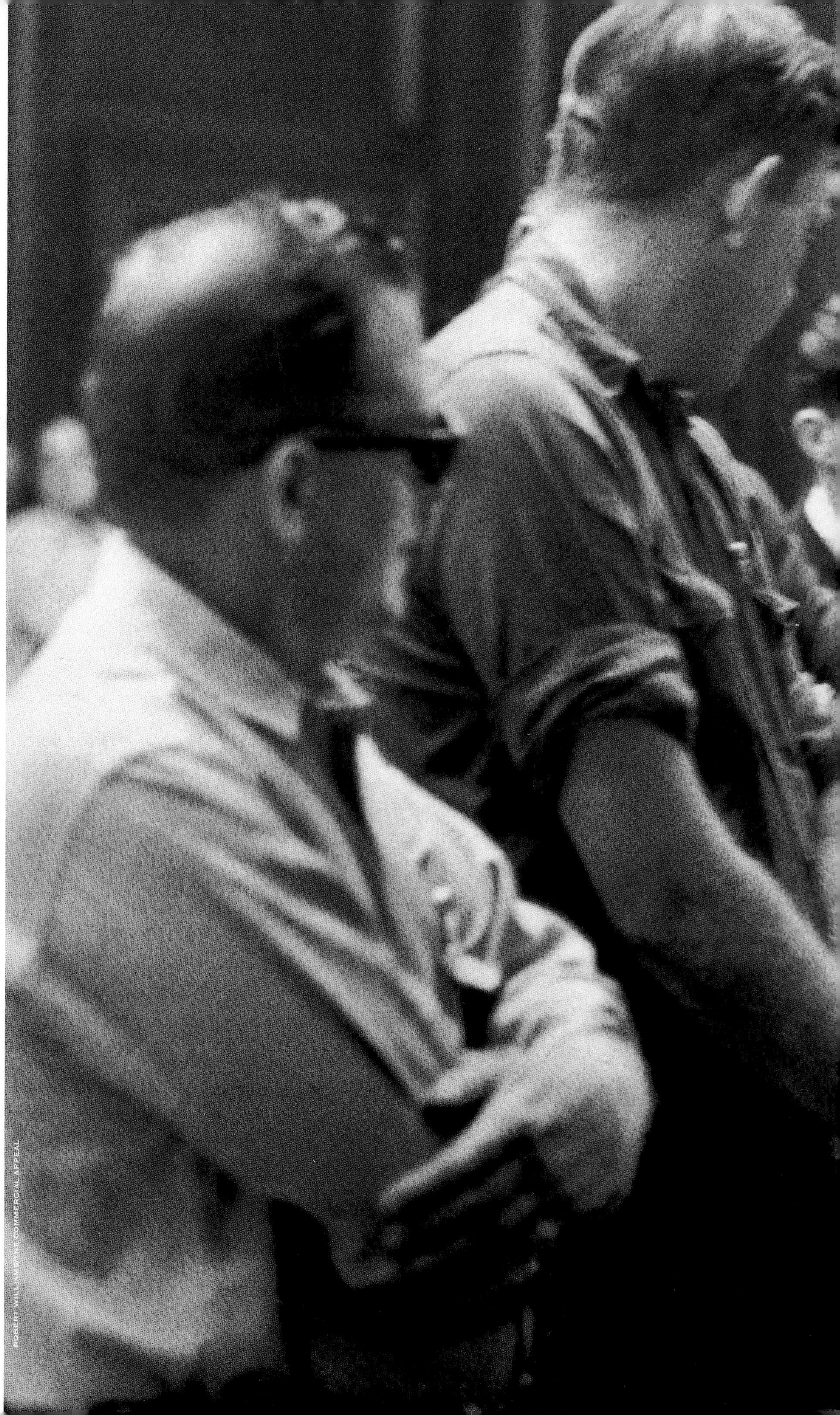

ROBERT WILLIAMS/THE COMMERCIAL APPEAL

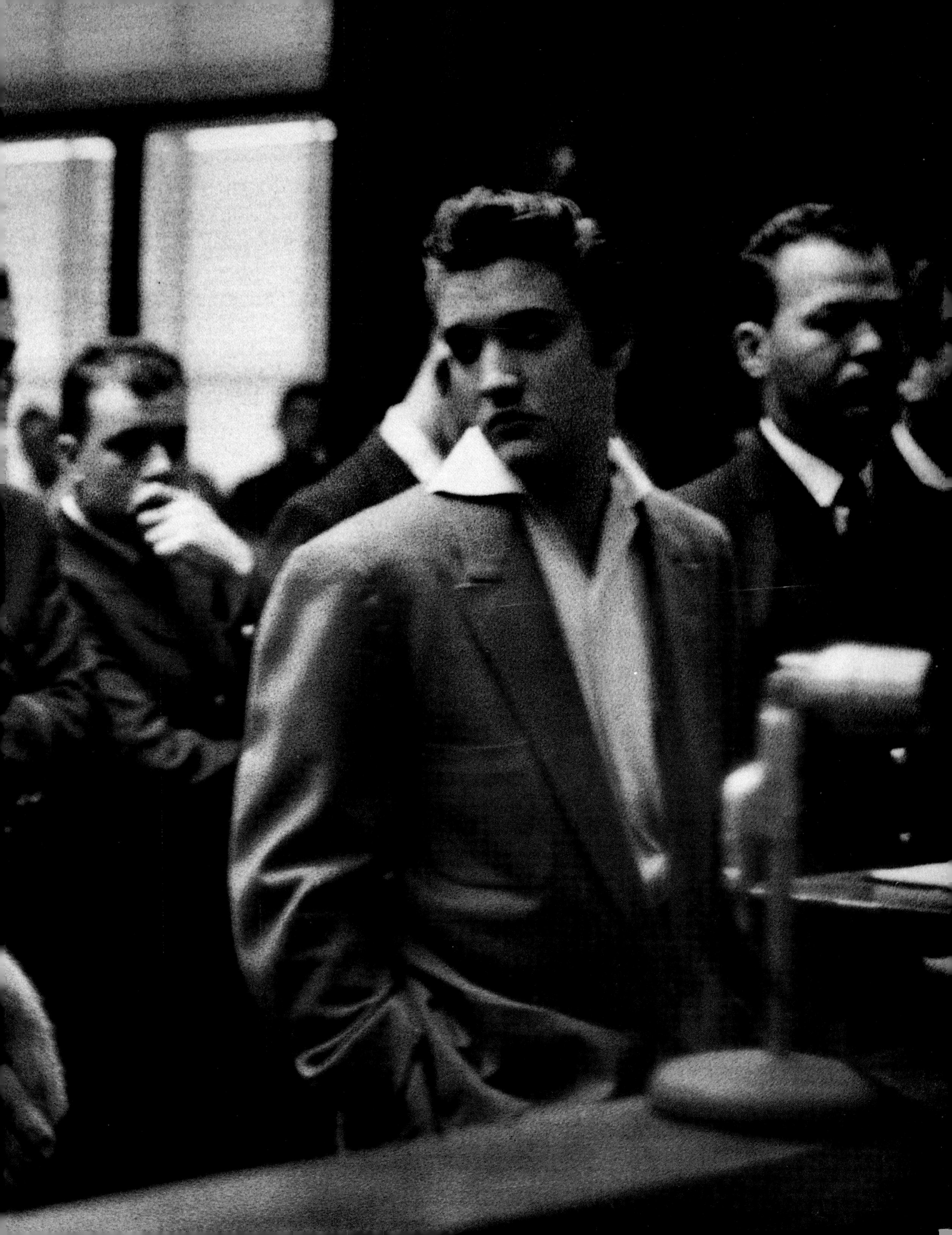

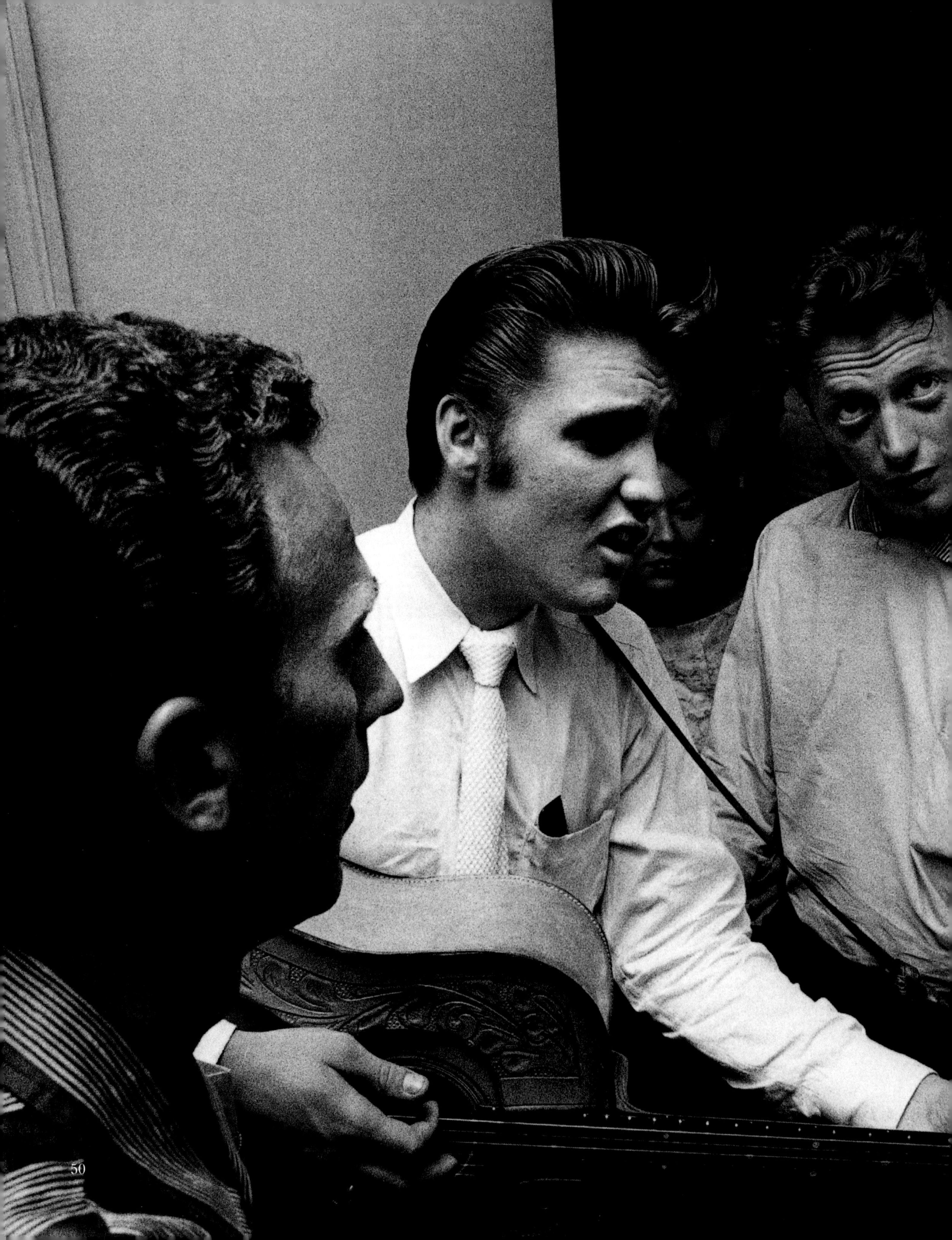

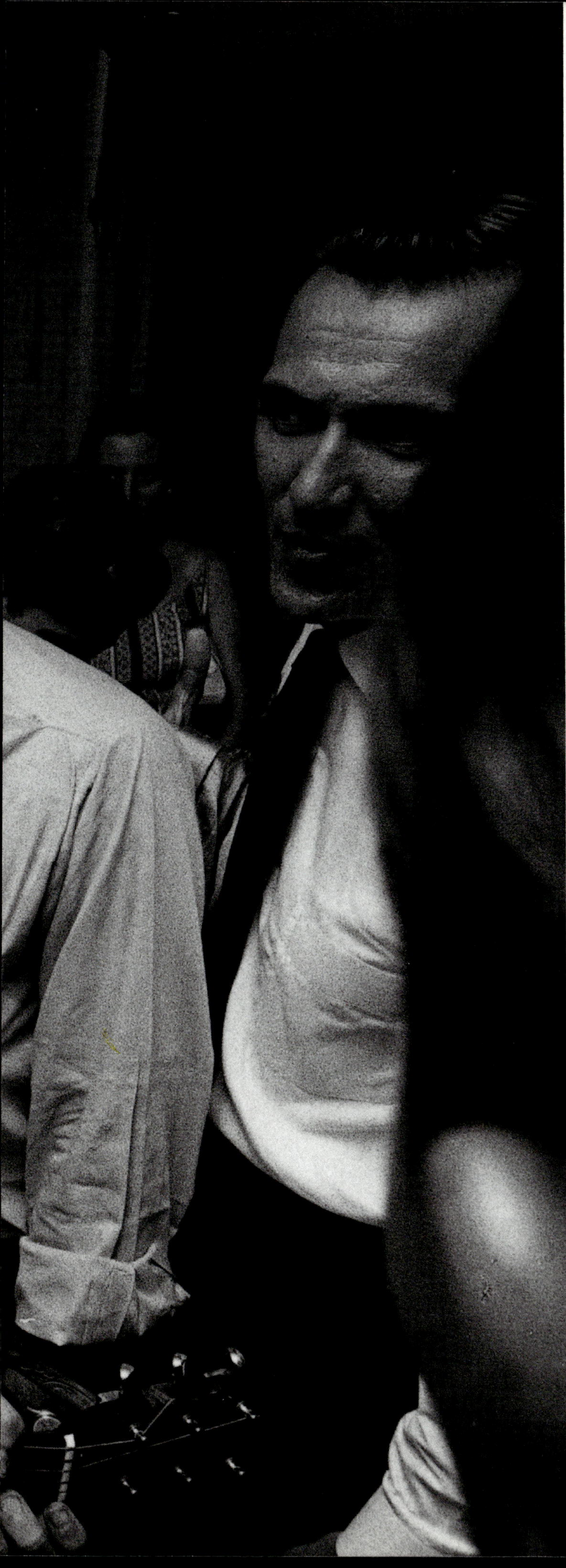

© JAY LEVITON-ATLANTA

ALMOST AS SOON AS HE HIT THE BIG TIME, ELVIS BEGAN TO ASSEMBLE A GANG OF FRIENDS, RELATIONS AND SYCOPHANTS THAT CAME TO BE KNOWN AS THE MEMPHIS MAFIA. ONE IMPORTANT TASK WAS HELPING ELVIS WARM UP, OR COOL DOWN, WITH GOSPEL HARMONIES BETWEEN SHOWS. HERE, RED WEST (CENTER) DID HIS DUTY WITH JORDANAIRES HOYT HAWKINS (FAR LEFT) AND HUGH JARRETT.

Elvis purchases his mansion, Graceland. A bubble-gum maker wants to strip the wood paneling off the walls of Elvis's old house, saw it into pieces, then sell it like baseball cards—with gum. Because this would conflict with other deals he has made, the Colonel declines.

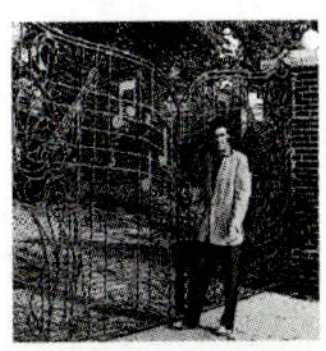

MARCH 1957

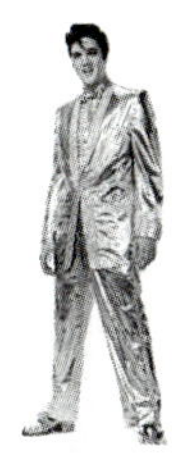

Elvis appears for the first time in his fabulous gold lamé suit designed by Nudie, a Brooklyn-born former boxer who had honed his sartorial skills by making costumes for burlesque dancers.

MARCH 1957

The night before he reports for induction into the U.S. Army, Elvis hosts a private blowout at Memphis's Rainbow Rollerdrome. Dividing his friends into two teams, he gives the signal, and each side tries to knock the daylights out of the other.

MARCH 1958

In September of 1957, Elvis got the shock of his life: The original Blue Moon Boys, guitarist Scotty Moore and bassist Bill Black, up and left him. He felt betrayed but shouldn't have. Scotty (near right) had played a crucial role in developing the unique fusion of blues and country known as the Presley Sound, but as Elvis had gotten richer, Scotty and Bill's share grew steadily smaller. They were put on salary instead of receiving a percentage of the profits and had been granted only one raise in two years. It was grossly unfair, but, according to Scotty, Elvis "kept saying he left the business side of it to Parker." Some weeks after their resignation, Scotty and Bill were offered a flat rate for each show. Reluctantly, they agreed. "Of course it stuck in my craw," said Scotty, who continued to play with Elvis off and on until 1969. "But we were still making more money than we could if we were driving trucks or something."

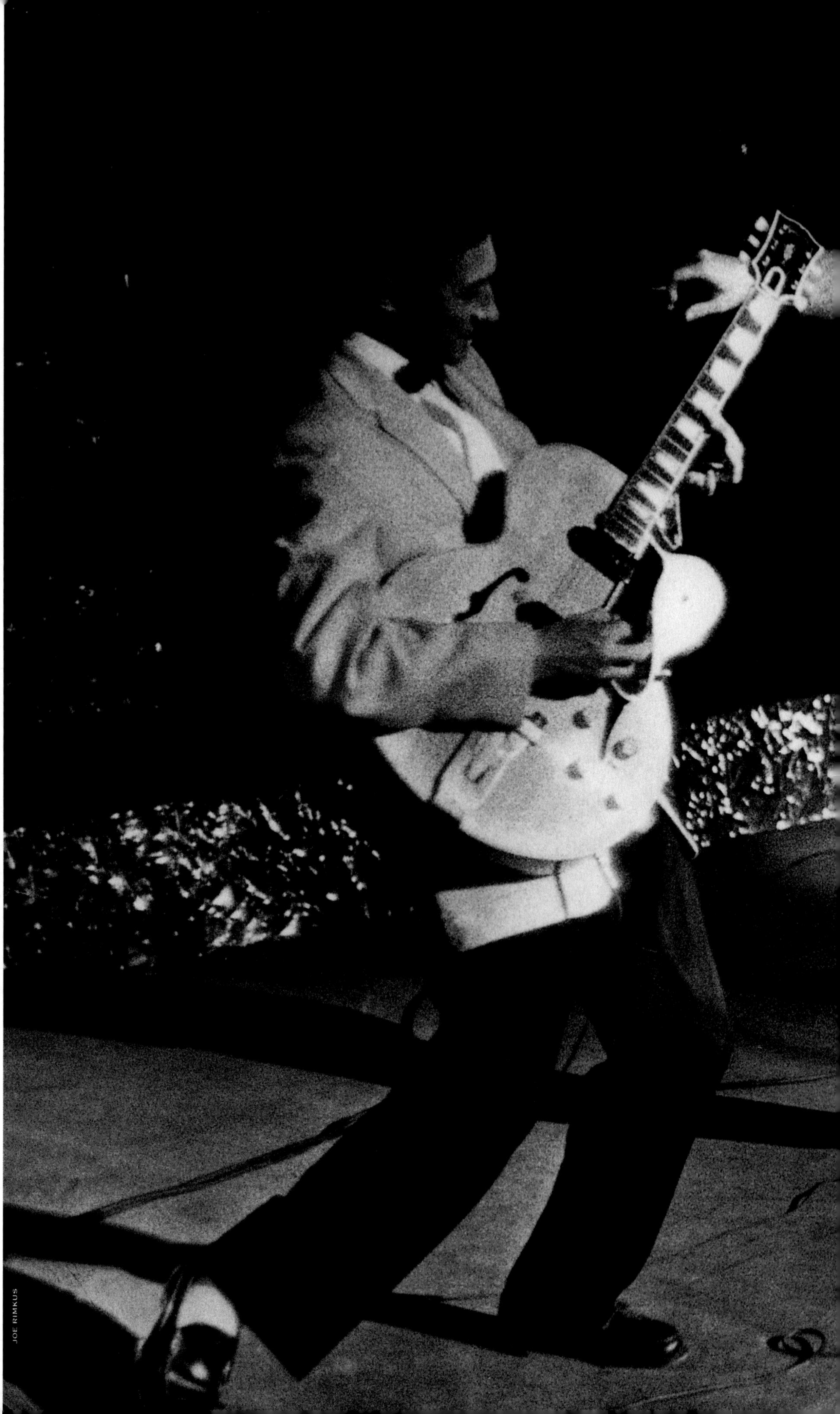
JOE RIMKUS

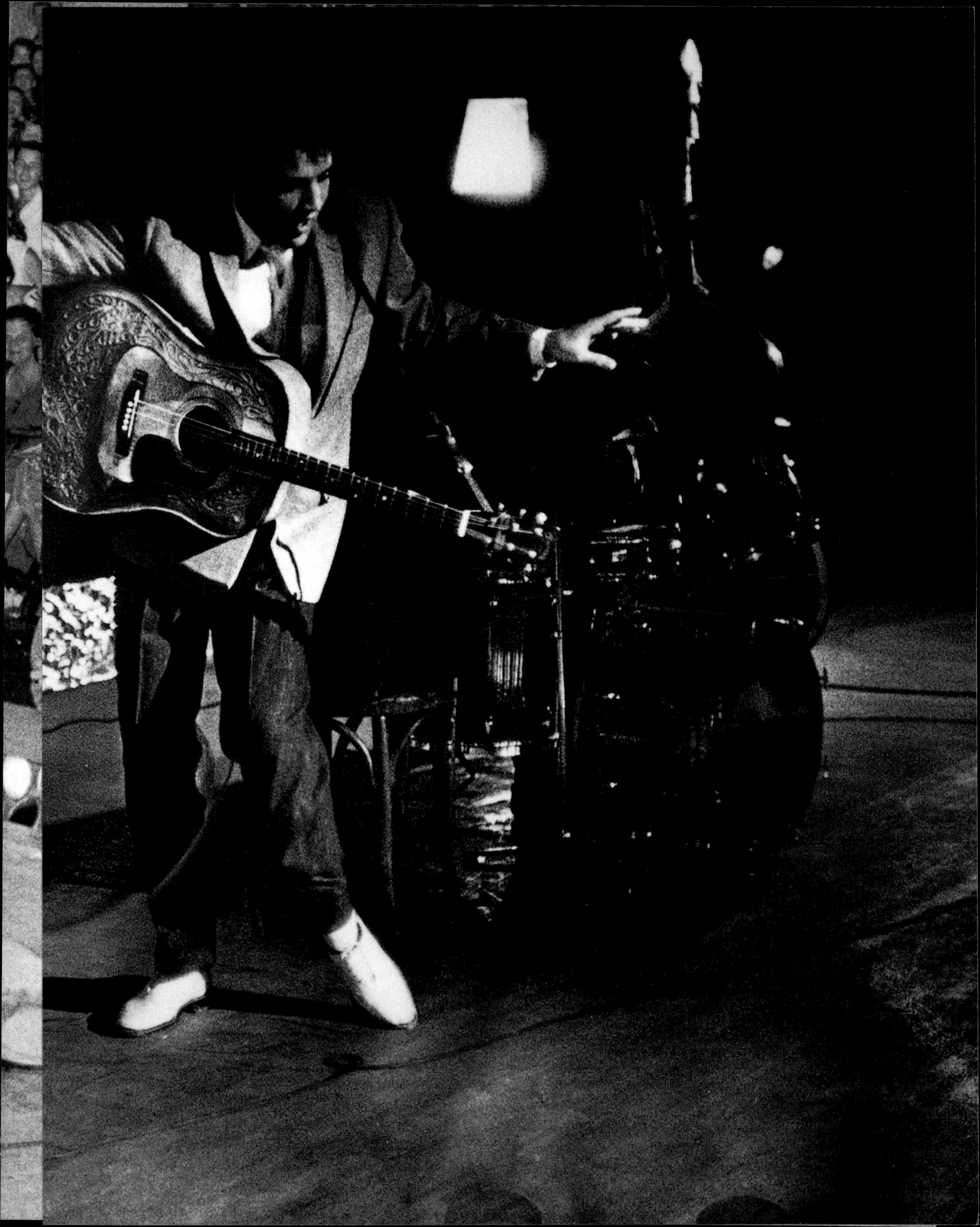

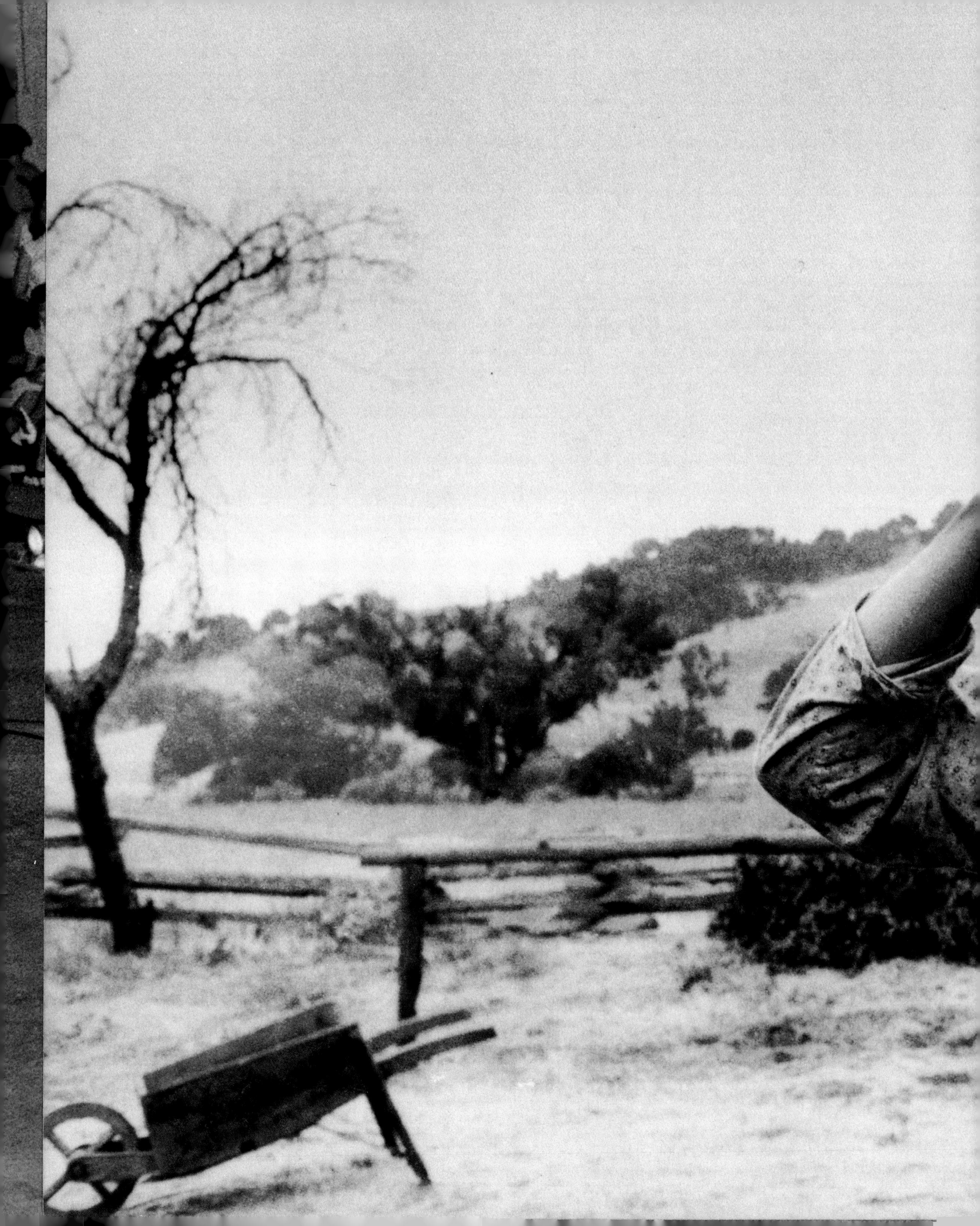

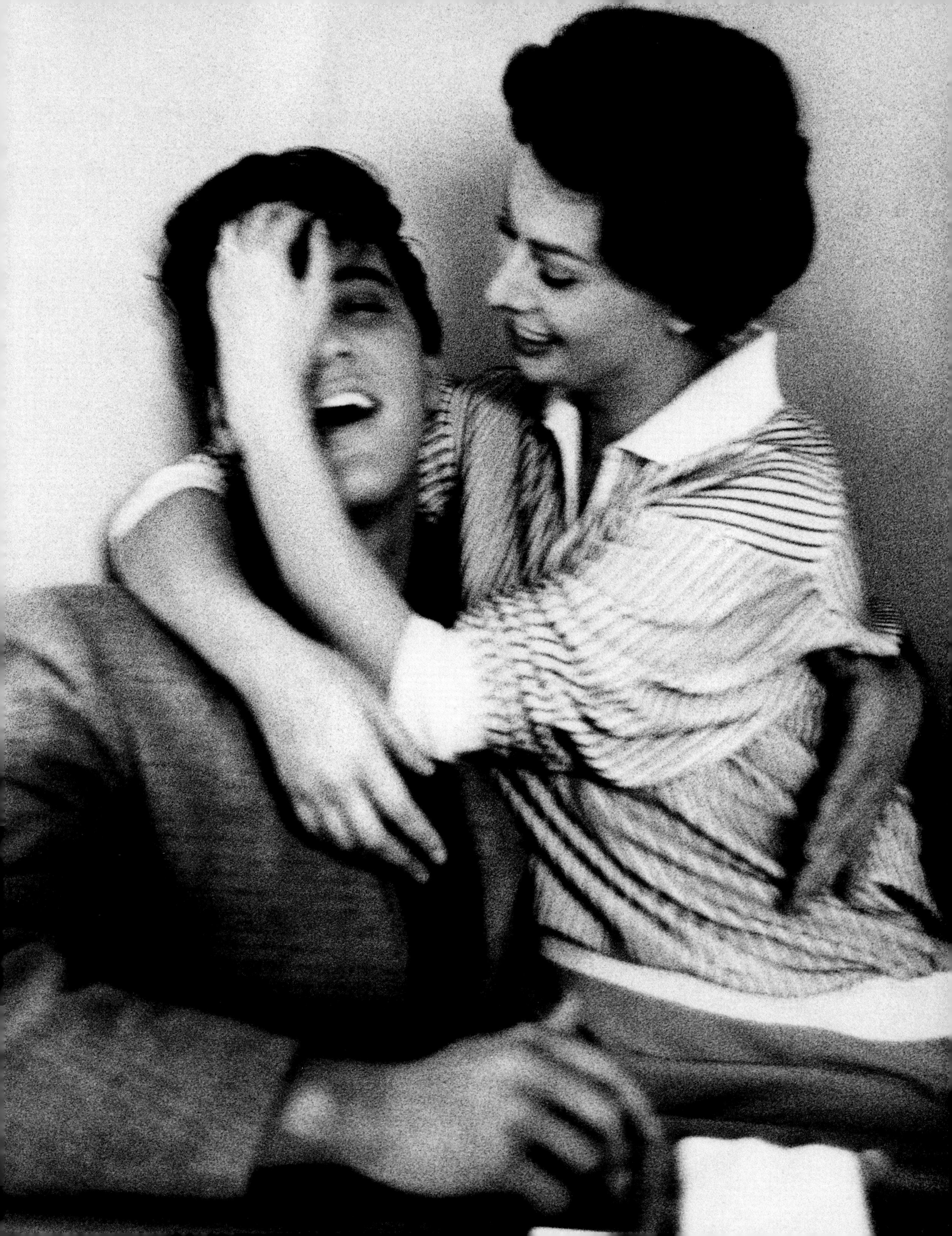

WILLIAM F. WARNECKE/CBS

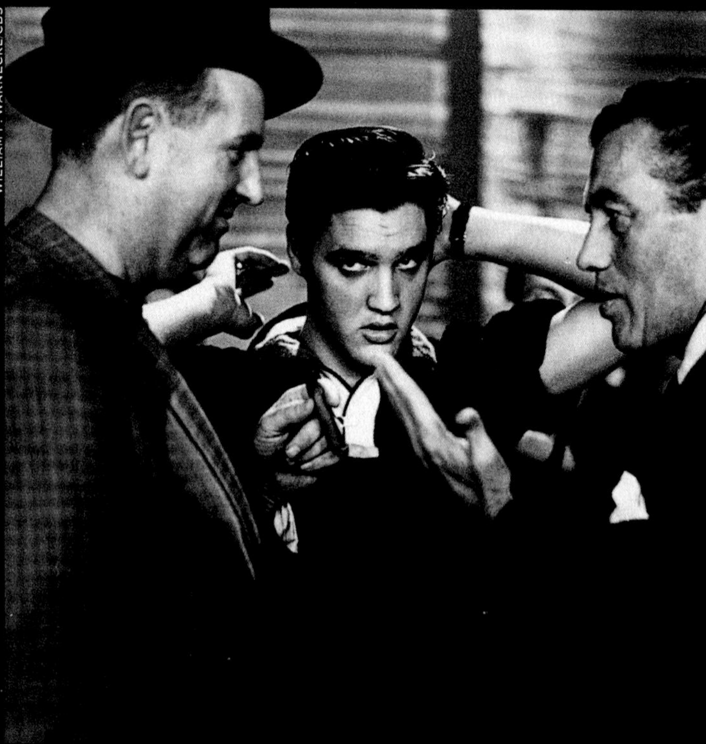

HE IS NOT MY CUP OF TEA," SAID ED SULLIVAN, AND INDEED IT IS HARD TO IMAGINE TWO SHOWMEN MORE UNALIKE THAN ELVIS AND ED. BUT WHEN THE PUBLIC DEMANDED IT, SULLIVAN OFFERED ELVIS A BOOKING ON HIS SHOW. COLONEL PARKER (LEFT, WITH THE STARS) STUNNED SULLIVAN BY DEMANDING A $50,000 FEE. THIS WAS 10 TIMES WHAT HAD BEEN OFFERED AND, IN FACT, MORE THAN ANYONE HAD EVER BEEN PAID FOR A TV APPEARANCE. STILL, SULLIVAN SWALLOWED HIS PRIDE AND SIGNED ELVIS FOR THREE SHOWS. GOOD MOVE: MORE THAN 80 PERCENT OF AMERICA TUNED IN TO THE FIRST PERFORMANCE. BY THE THIRD, SULLIVAN'S CONVERSION WAS COMPLETE. "THIS IS A REAL DECENT, FINE BOY," HE SAID. "WE'VE NEVER HAD A PLEASANTER EXPERIENCE WITH A BIG NAME."

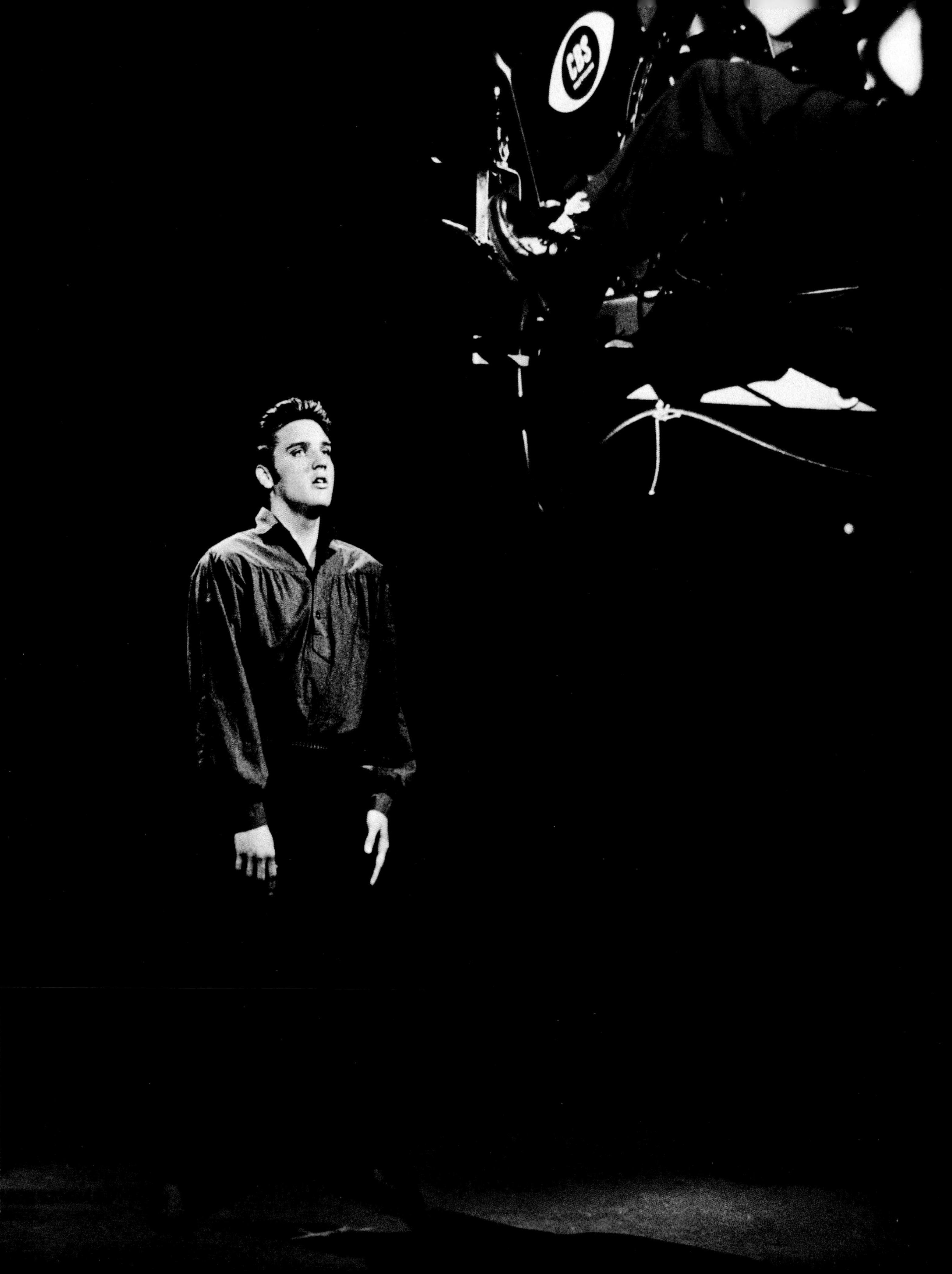
CBS

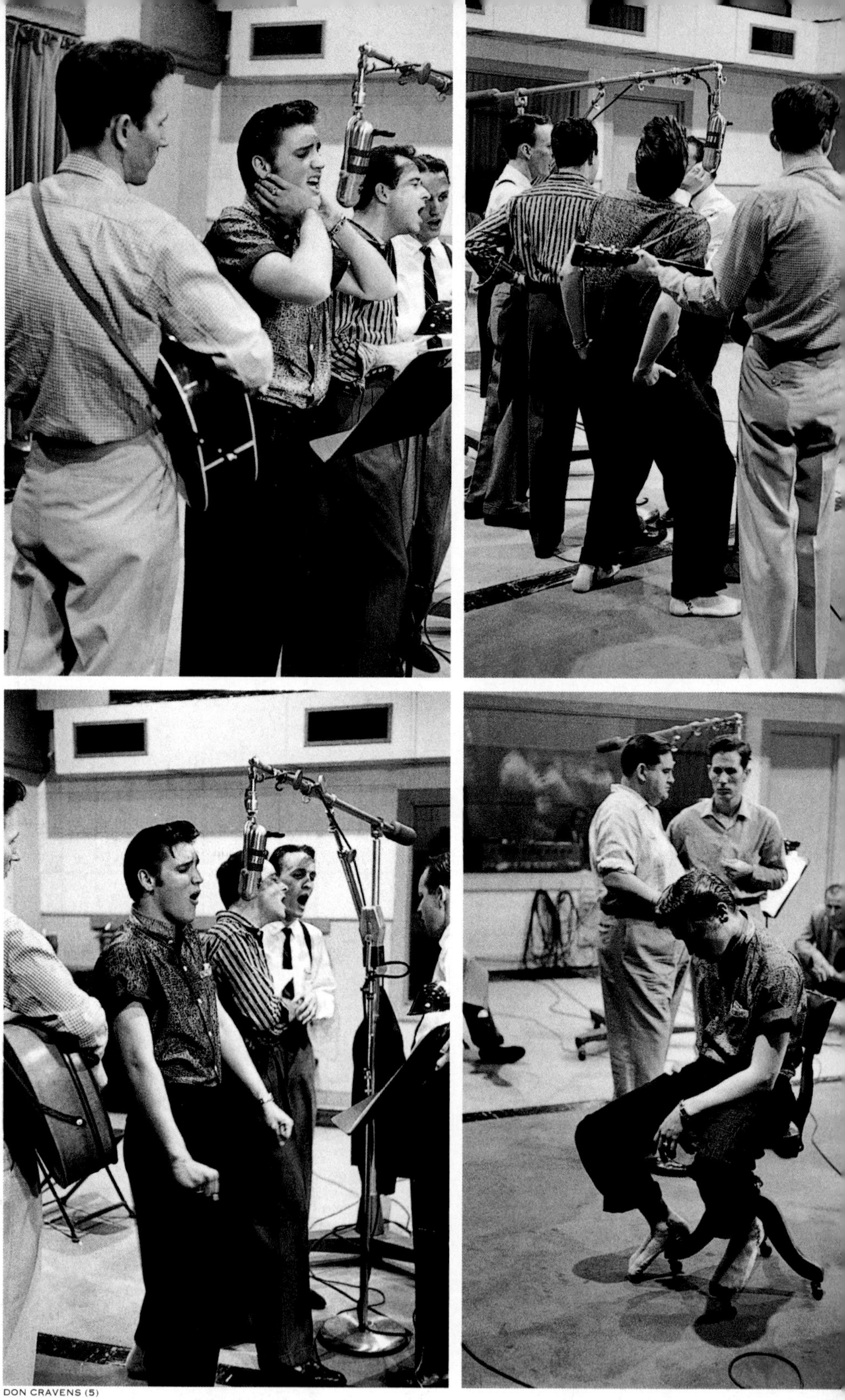

DON CRAVENS (5)

ELVIS CROONED (PROBABLY "I WANT YOU, I NEED YOU, I LOVE YOU") AND CONCENTRATED AT ONE OF HIS FIRST SESSIONS FOR RCA IN NASHVILLE. CHET ATKINS PLAYED GUITAR WHILE GORDON STOKER AND BEN AND BROCK SPEER ADDED BACKGROUND VOCALS. ELVIS WAS SHOELESS, ATKINS LATER SAID, BECAUSE "HE HAD SPLIT HIS PANTS AND HAD TO CHANGE 'EM. A RECEPTIONIST FOUND THE OLD ONES—THEY WERE PINK AND BLUE AND BLACK—AND ASKED, 'WHAT DO YOU WANT ME TO DO WITH THESE?' I SAID, 'YOU BETTER SAVE 'EM. HE'S GONNA BE THE BIGGEST THING EVER.' SHE KINDA TURNED UP HER NOSE. BUT TWO OR THREE MONTHS LATER SHE WAS TRYING TO GET ON *I'VE GOT A SECRET* BECAUSE SHE HAD ELVIS'S PANTS."

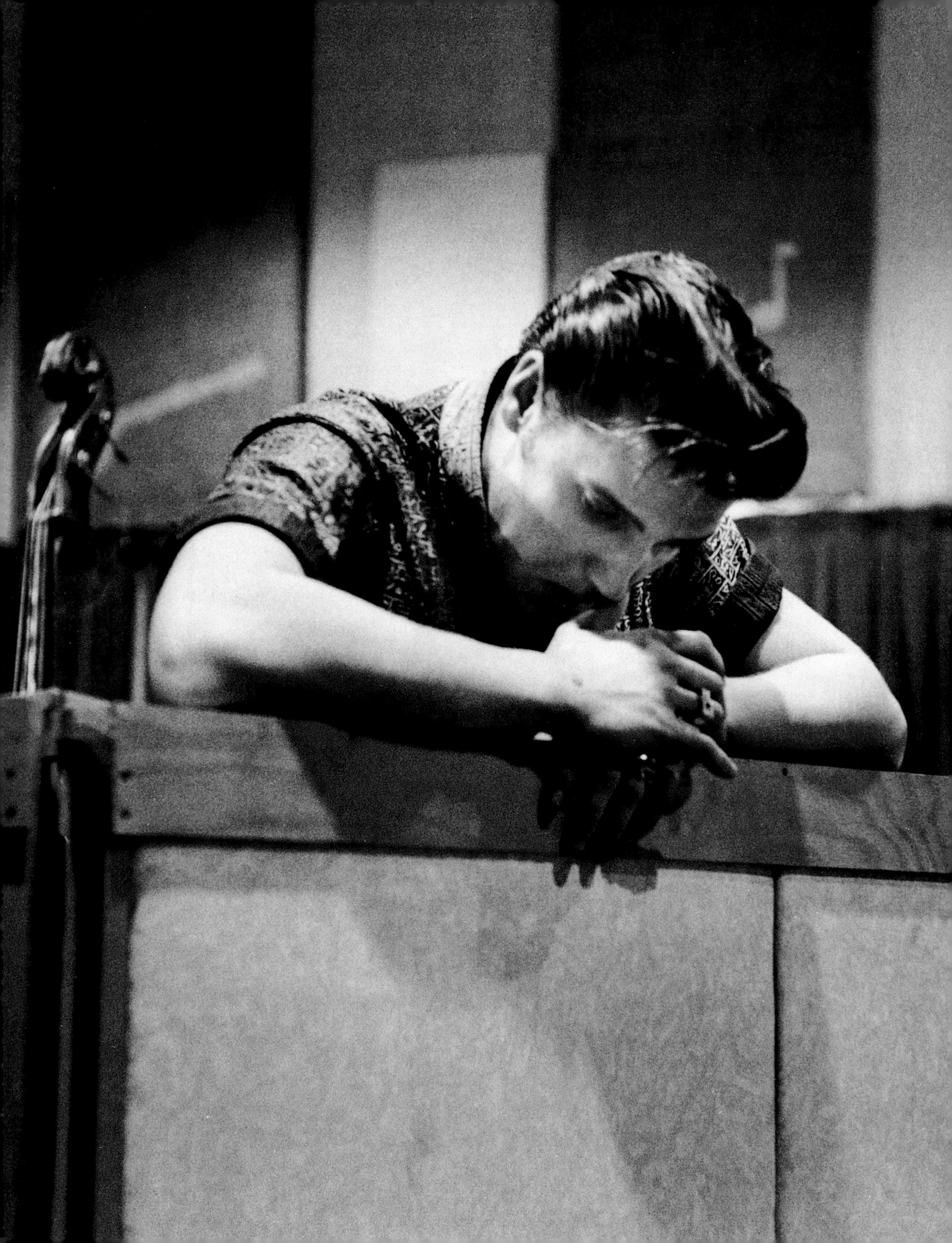

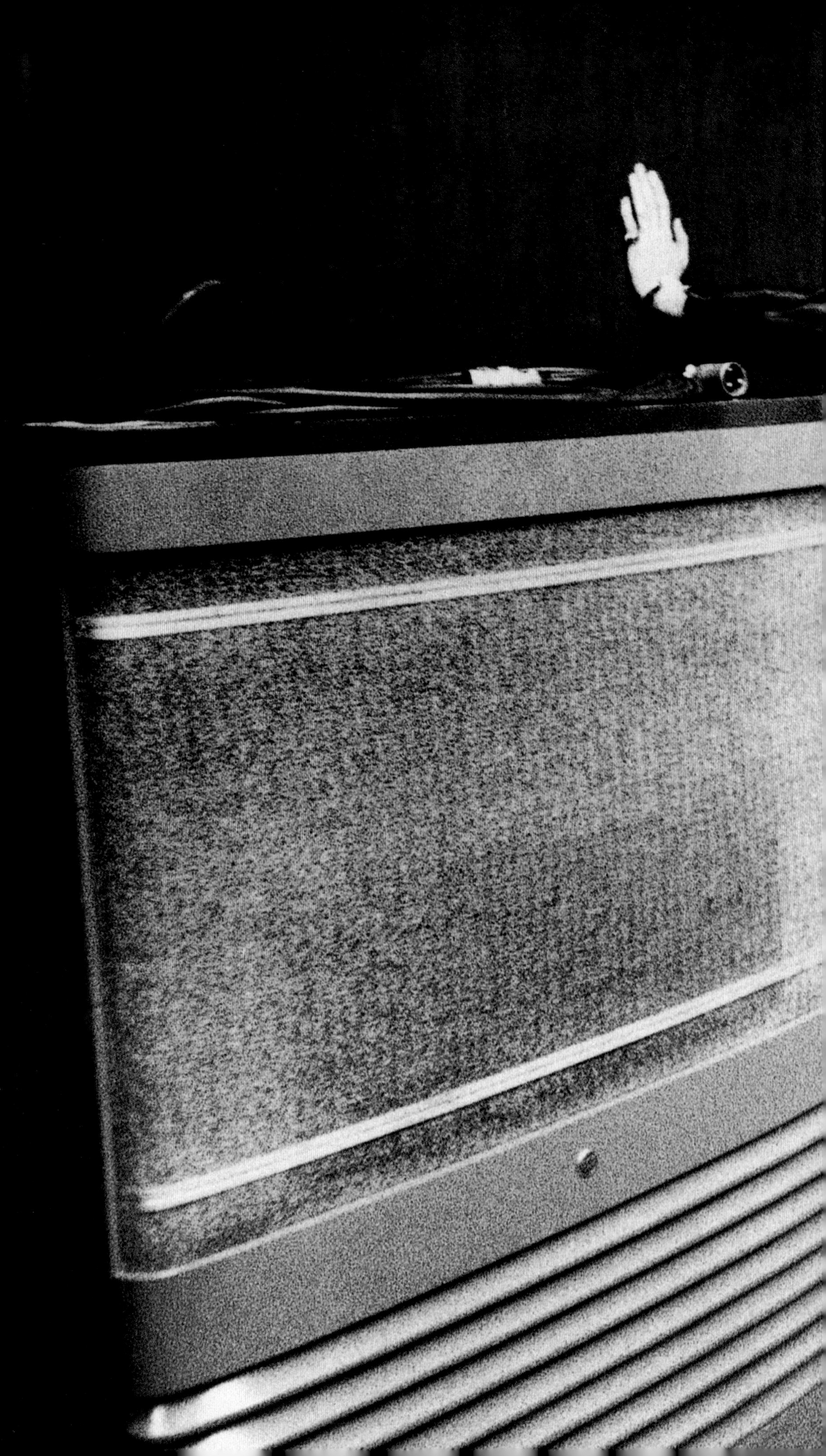

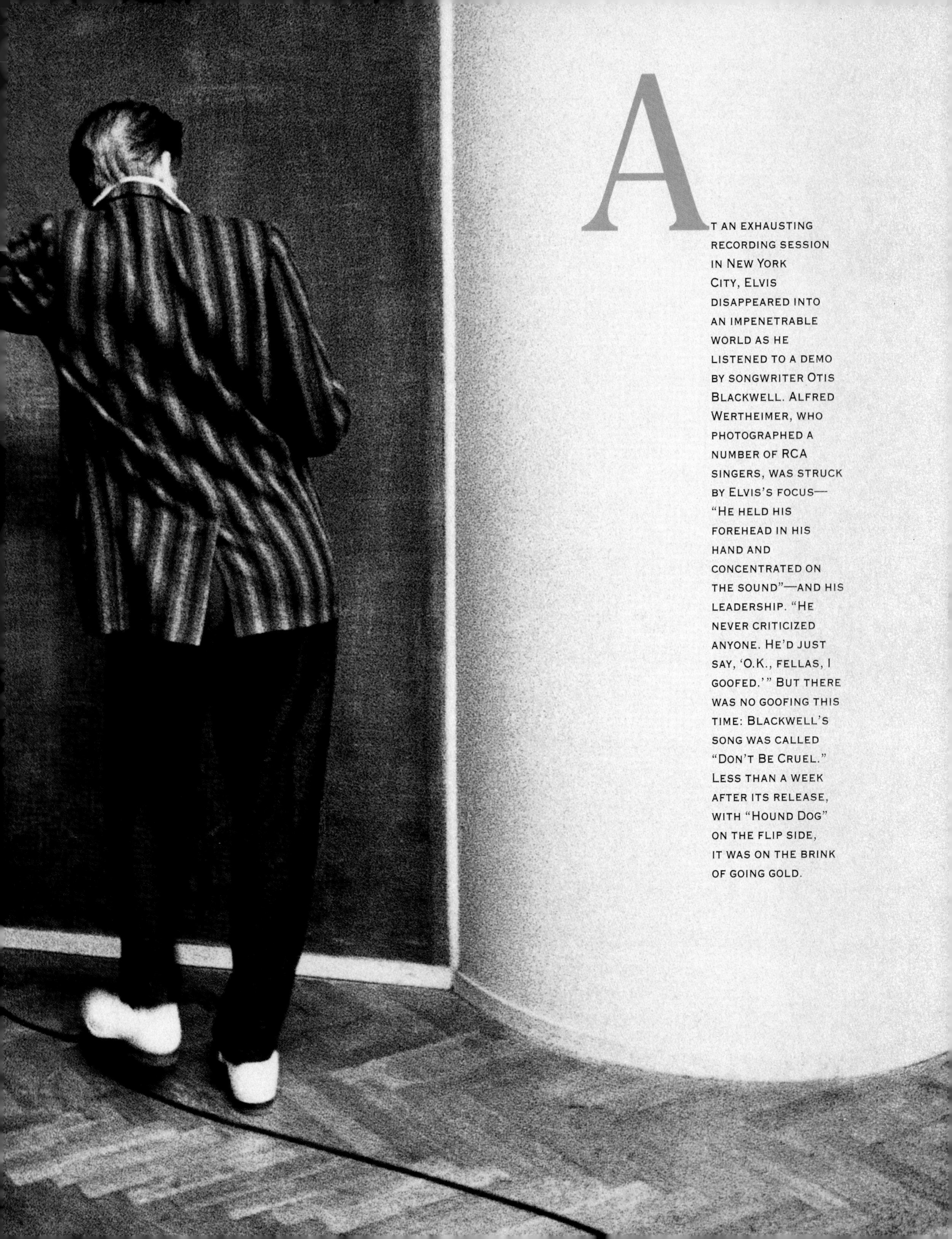

At an exhausting recording session in New York City, Elvis disappeared into an impenetrable world as he listened to a demo by songwriter Otis Blackwell. Alfred Wertheimer, who photographed a number of RCA singers, was struck by Elvis's focus—"He held his forehead in his hand and concentrated on the sound"—and his leadership. "He never criticized anyone. He'd just say, 'O.K., fellas, I goofed.'" But there was no goofing this time: Blackwell's song was called "Don't Be Cruel." Less than a week after its release, with "Hound Dog" on the flip side, it was on the brink of going gold.

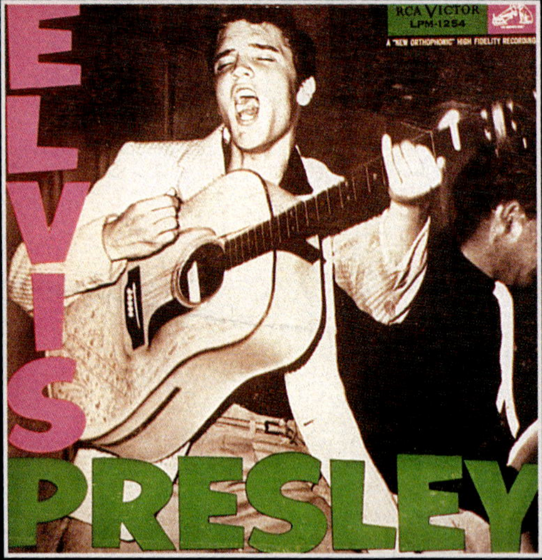
RCA VICTOR
LPM-1254
A "NEW ORTHOPHONIC" HIGH FIDELITY RECORDING
ELVIS
PRESLEY

1956

THE BETTER TO DISPLAY HIS COLLECTION OF GOLD AND PLATINUM RECORDS, HE BUILT AN 80-FOOT HALLWAY AT GRACELAND. NOWADAYS, TOUR GUIDES LOVE TO TELL VISITORS THAT MORE THAN A BILLION ELVIS RECORDINGS HAVE BEEN SOLD. LAID END TO END, THE GUIDES LIKE TO SAY, THESE WOULD CIRCLE THE EARTH TWICE. THIS NEVER FAILS TO AMAZE.

PICTURED HERE ARE THE COVERS OF ALL OF ELVIS'S ALBUMS— EXCEPT *GREATEST HITS* COLLECTIONS, BUDGET KNOCKOFFS AND OTHER REGURGITATIONS OF THESE ORIGINALS.

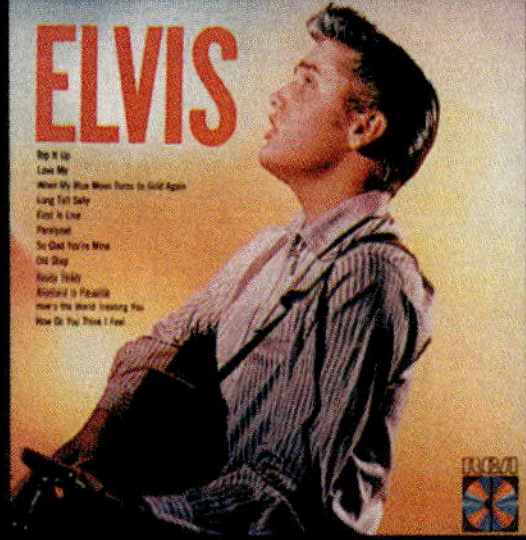

1957

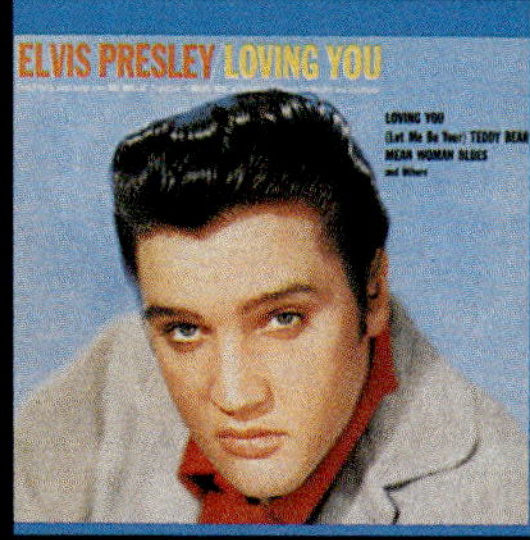

1957

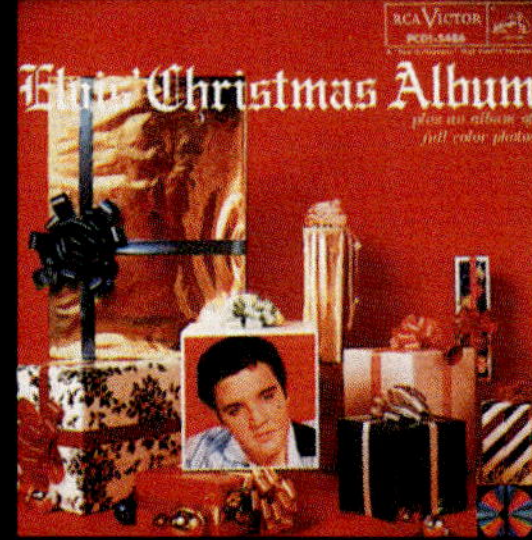

1957

IN 1957, WHEN SOME CONSIDERED CHRISTMAS AND ROCK POLAR OPPOSITES, *ELVIS' CHRISTMAS ALBUM* WAS BANNED BY MANY RADIO STATIONS. SINCE THEN, IT HAS SOLD MORE THAN THREE MILLION COPIES.

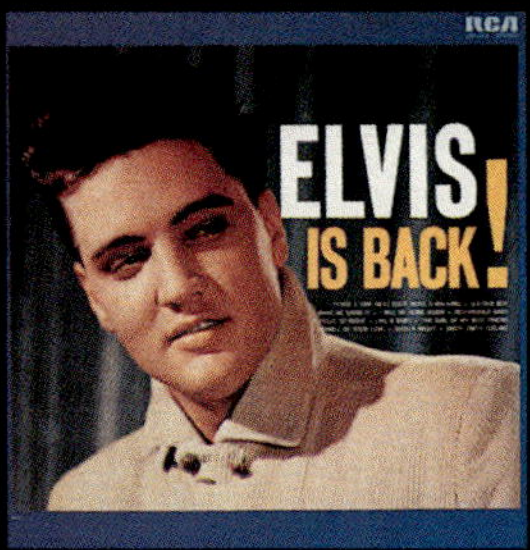

1960

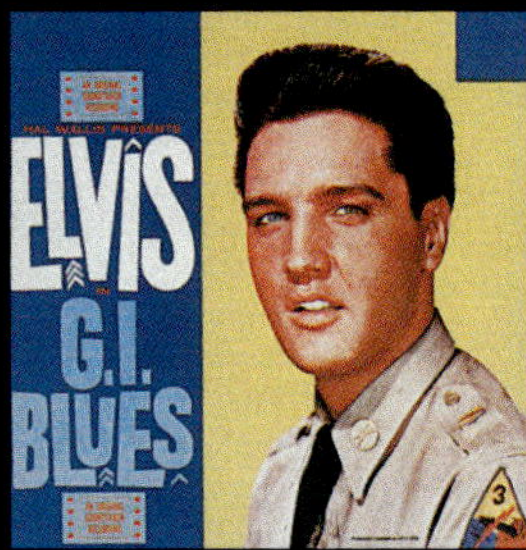

1960

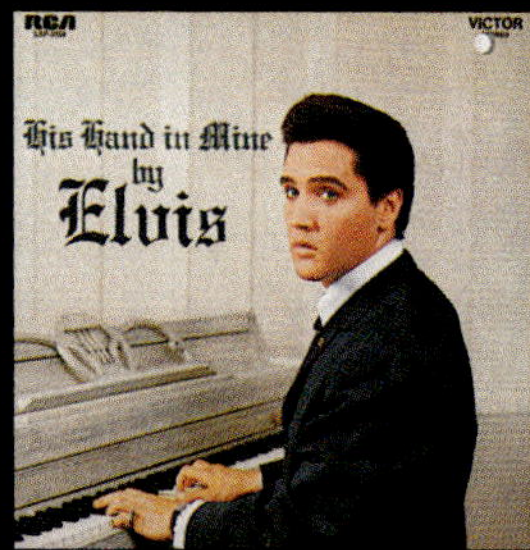

1960

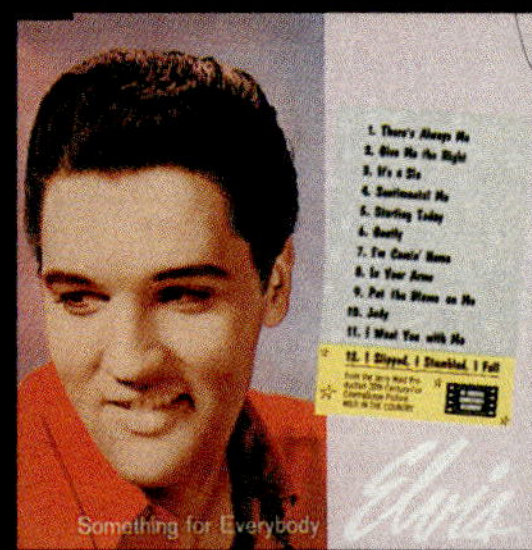

1961

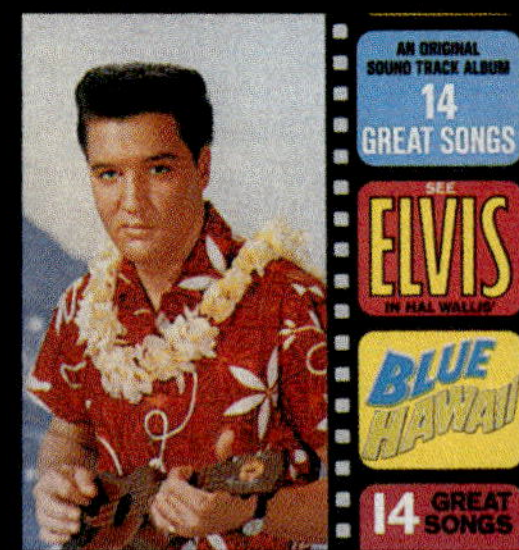

1961

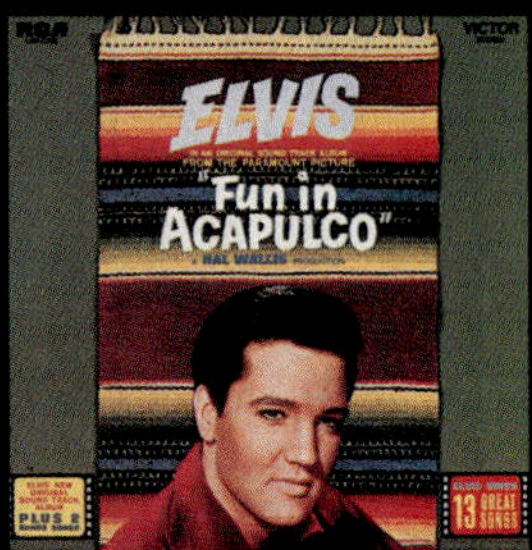

1963

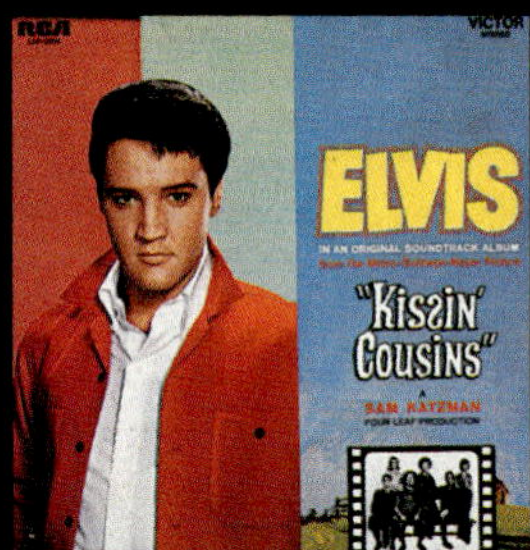

1964

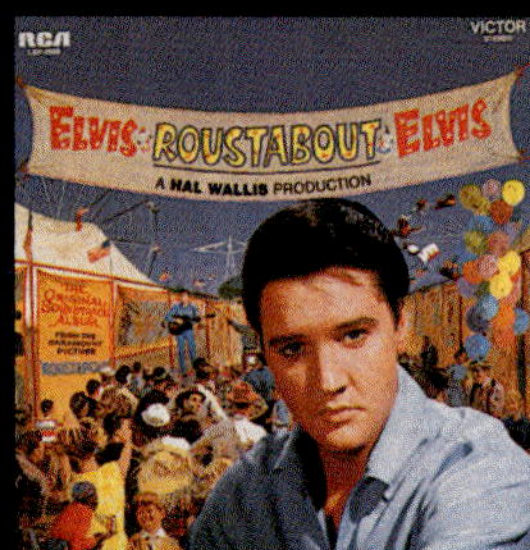

1964

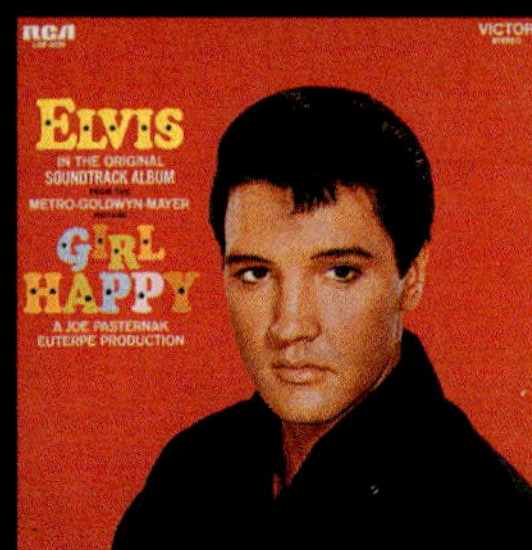

1965

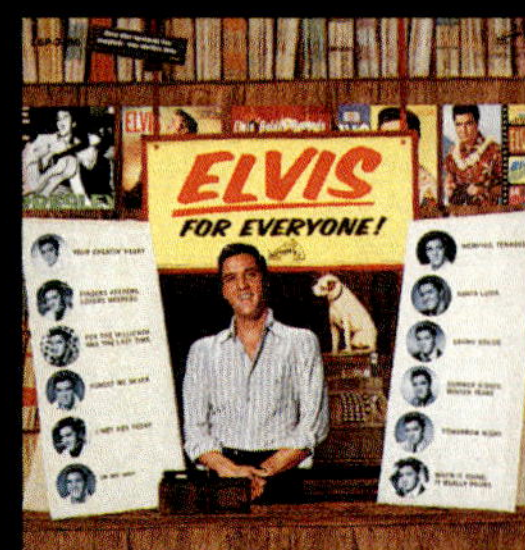

1965

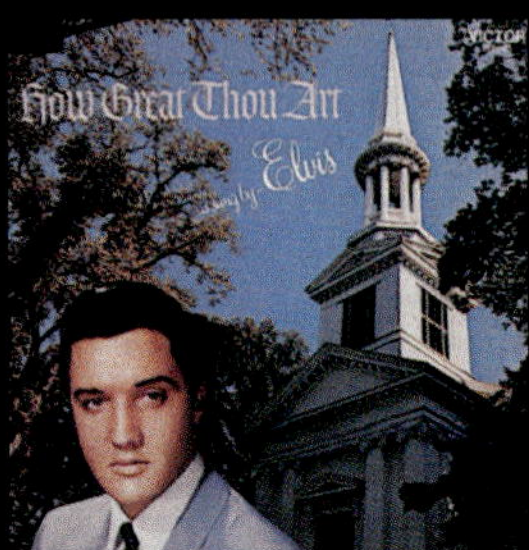

1967

ELVIS WON HIS FIRST GRAMMY FOR *HOW GREAT THOU ART* IN 1967. ALL THREE OF HIS GRAMMYS WERE FOR GOSPEL RECORDINGS.

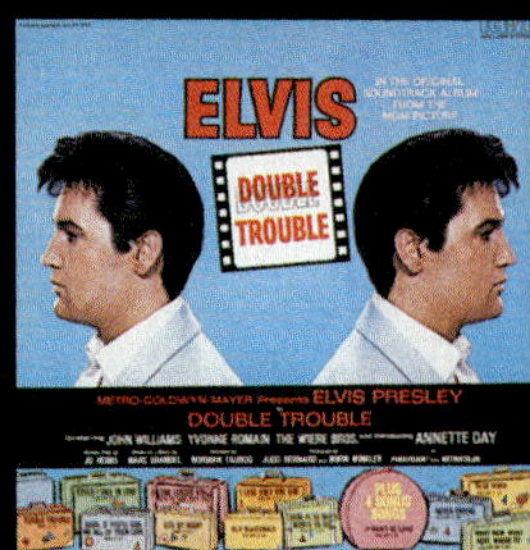

1967

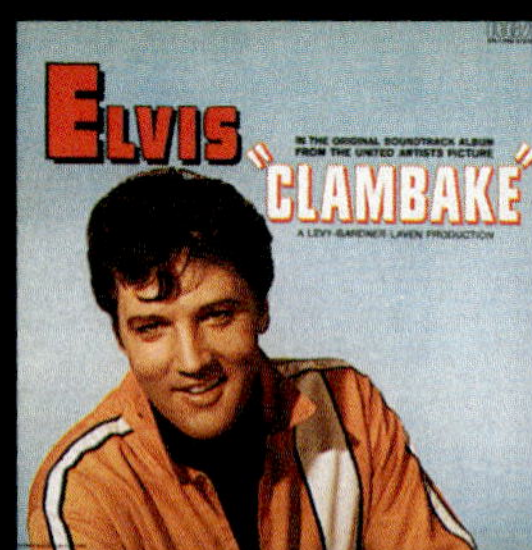

1968

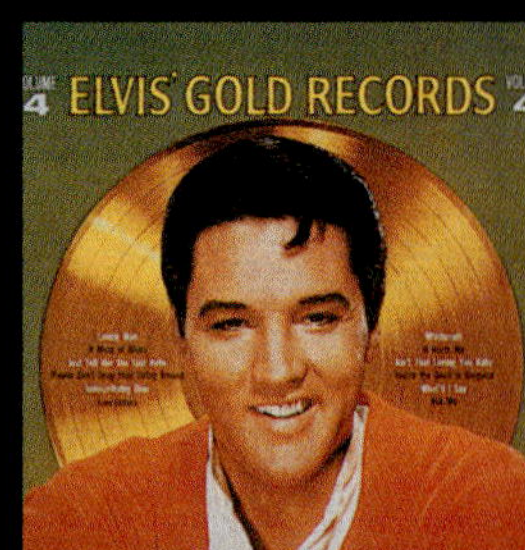

1968

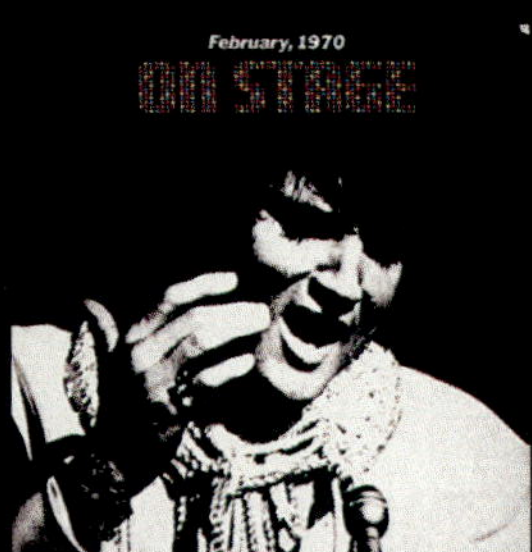

1970

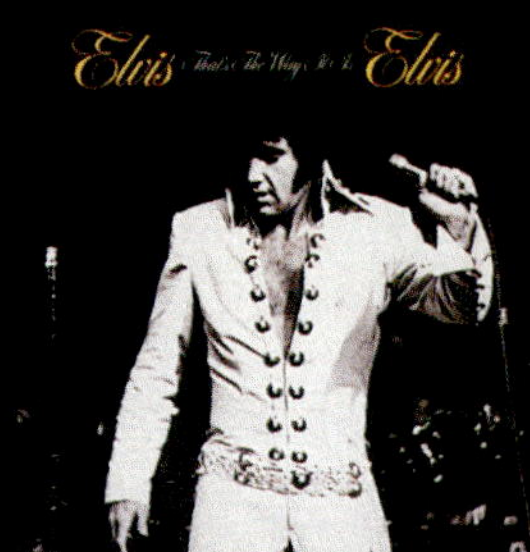

1970

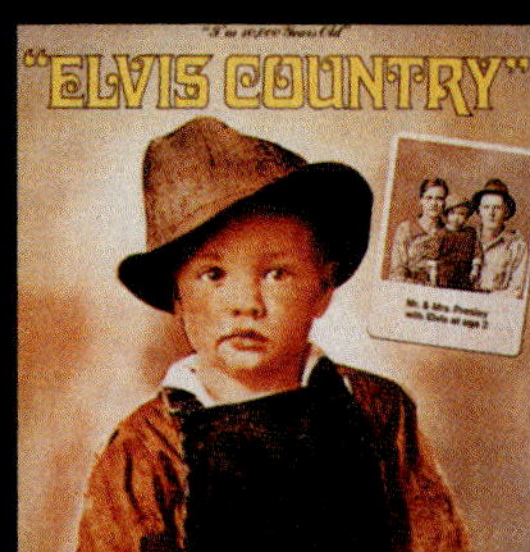

1971

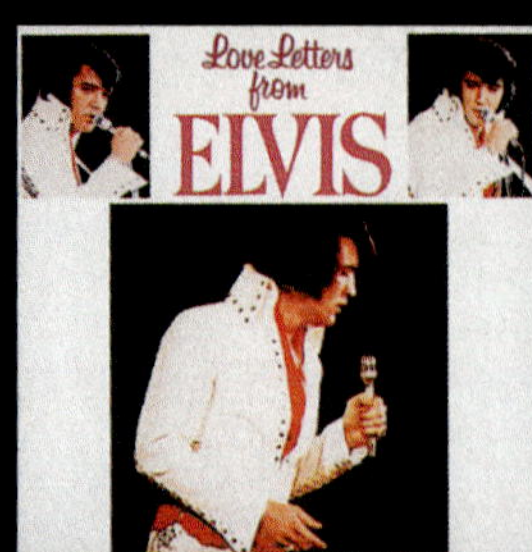

1971

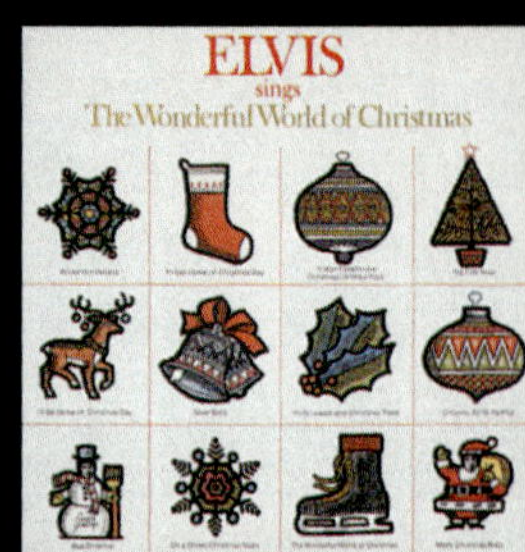

1971

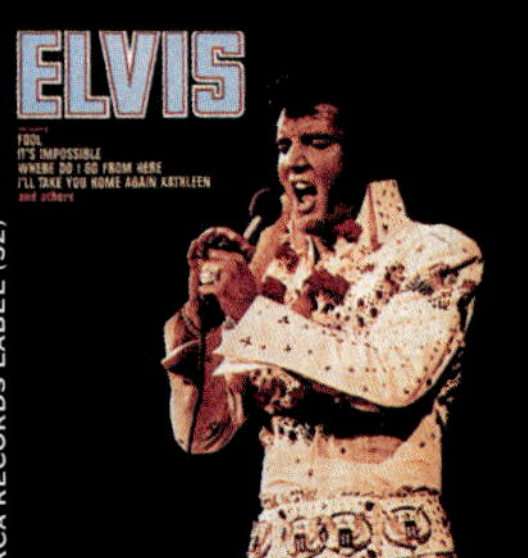

1973

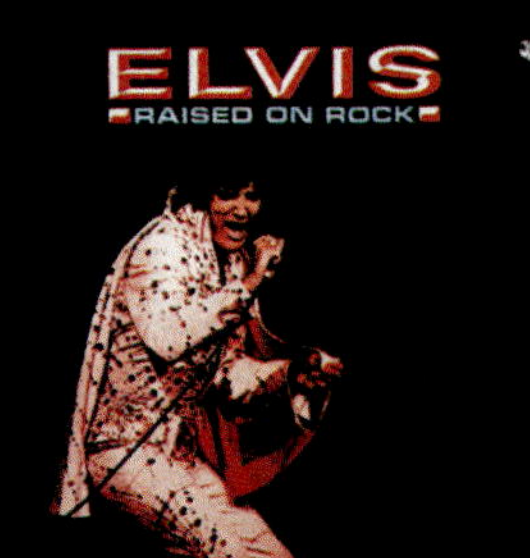

1973

ELVIS PRESLEY (PAGE 66) WAS RCA'S FIRST POP ALBUM CERTIFIED AS A GOLD RECORD BY THE RECORDING INDUSTRY ASSOCIATION OF AMERICA.

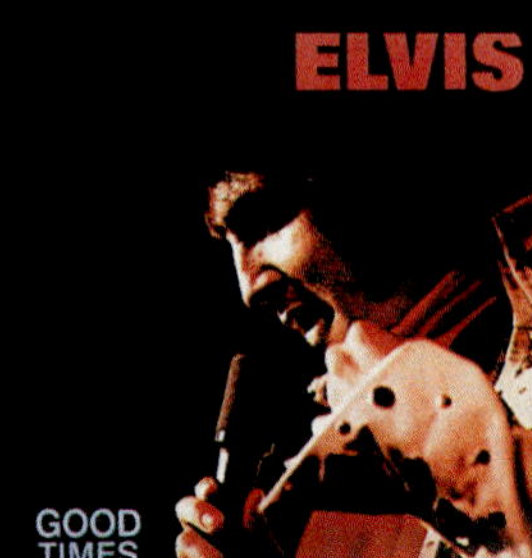

1974

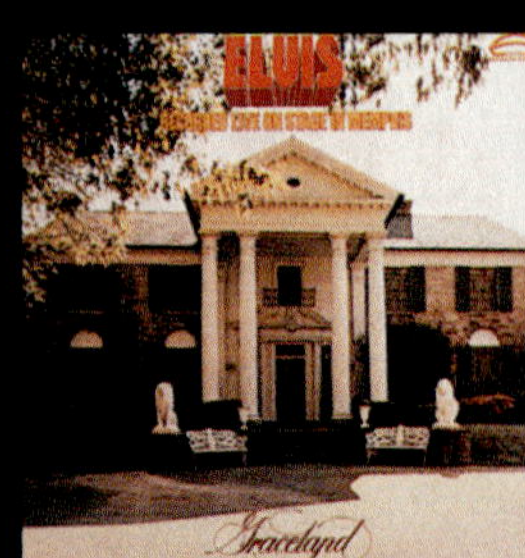

1974

RCA RECORDS LABEL (52)

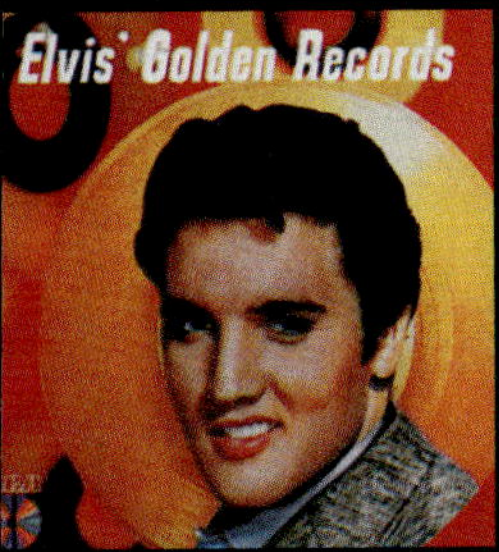

1958

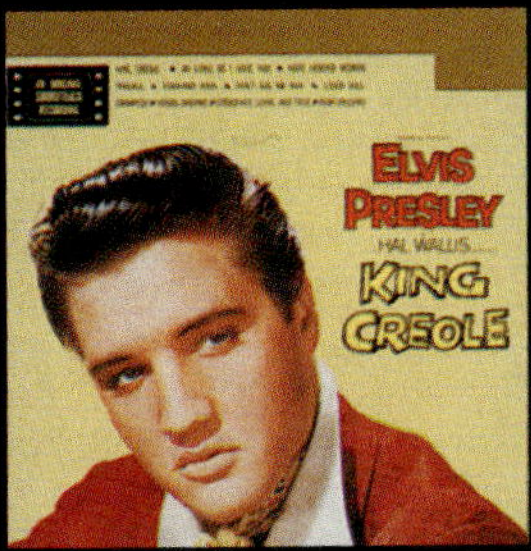

1958

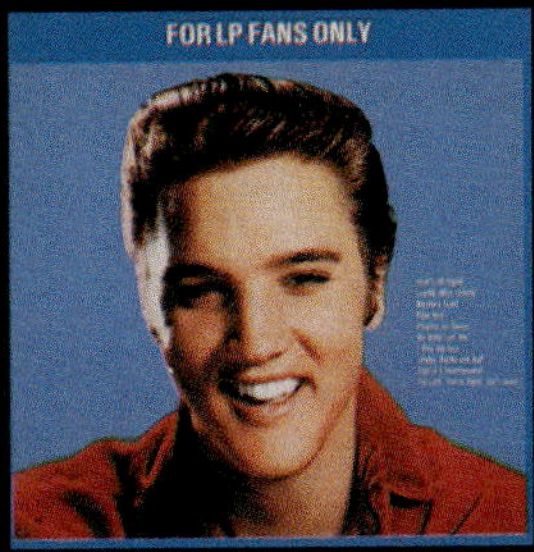

1959

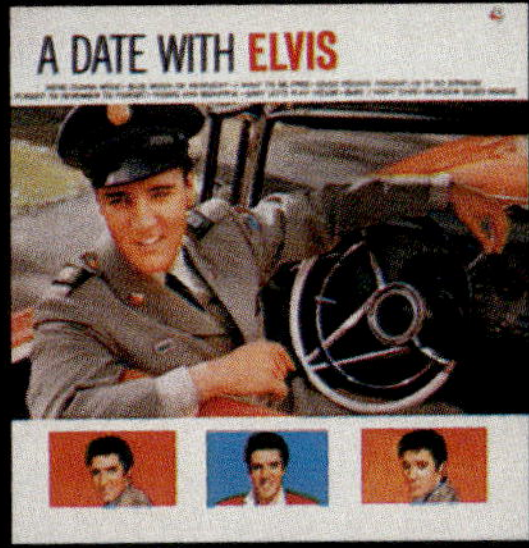

1959

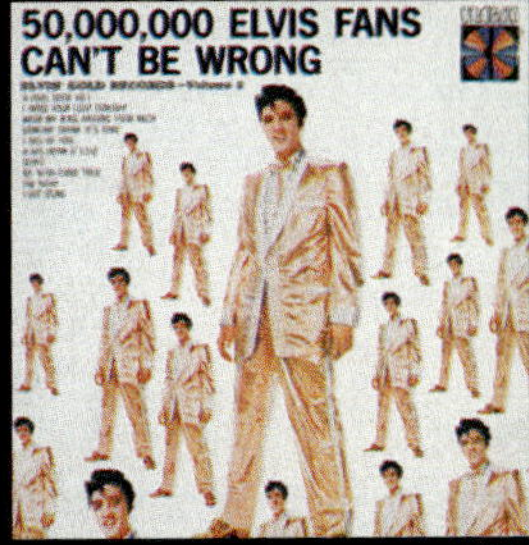

1959

JUST SIX MONTHS AFTER THE RELEASE OF *BLUE HAWAII*, IT HAD SOLD MORE COPIES THAN ANY PRESLEY ALBUM UP TO THAT TIME—TWO MILLION.

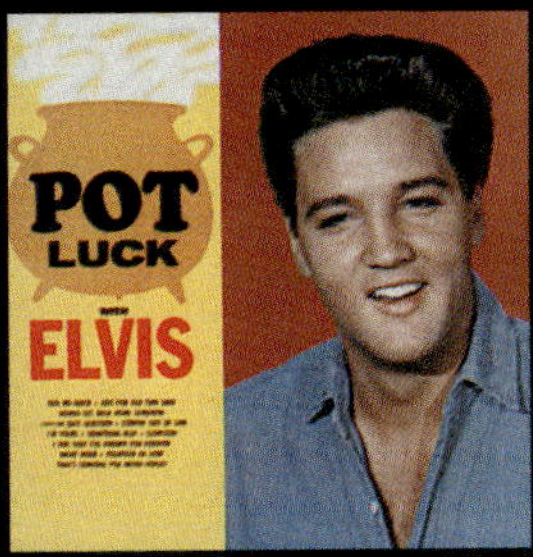

1962

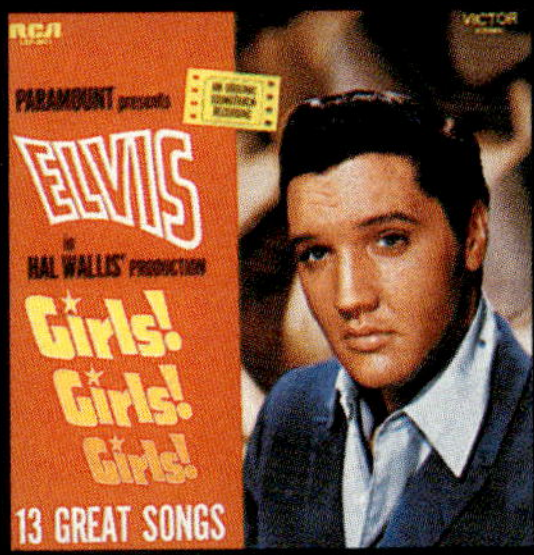

1962

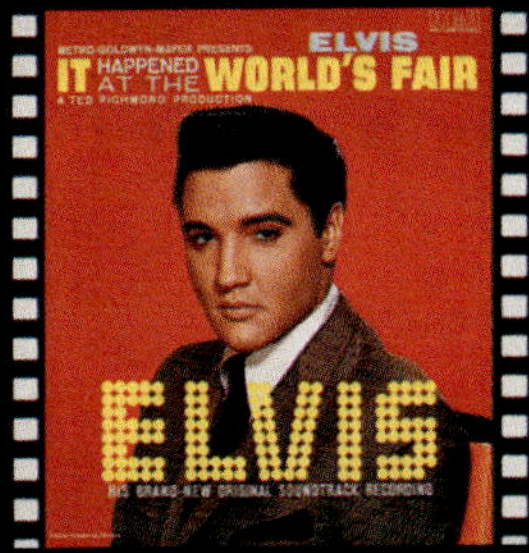

1963

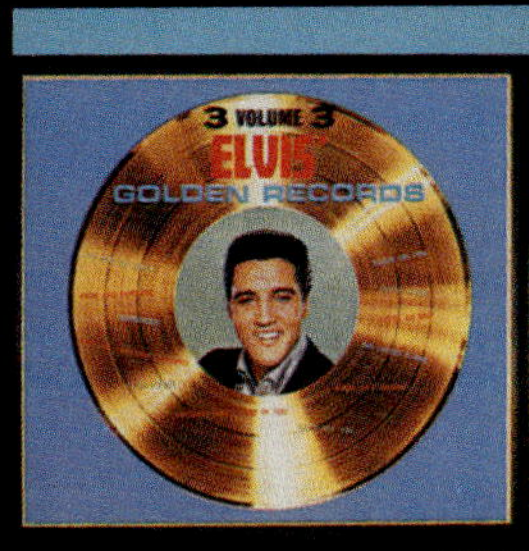

1963

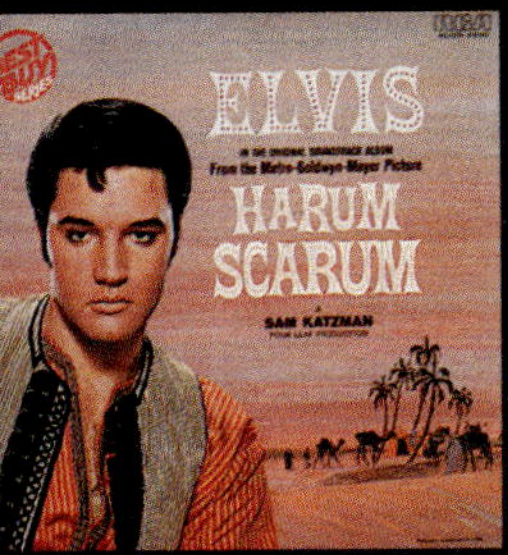

1965

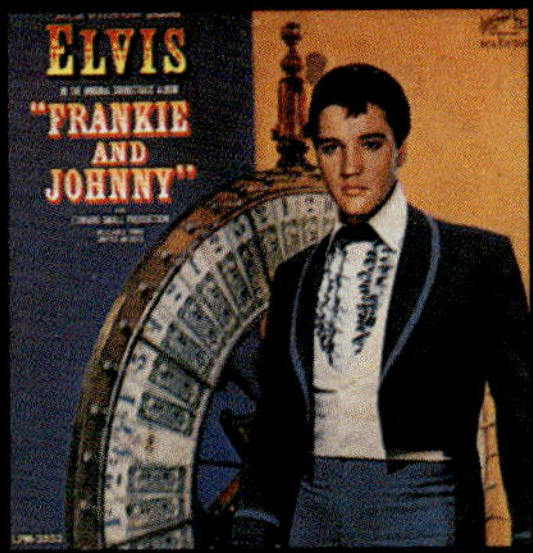

1966

SO FAR, ELVIS HAS 61 GOLD AND PLATINUM ALBUMS, MORE THAN ANY OTHER ARTIST. THE ROLLING STONES ARE SECOND WITH 34.

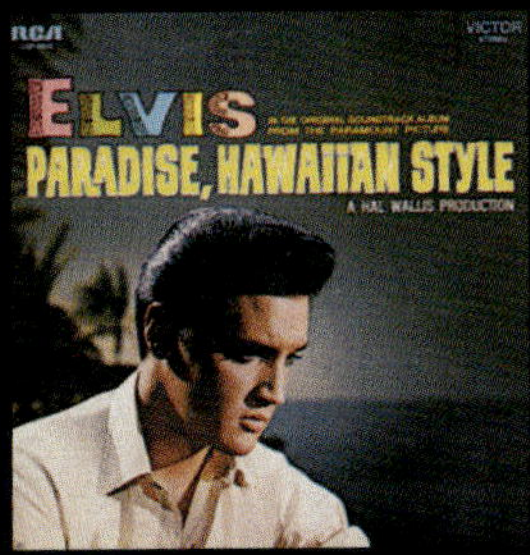

1966

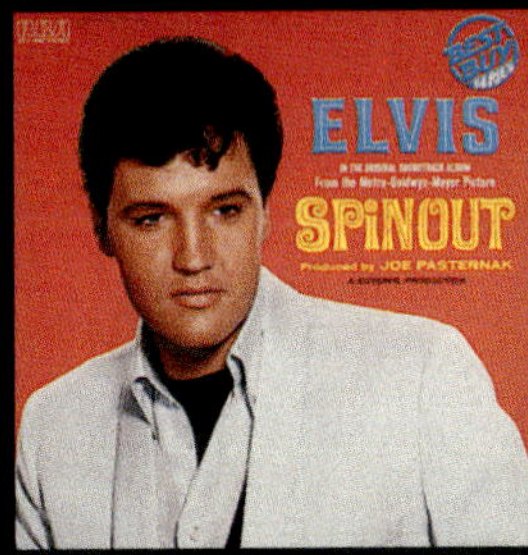

1966

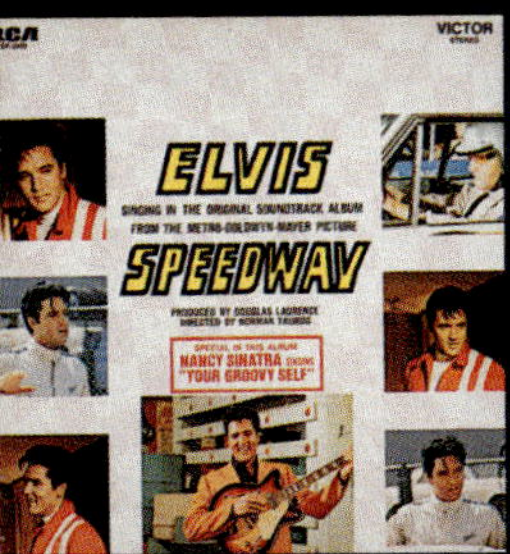

1968

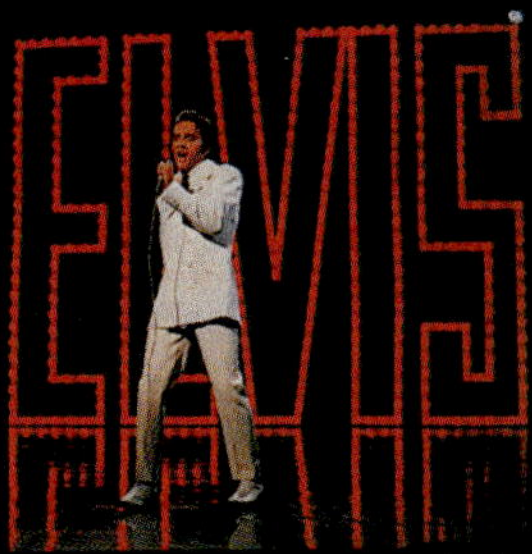

1968

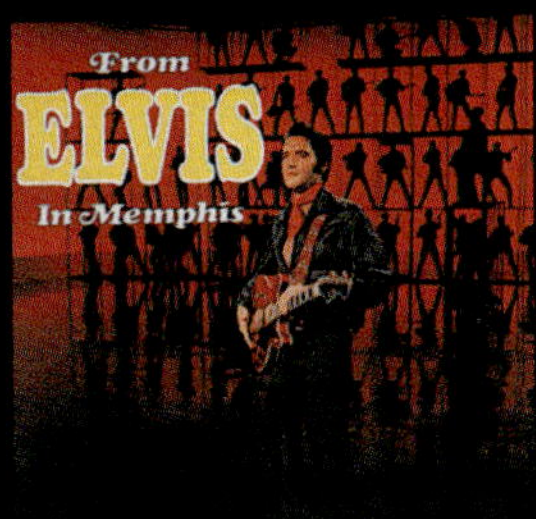

1969

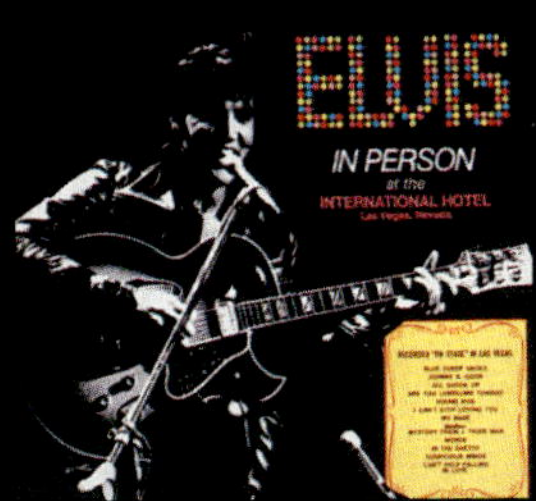

1969

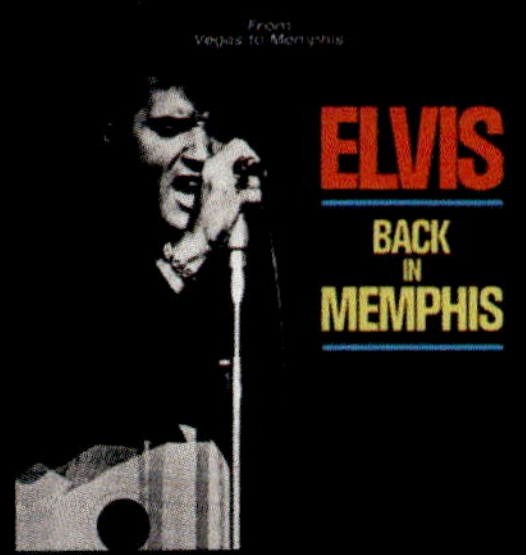

1969

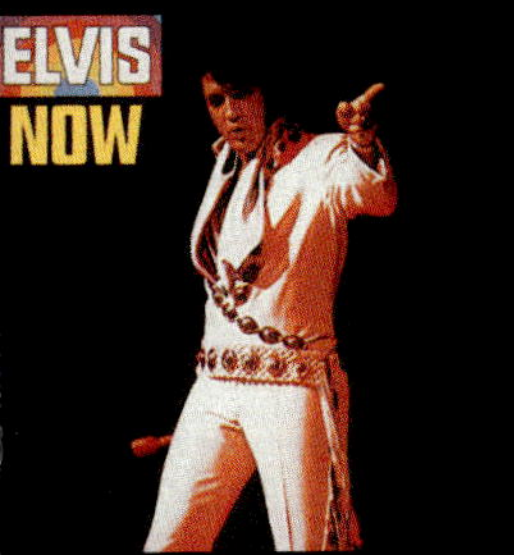

1972

IN THE FOUR MONTHS AFTER HIS DEATH, AN ESTIMATED 200 MILLION ELVIS RECORDS WERE SOLD WORLDWIDE.

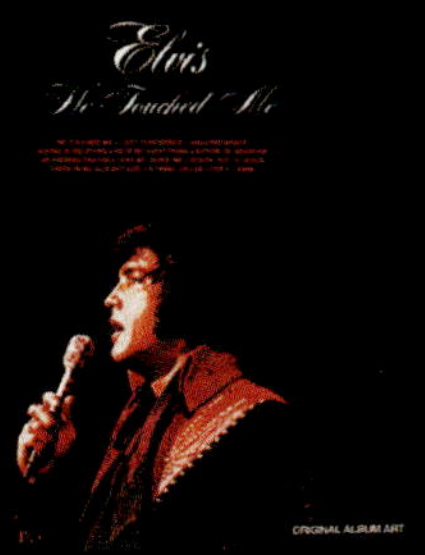

1972

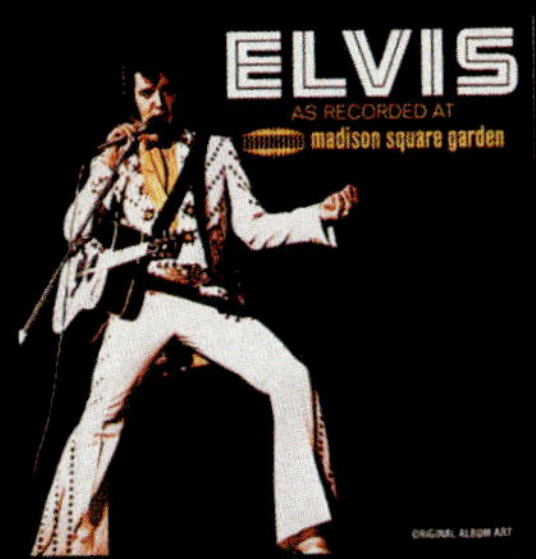

1972

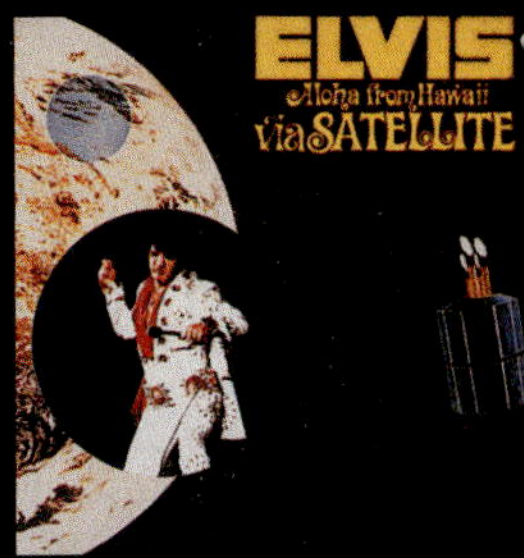

1973

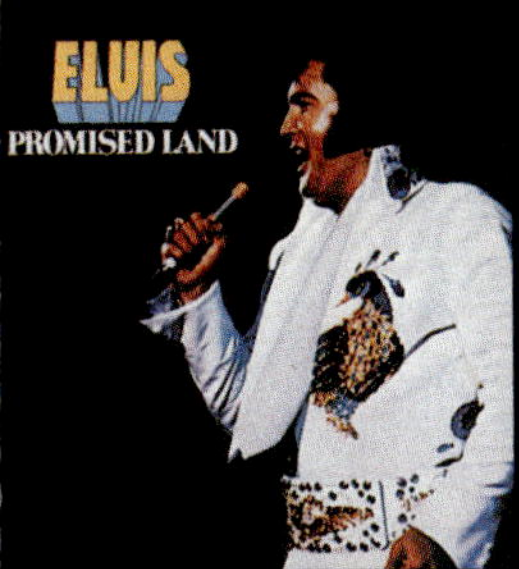

1975

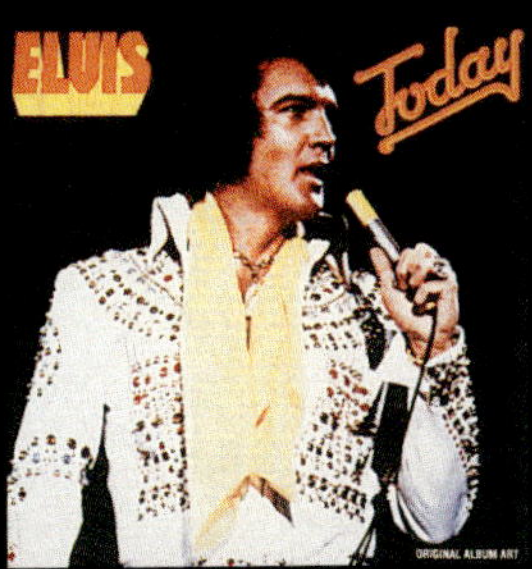

1975

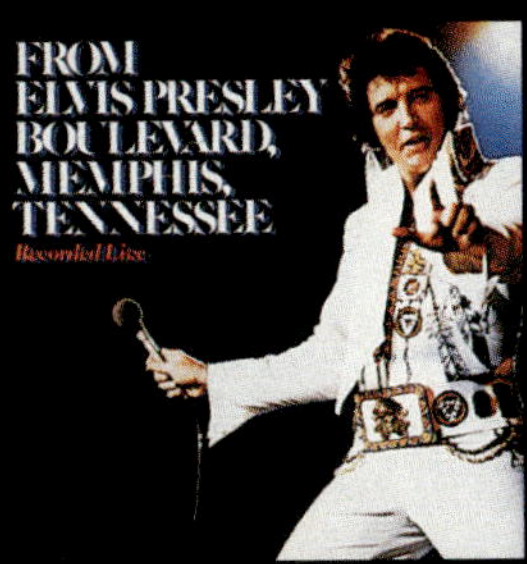

1976

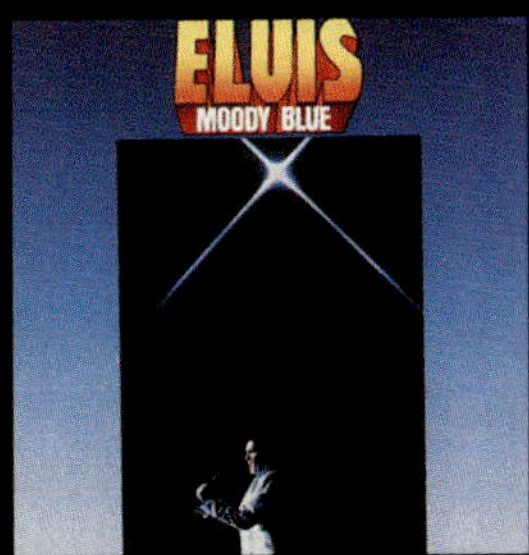

1977

ACCORDING TO *THE OFFICIAL PRICE GUIDE TO ELVIS PRESLEY RECORDS AND MEMORABILIA*, AN ORIGINAL COPY OF HIS FIRST LP, *ELVIS PRESLEY*, IS WORTH FROM $8 TO $300; HIS LAST, *MOODY BLUE*, $6 TO $3,500.

ROCKIN' THE ARMY

WHEN THE DRAFT NOTICE CAME, ALL HIS FRIENDS TRIED TO CHEER HIM UP. "ELVIS, THEY'LL NEVER TAKE YOU," CLIFF GLEAVES SAID. "YOU'RE TOO BIG." BUT IT WASN'T JUST UNCLE SAM WHO WANTED HIM TO GO. SO DID COLONEL PARKER. THE DRAFT WAS A FREE PUBLIC-RELATIONS BONANZA. WHEN THE ARMY OFFERED ELVIS A PERFORMER'S POST IN SPECIAL SERVICES, THE COLONEL WOULD HAVE NONE OF IT. "IF THEY WANT MY BOY TO SING," HE SAID, "THEY ARE GOING TO HAVE TO PAY FOR IT LIKE ANYONE ELSE." ELVIS'S

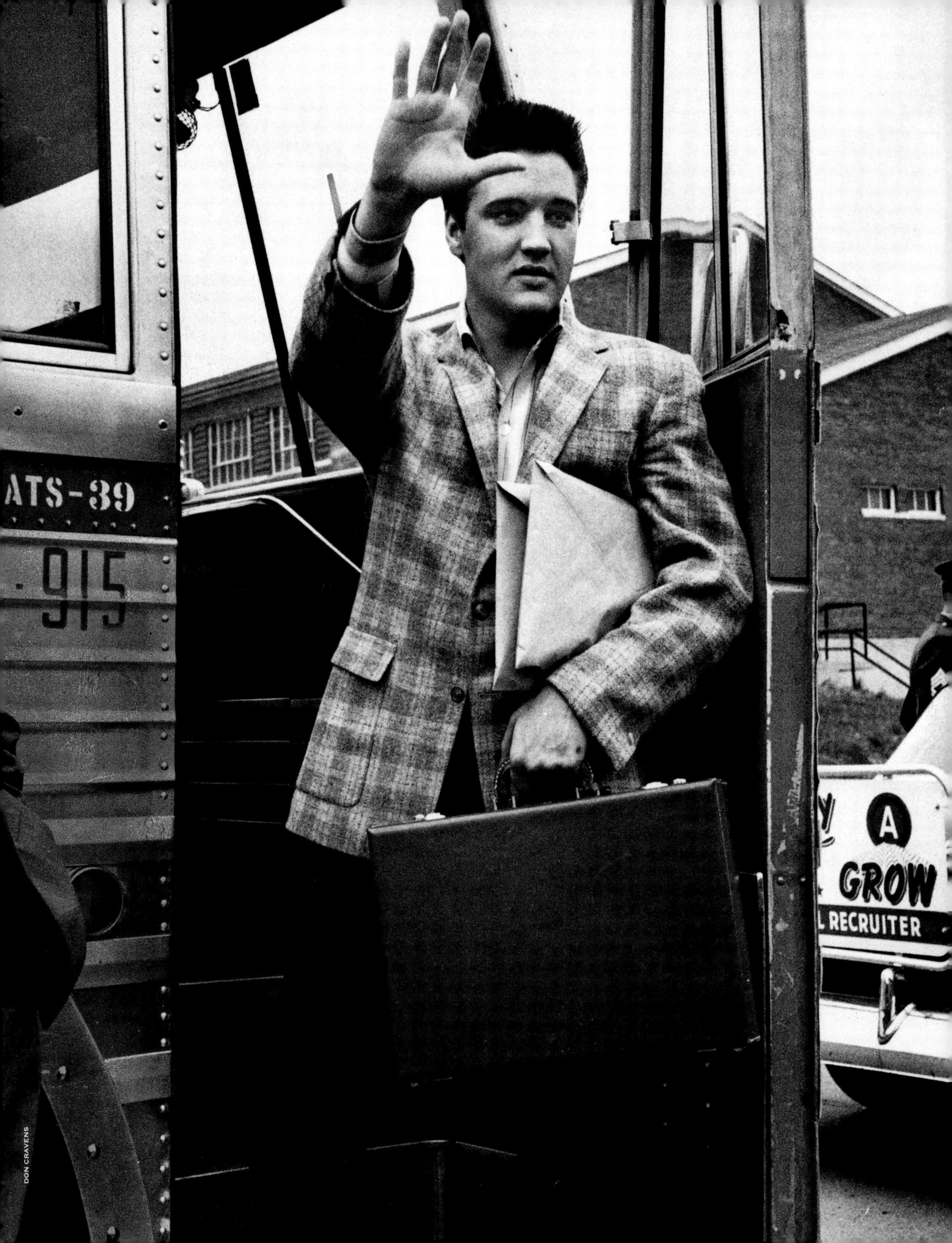

DON CRAVENS

Why me?" he had wept in the lap of his old friend Barbara Pittman a few days before reporting for induction in March of 1958. He saw no reason to believe there would be anything left of his career when his two years of GI blues were done. Worse, his mother, Gladys (top left, weeping), whom he loved above all else, was suffering mightily from hepatitis, and he couldn't bear to leave her. For three days, a media parade with Colonel Tom as Grand Marshall followed Elvis through the induction process (bottom left: Parker breakfasting with Elvis shortly before his trip to the Army barber). The press had always made much of Elvis's hair (*Time* reported that it swam with "sweat and goose grease"), and flashbulbs popped like mad during his shearing. "I know a lot of people who would pay a lot of money for that hair!" the colonel crowed.

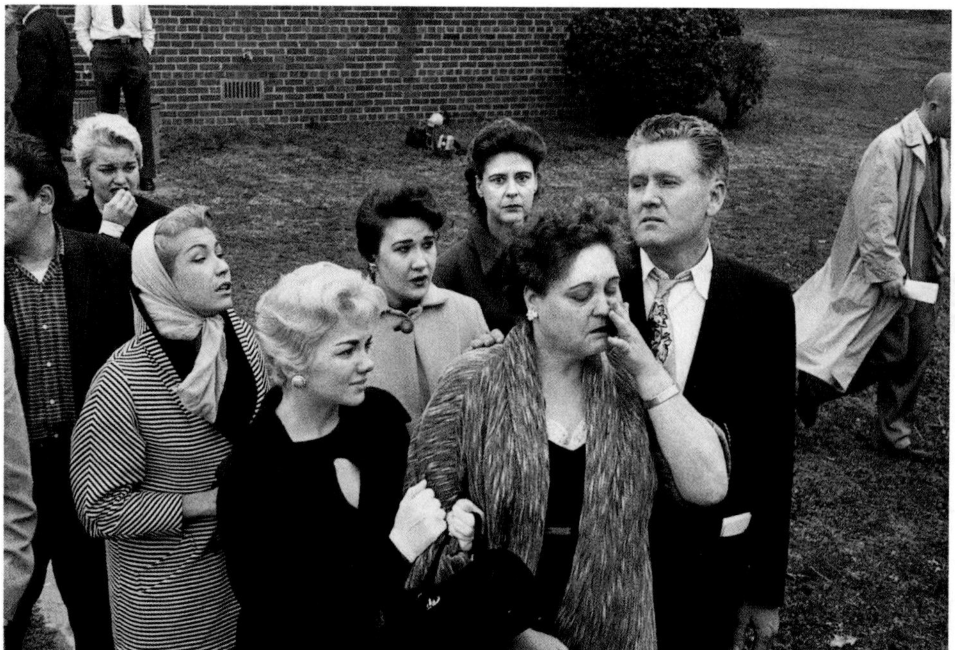

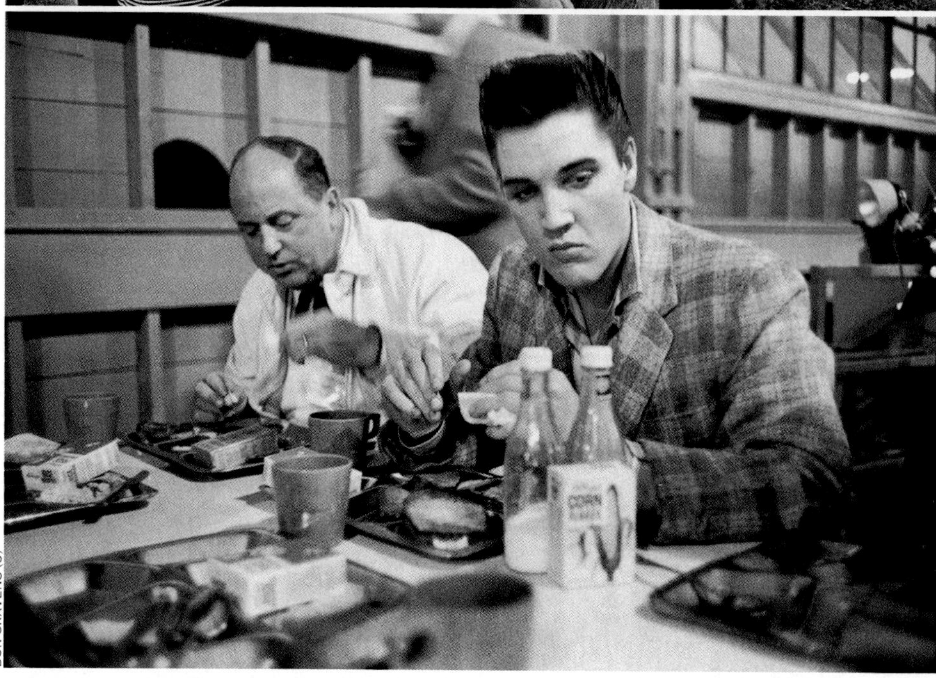

DON CRAVENS (3)

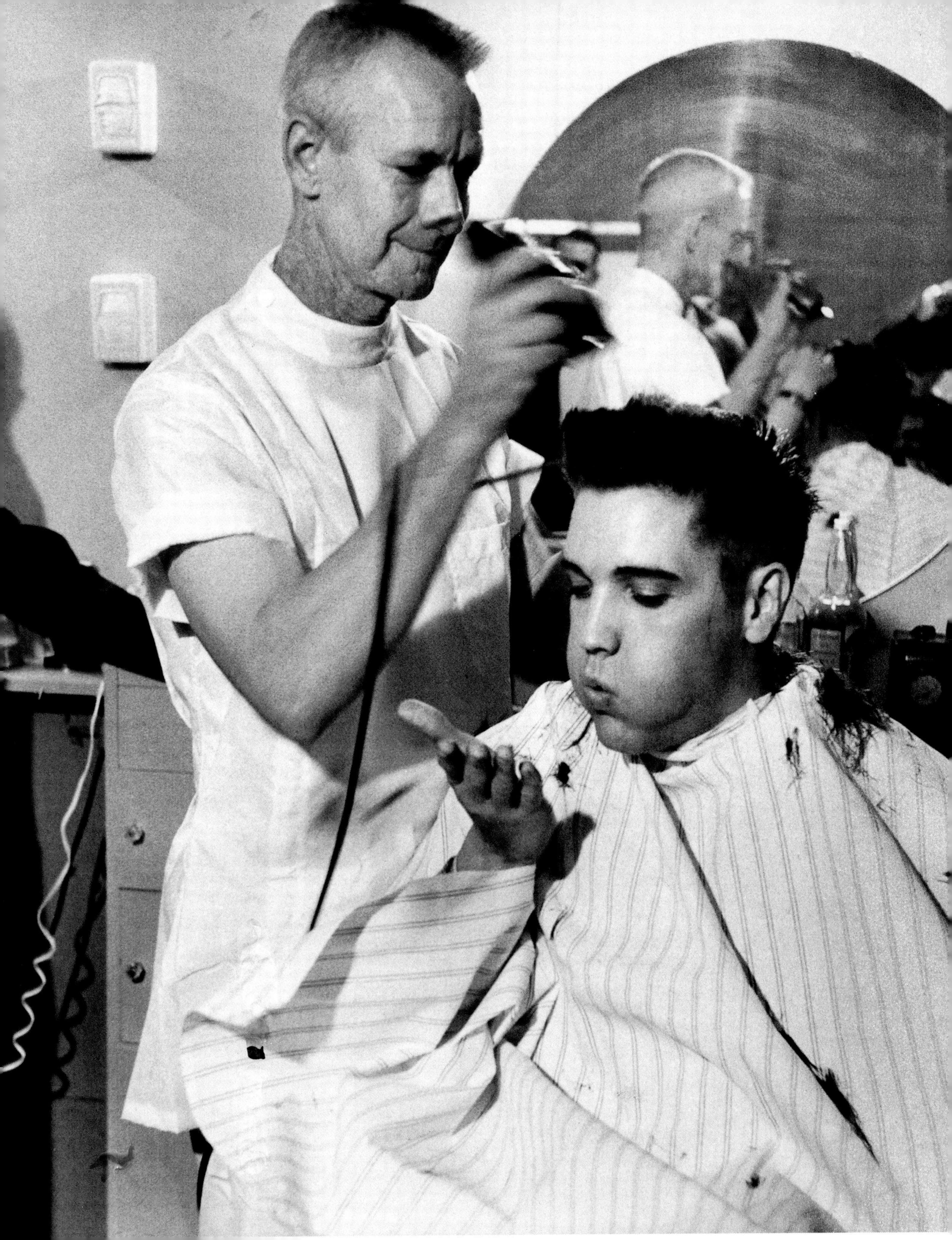

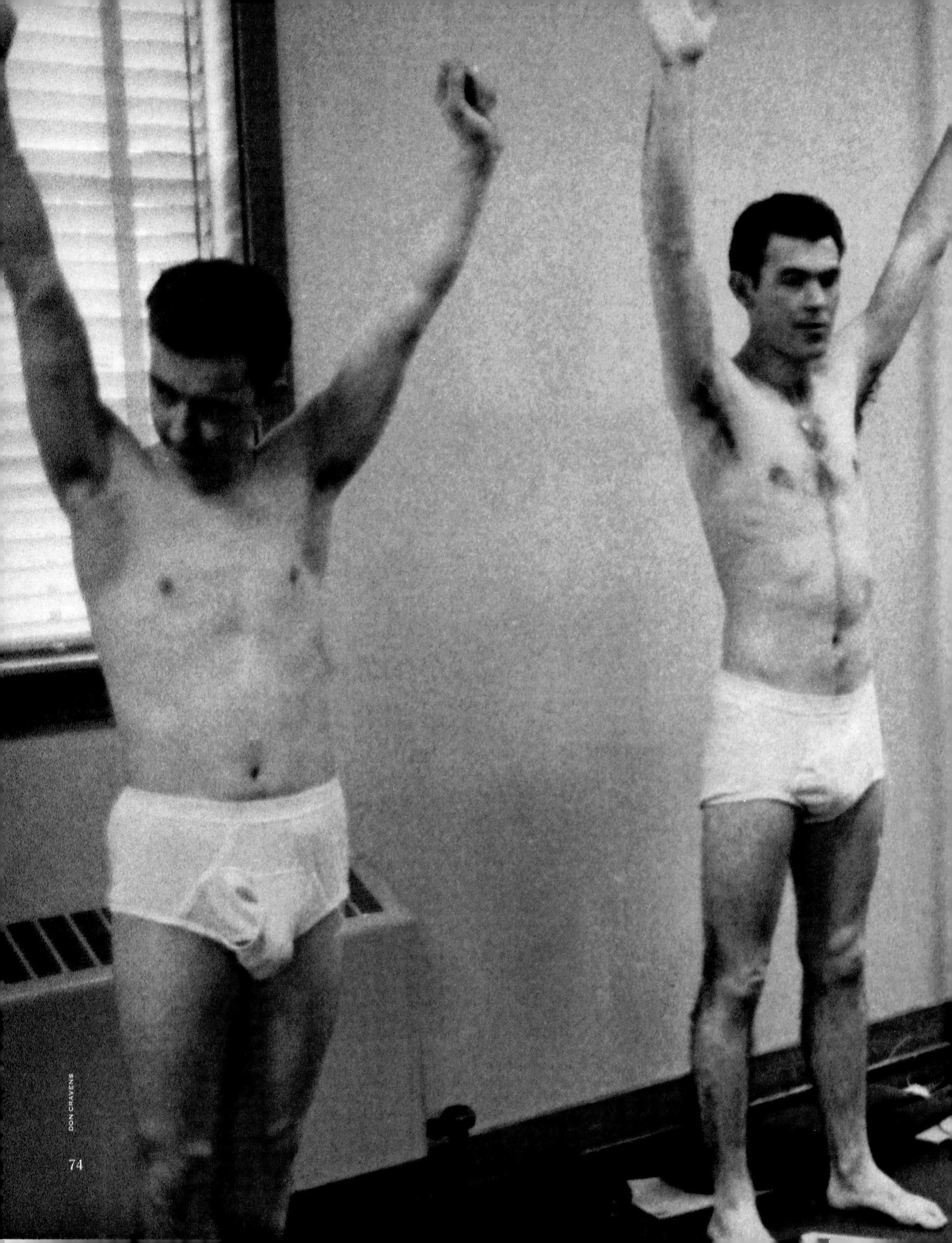
DON CRAVENS

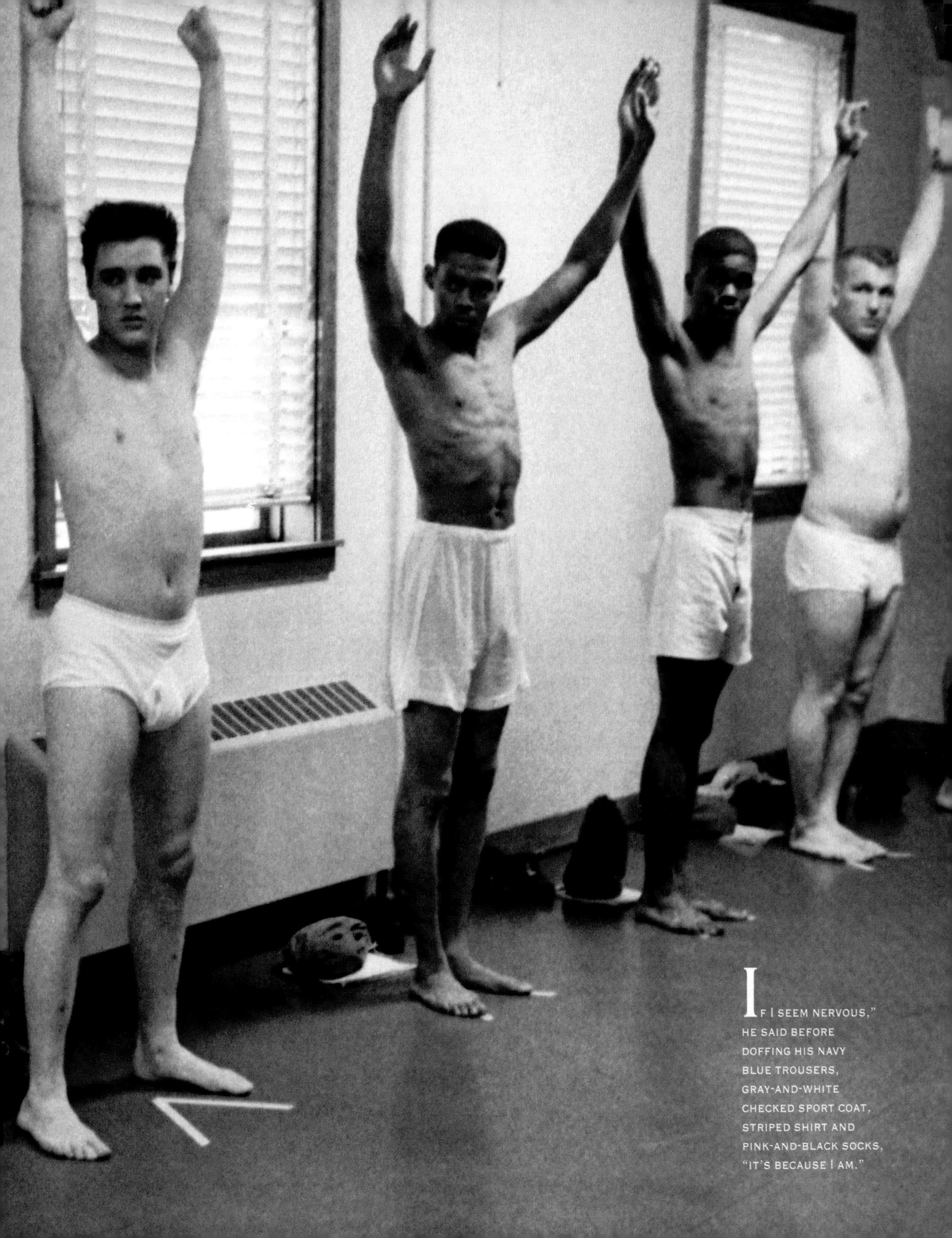

"IF I SEEM NERVOUS," HE SAID BEFORE DOFFING HIS NAVY BLUE TROUSERS, GRAY-AND-WHITE CHECKED SPORT COAT, STRIPED SHIRT AND PINK-AND-BLACK SOCKS, "IT'S BECAUSE I AM."

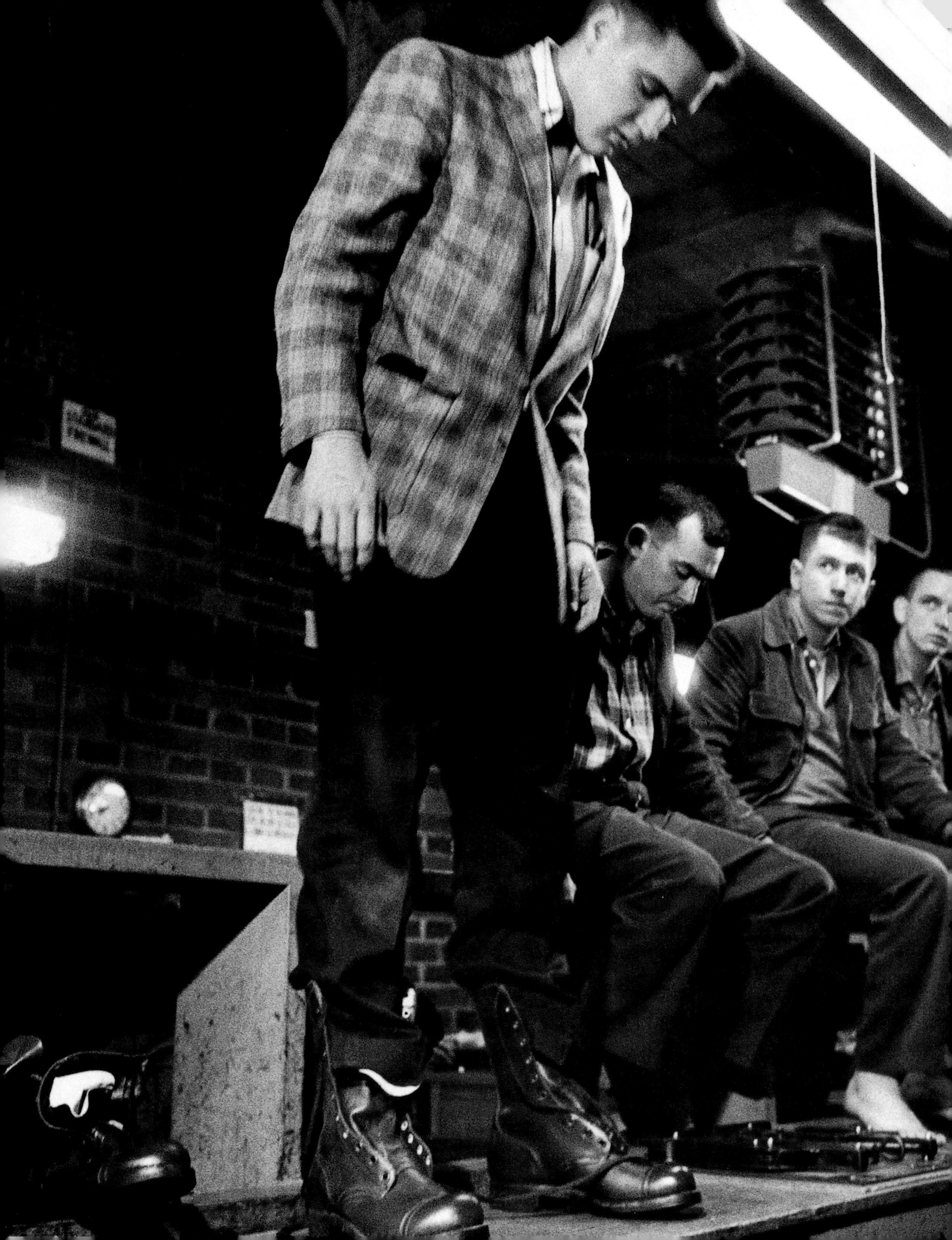

AFTER COMPLETING HIS PHYSICAL AT KENNEDY VETERAN'S HOSPITAL IN MEMPHIS, ELVIS SOMBERLY KISSED HIS PARENTS (AS WELL AS A GIRLFRIEND OR TWO) AND TOOK ONE LAST LOVING LOOK AT HIS CADILLAC. "GOODBYE, YOU LONG BLACK SONOFABITCH," HE TOLD THE CAR. THE OTHER INDUCTEES LAUGHED, AND ELVIS BOARDED A BUS FOR FORT CHAFFEE, ARK., WHERE HE WAS ISSUED A PAIR OF SIZE 12 ARMY BOOTS (OPPOSITE) ALONG WITH THE REST OF HIS MILITARY TOGS. MEANWHILE, COLONEL PARKER, WHO HAD FOLLOWED ALONG WITH THE PACK OF REPORTERS, SEEMED HAPPIER THAN EVER. HE CHATTED WITH ARMY BRASS (TOP RIGHT) AND NEWSHOUNDS (BOTTOM RIGHT) AND EVEN HANDED OUT BALLOONS ADVERTISING ELVIS'S NEW FILM, *KING CREOLE*. ONE PHOTOGRAPHER ACTUALLY HID IN THE BARRACKS HOPING FOR A SHOT OF ELVIS IN HIS BUNK, BUT THE ARMY THREW HIM OUT. KING ELVIS HAD BECOME PRIVATE PRESLEY.

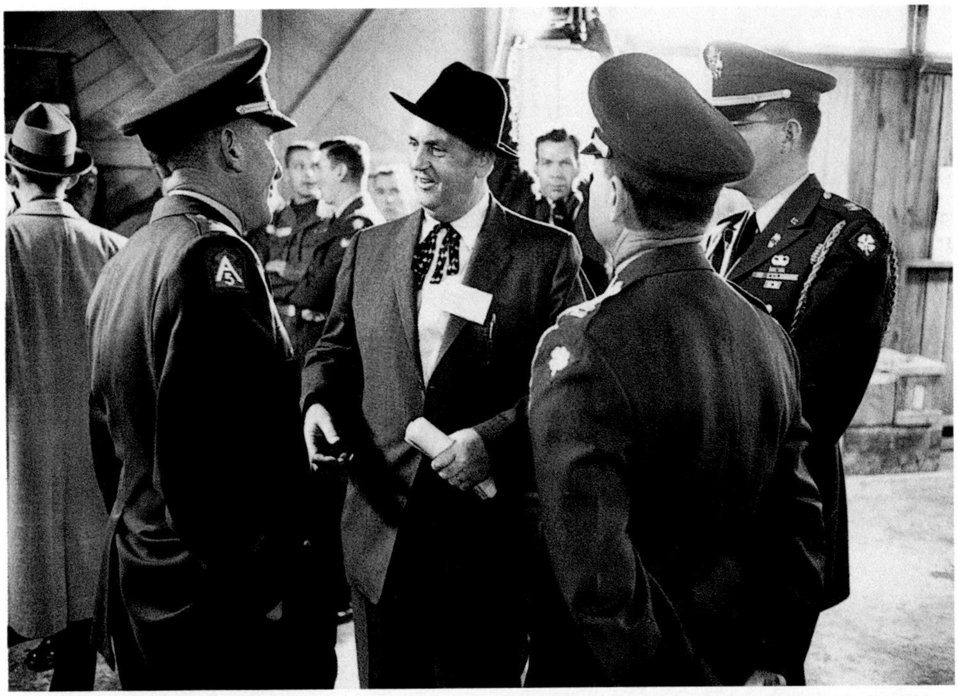

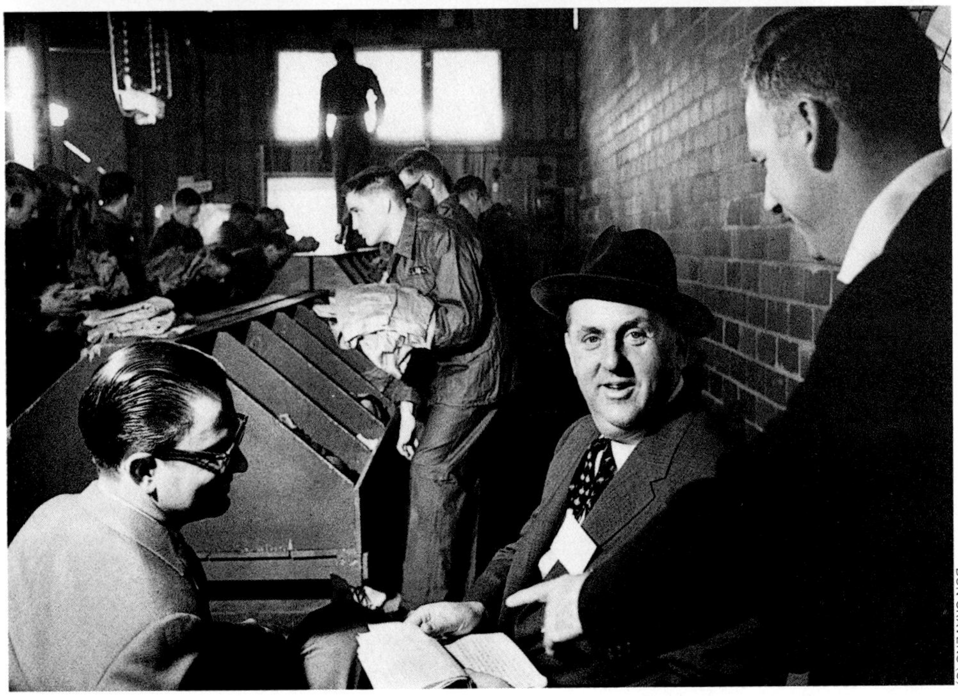

DON CRAVENS (3)

"Miss your teddy bear, Elvis?" the other soldiers chided him shortly after he was posted to Fort Hood, Tex. Actually, it was Gladys whom he missed. As soon as he could get off base, he retreated to his old friend Eddie Fadal's house in Waco to call her. "For a solid hour, they were crying, weeping, moaning on the telephone," Fadal recalled. "Not hardly a word was spoken. " But like most privates, Elvis began to grow accustomed to Army life. The men began to accept him, too. It didn't hurt that he bought everyone in his unit a spare uniform and sometimes paid as much as 20 bucks to have someone take KP duty in his stead. Then, on August 11, he received terrifying news: Gladys's health had taken a turn for the worse. Though he was due for overseas posting in six weeks, he was granted an emergency furlough to see her.

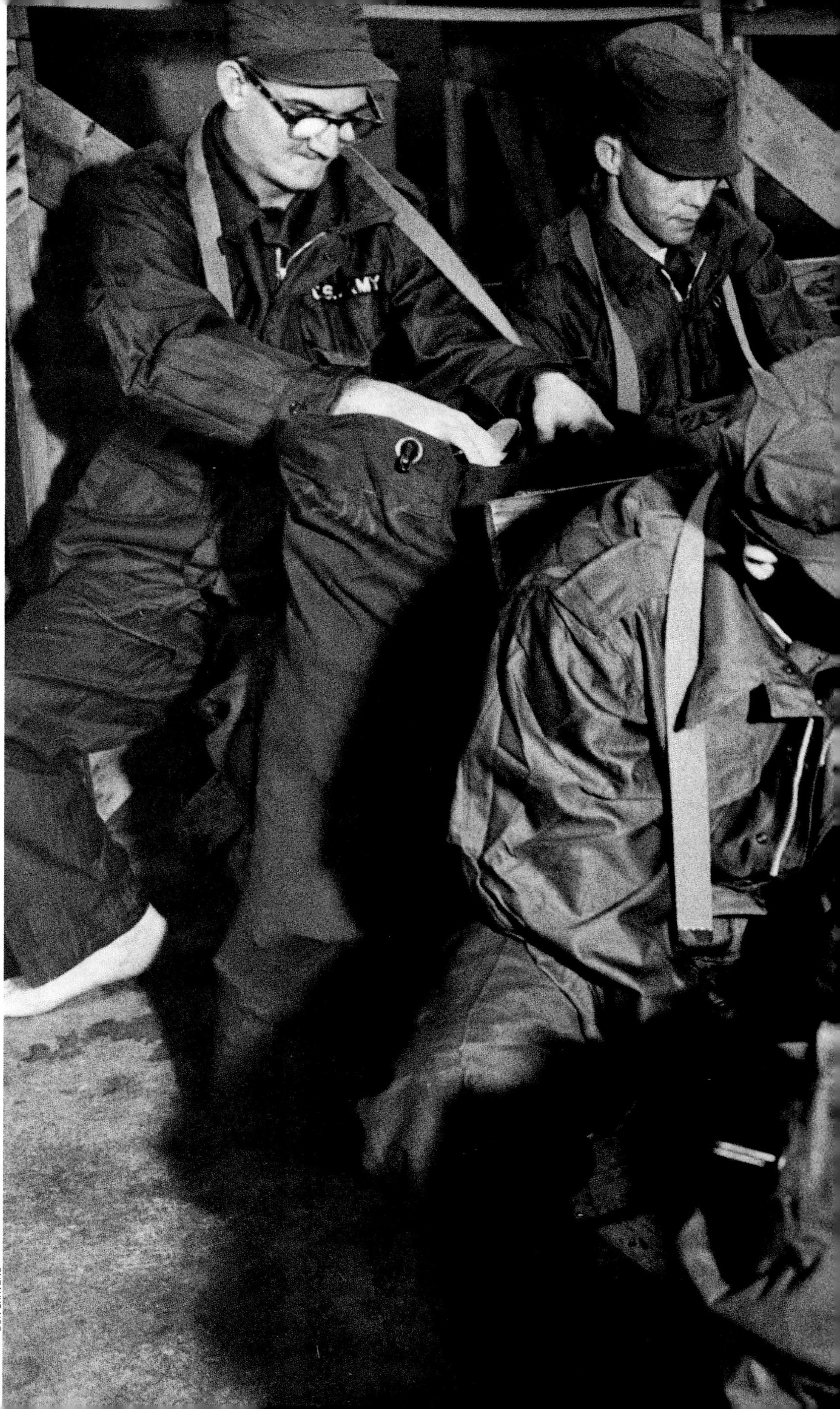

DON CRAVENS

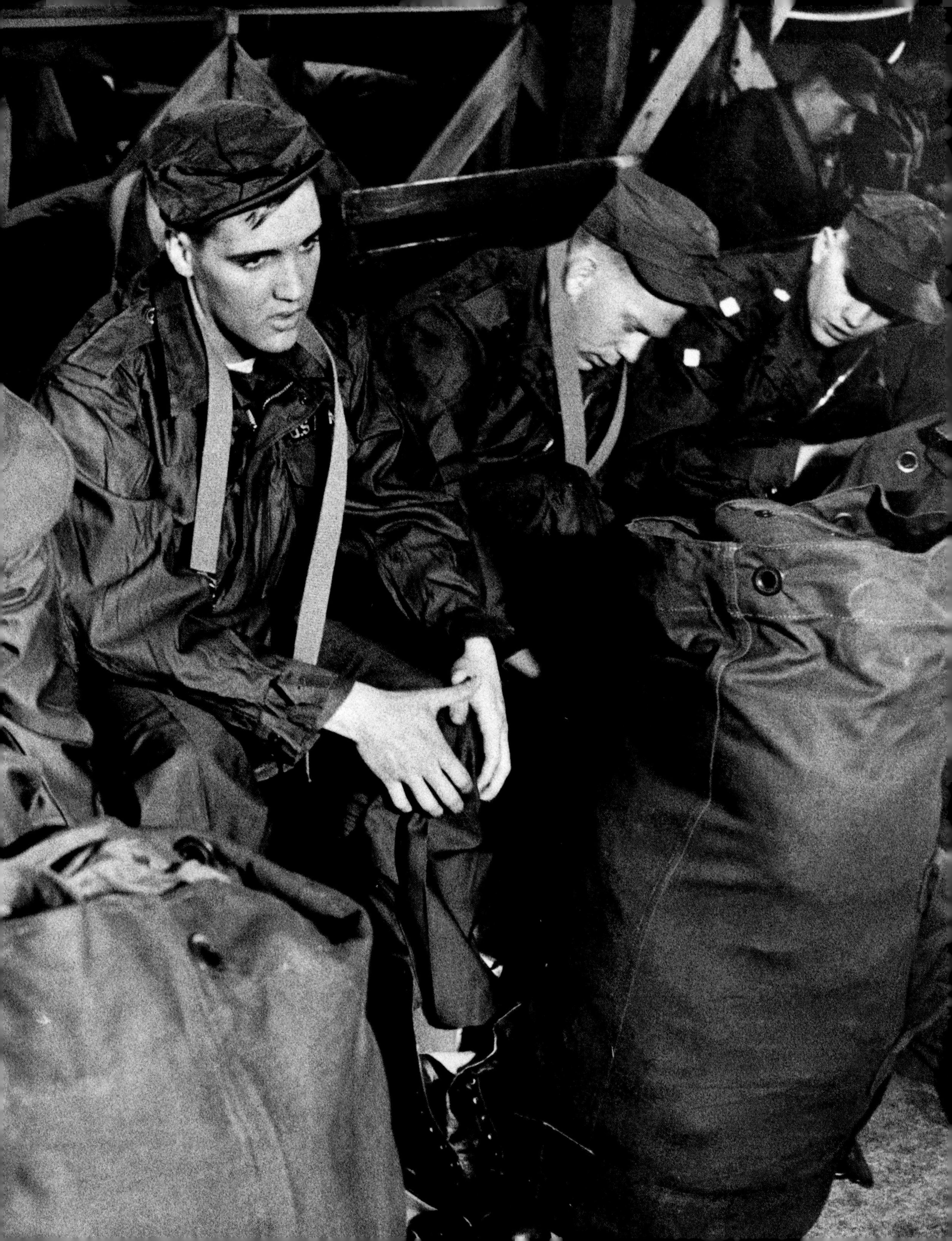

She's all I lived for," Elvis wailed. "She was always my best girl." Wearing a white frilled shirt his dead mother had often admired, he sat with his father on the steps of Graceland and cried inconsolably (right), rising only to bury himself in the arms of visiting loved ones. Then, he would lead these friends and relations to his mother's open coffin and gently stroke her corpse. "Wake up, mama," he whimpered. "Wake up, Baby, and talk to Elvis." When her body was laid in its grave, he tried to leap in after it. For days, he clutched her pink housecoat to his breast and kissed it lovingly. One witness called it "the most pitiful sight you ever saw."

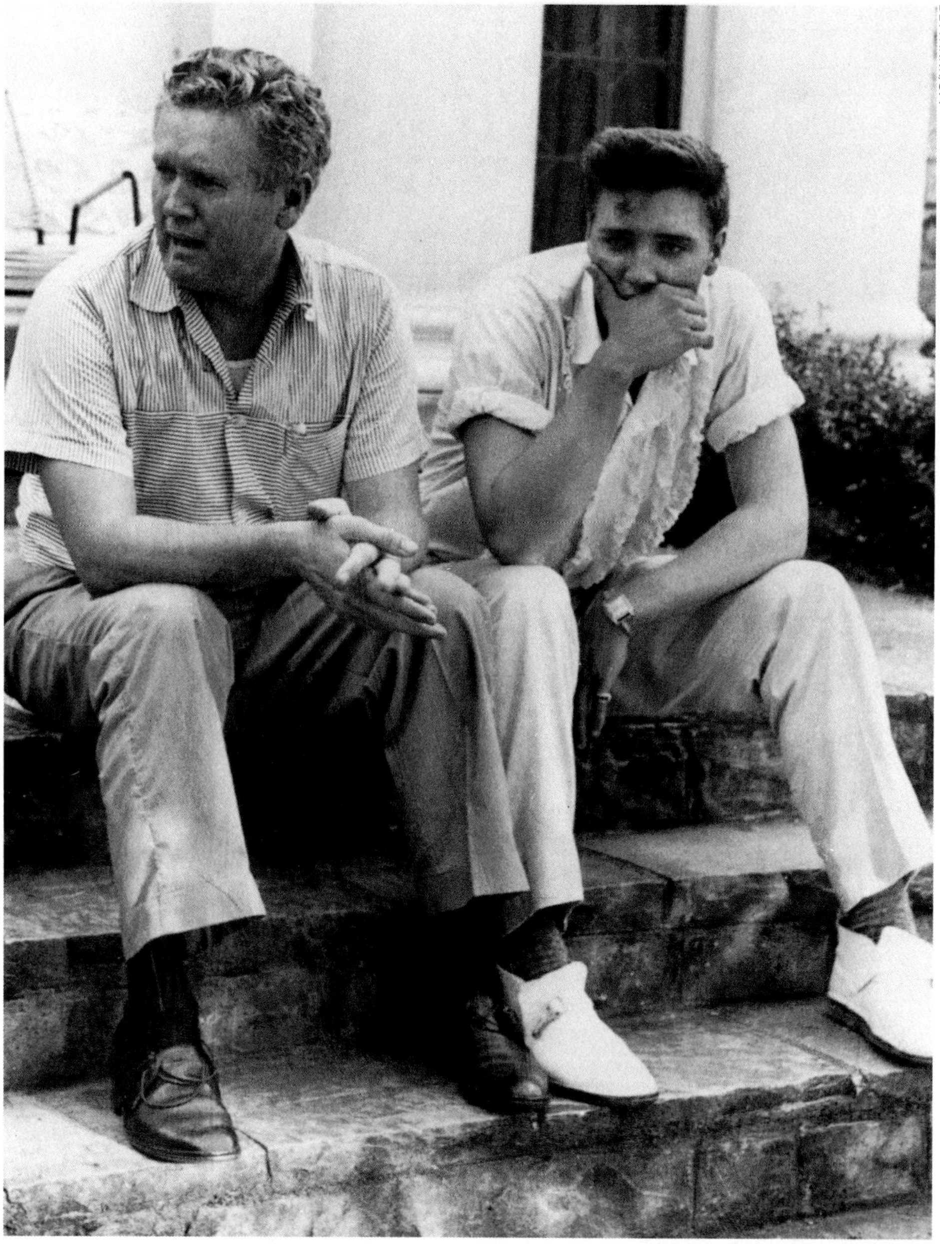

BETTMANN/UPI

A month later at Brooklyn Army Terminal, he stood before 125 reporters (opposite), polite and charming as ever. He answered all the usual questions in the usual way: No, he didn't think his music caused juvenile delinquency and, no, he wasn't engaged to be married. But when asked about his mother, he struggled to express his feelings. "I was an only child, and Mother was always right with me," he said. "I could wake her up any hour of the night if I was worried or troubled." He would never sell Graceland, he added, "because that was my mother's home." In truth, Elvis never recovered from Gladys's death. "He changed completely," said Lillian Mann Smith, an aunt who had known him from childhood. "He didn't seem like Elvis ever again."

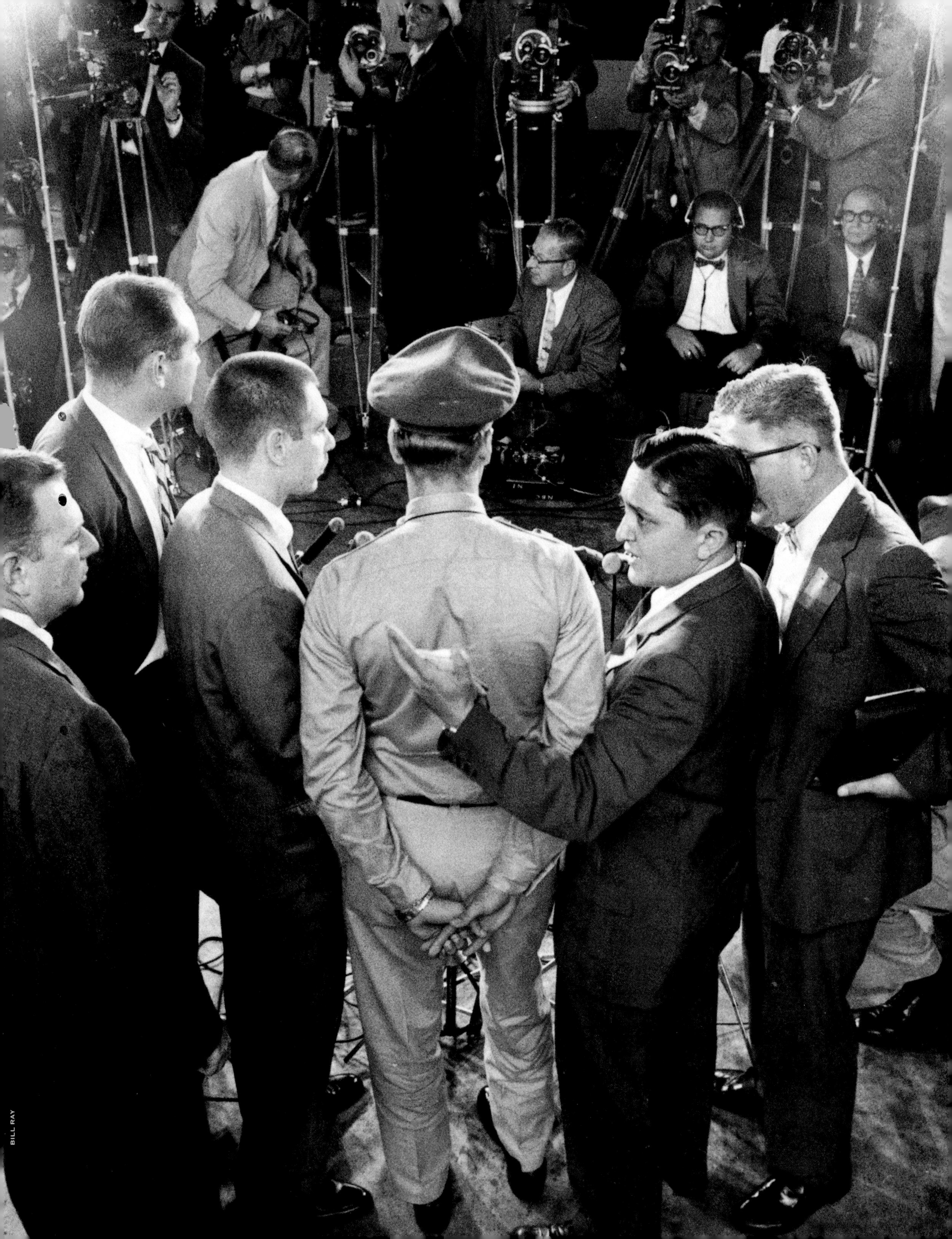
BILL RAY

Although 2,000 yearning fans showed up at the Brooklyn pier (right) to see him off, Elvis's departure was far more excruciating for him than it was for them. Once again Colonel Parker and the media turned the event into a carnival. As photographers held their cameras at the ready and a military band played a brassy version of "Tutti Frutti," Elvis was ordered up the gangplank eight times carrying a duffel bag that wasn't even his. Finally, as the band struck up "Don't Be Cruel," the USS *General Randall* set sail for Germany. But for many nights after, Elvis's bunkmate, Charlie Hodge, lay in the ship's dark hold and listened "as Elvis quietly moaned."

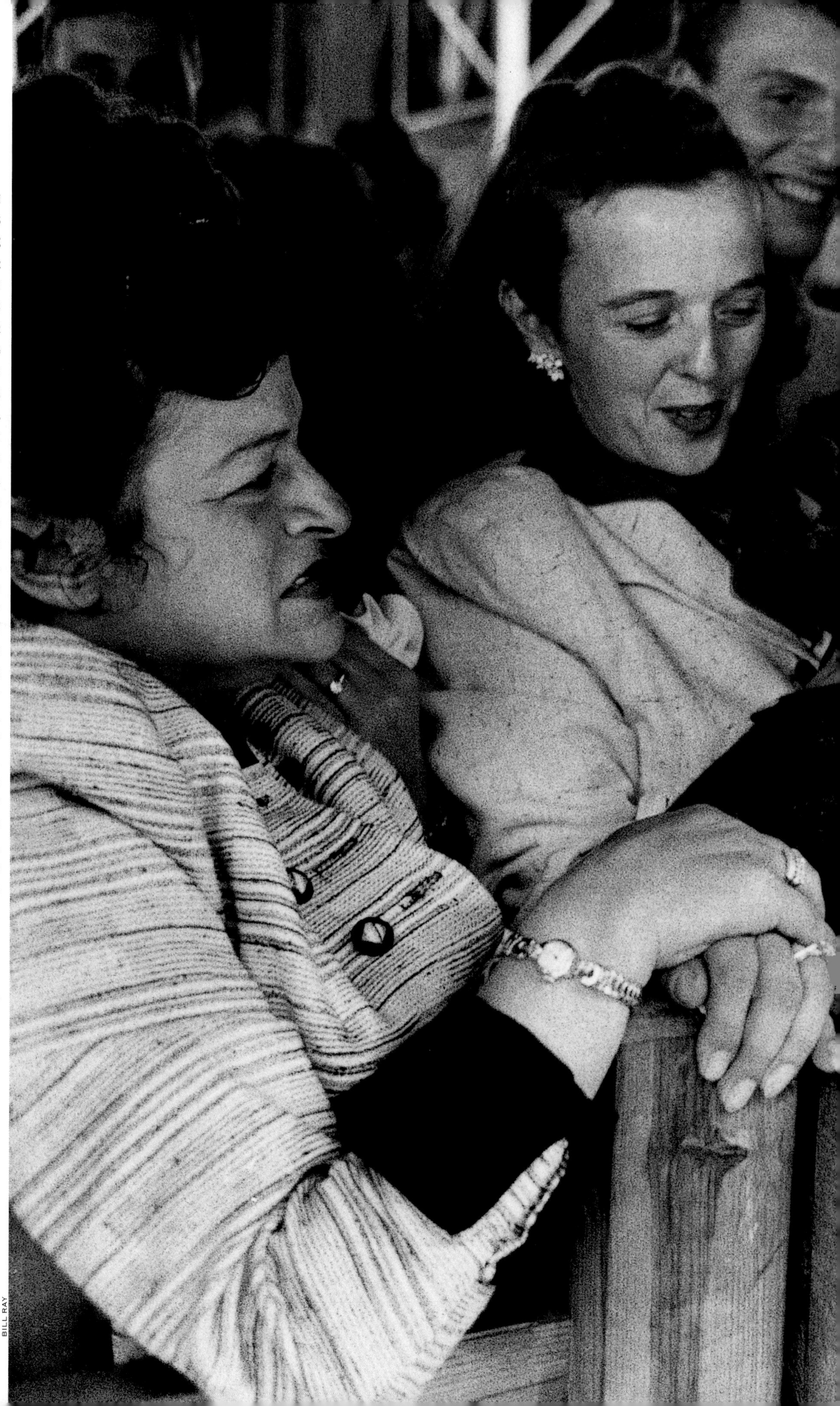

BILL RAY

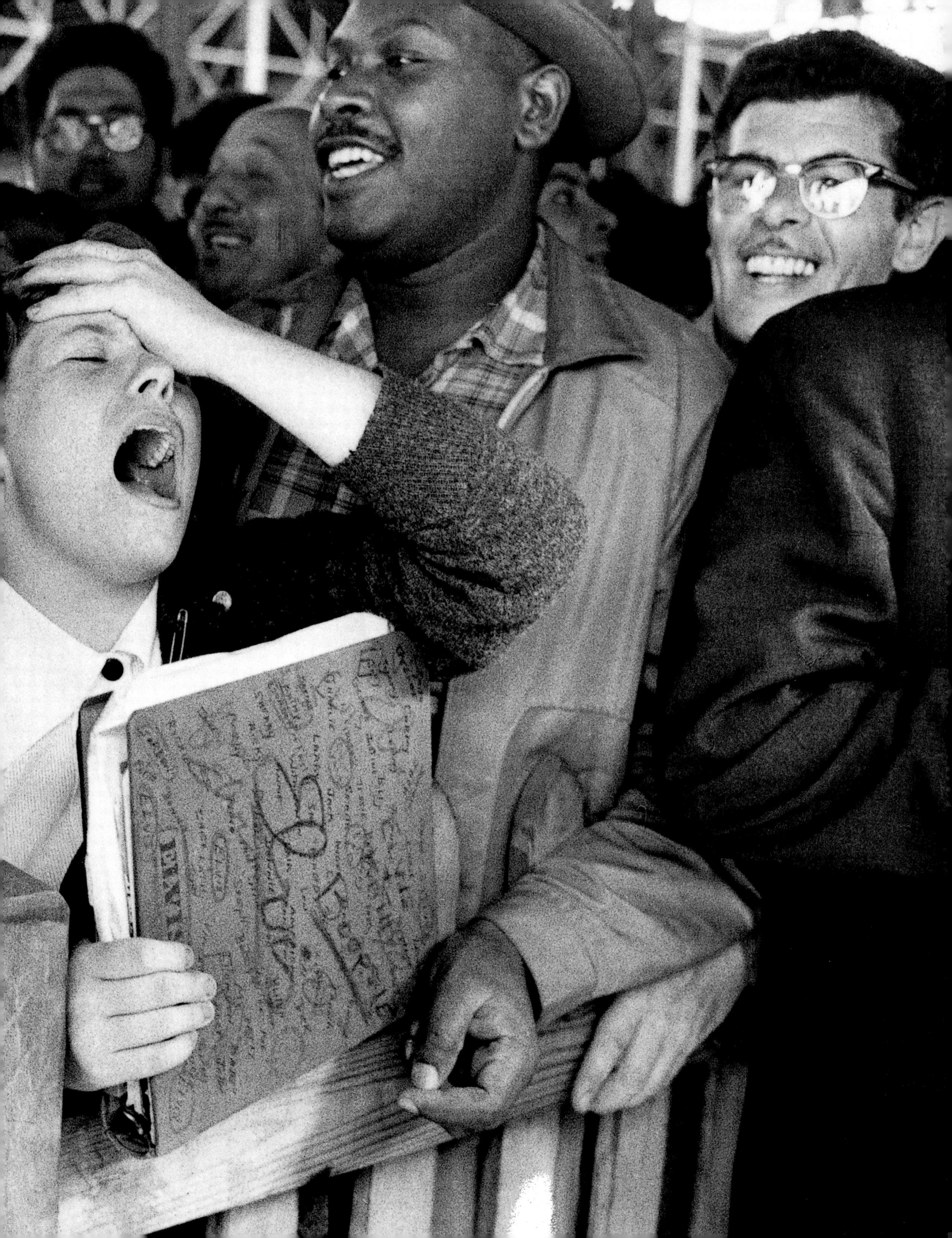

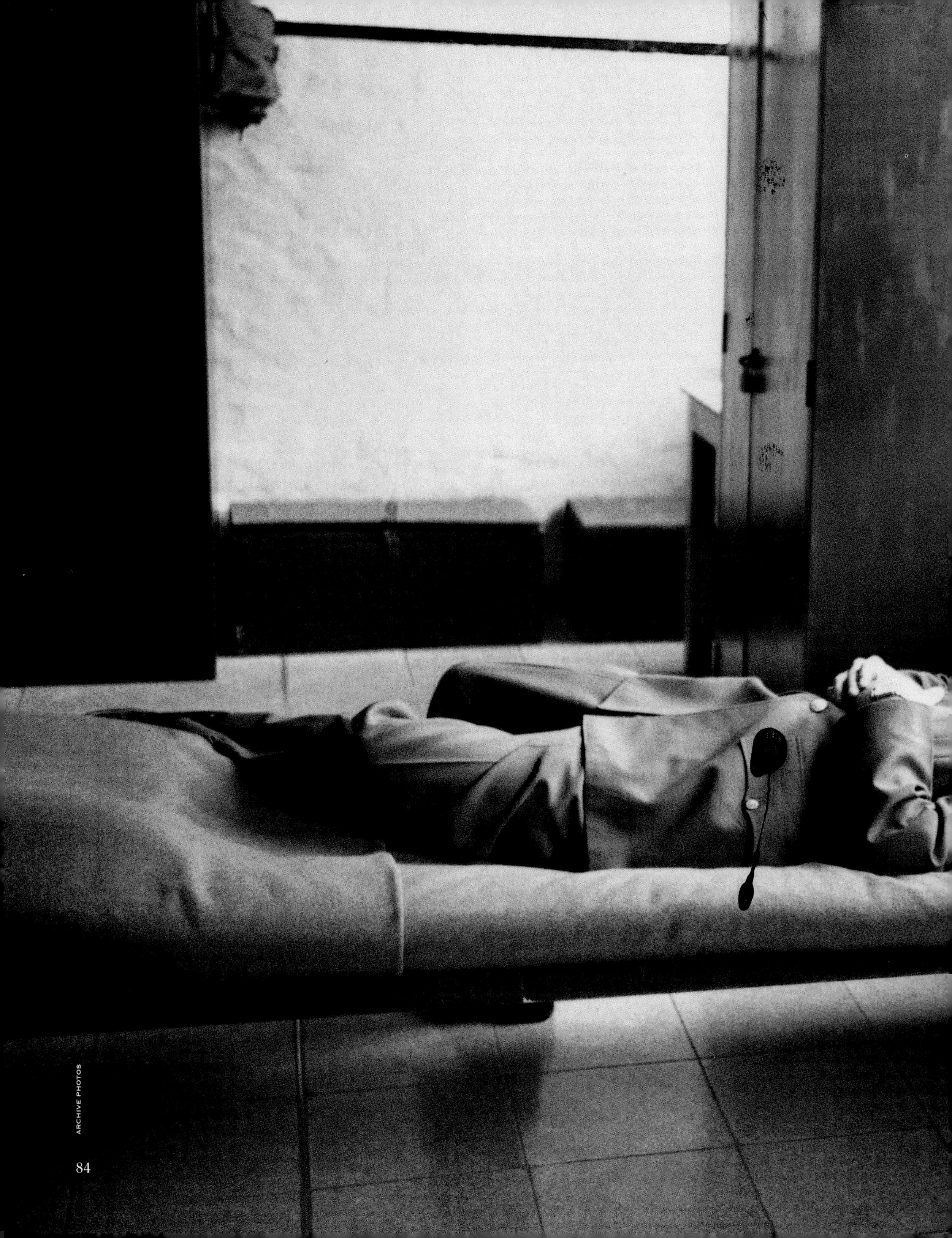

ARCHIVE PHOTOS

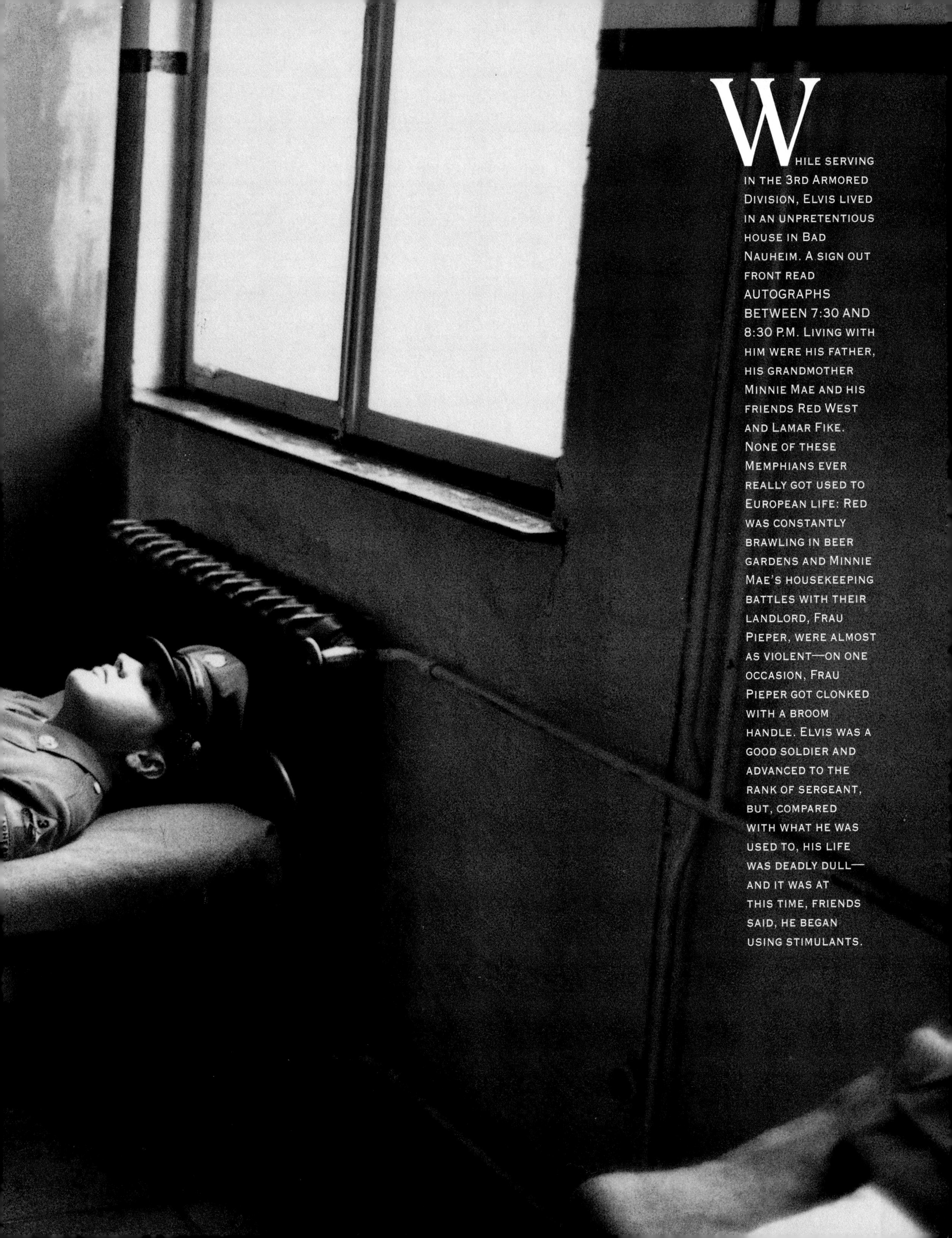

While serving in the 3rd Armored Division, Elvis lived in an unpretentious house in Bad Nauheim. A sign out front read AUTOGRAPHS BETWEEN 7:30 AND 8:30 P.M. Living with him were his father, his grandmother Minnie Mae and his friends Red West and Lamar Fike. None of these Memphians ever really got used to European life: Red was constantly brawling in beer gardens and Minnie Mae's housekeeping battles with their landlord, Frau Pieper, were almost as violent—on one occasion, Frau Pieper got clonked with a broom handle. Elvis was a good soldier and advanced to the rank of sergeant, but, compared with what he was used to, his life was deadly dull—and it was at this time, friends said, he began using stimulants.

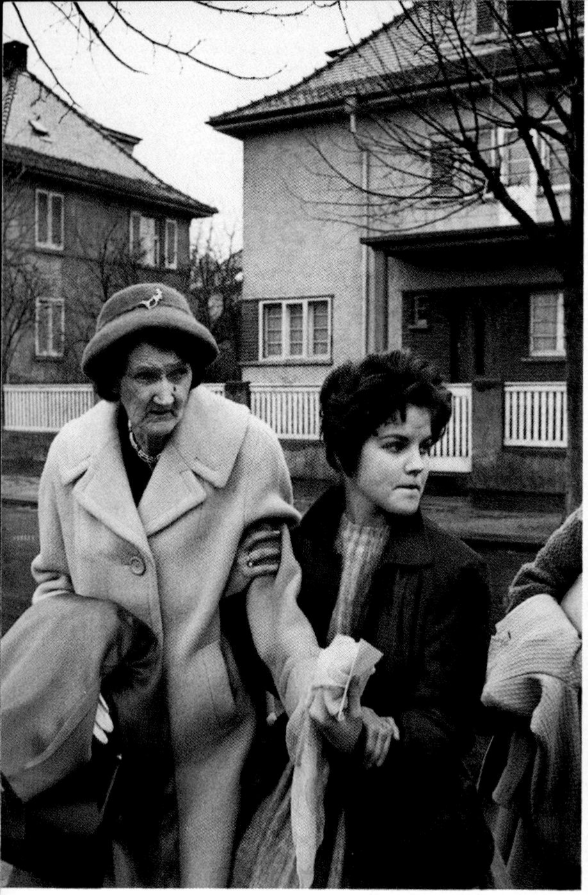

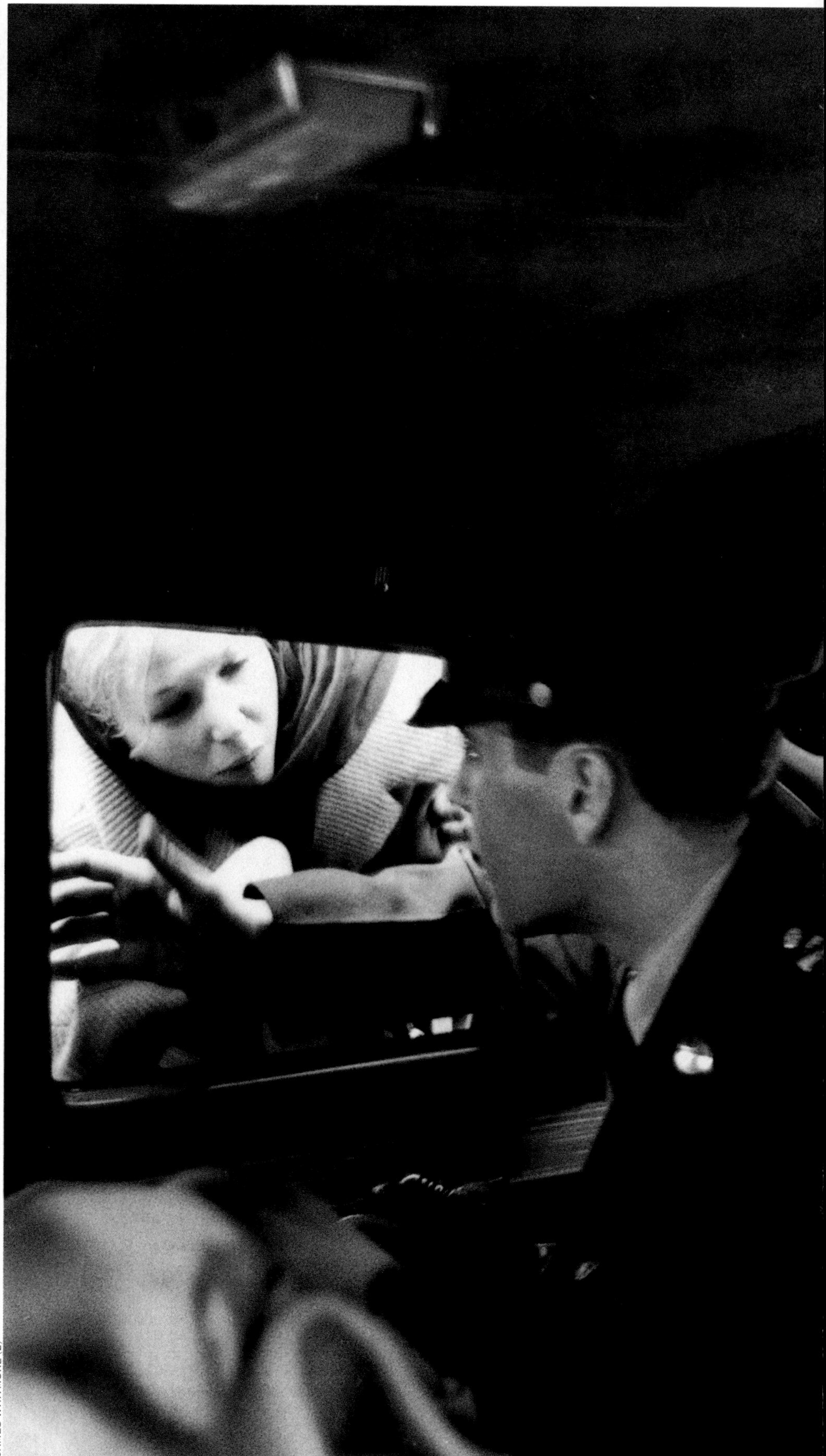

JAMES WHITMORE (2)

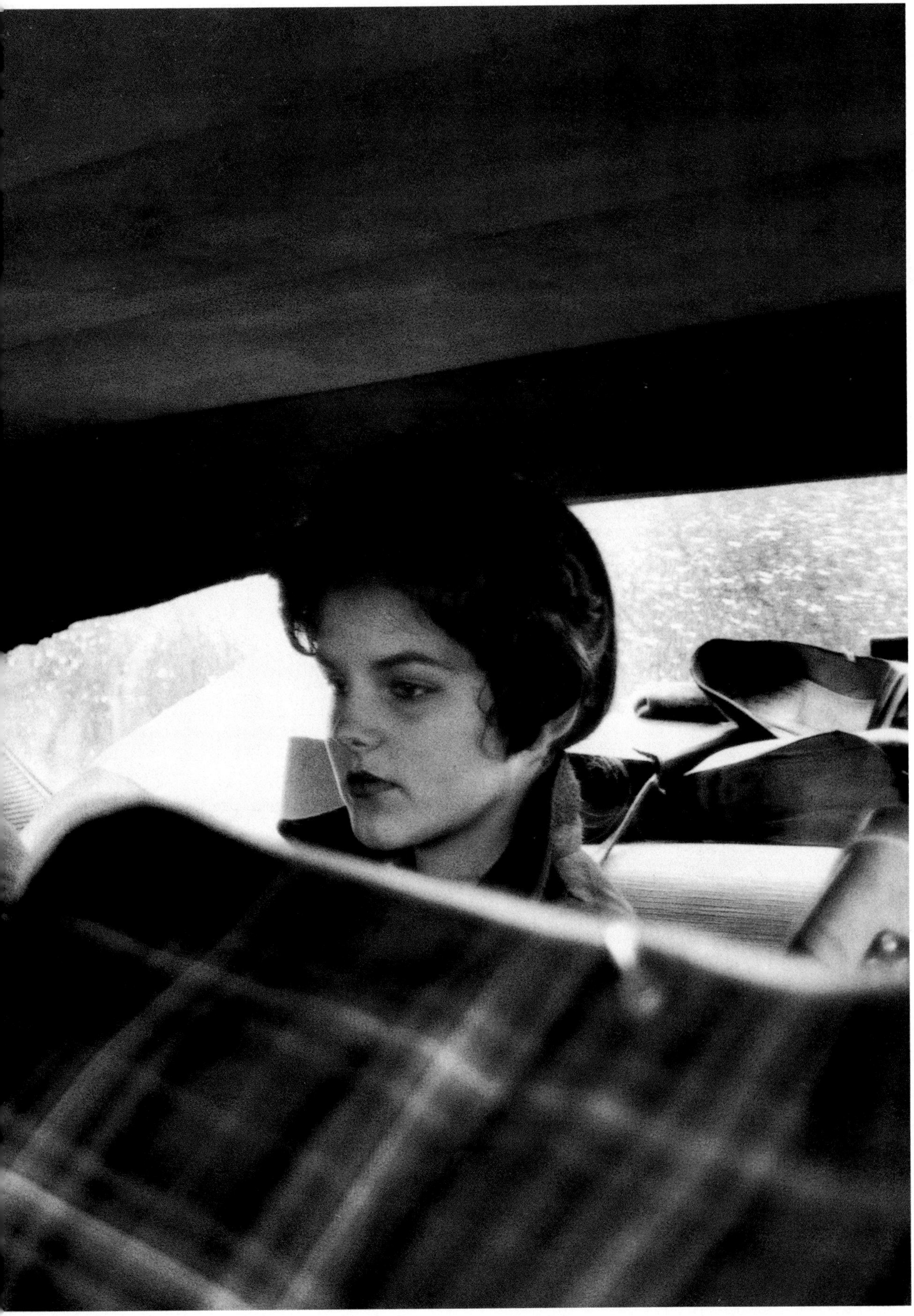

Both Elvis and his father, desperate to fill the void left by Gladys, met their future brides in Germany, but two more different females cannot be imagined. Dee Stanley was worldly—in fact, she was married when she started dating Vernon. Priscilla Beaulieu was the picture of innocence, a 14-year-old in a sailor suit, when Elvis first laid eyes on her. For six months, Priscilla and Elvis spent long evenings in his bedroom, talking intimately and smooching passionately. The night before he was to return to the States, she later wrote, "I begged him to consummate our love," but Elvis declined. She was too young, and besides, he said, "I'm torn with the feelings I have for you." The next morning, after leading Minnie Mae to her car (far left), Priscilla rode with Elvis to the airport (near left.) He gave her his combat jacket ("It shows you belong to me") and told her to write him letters on pink stationery. "Then he disappeared. Just like that."

Despite his tender farewell to his future bride, Elvis was all business later that afternoon at a Fort Dix press conference before some 200 reporters. "I am fond of Priscilla," he said firmly, "but I have no plans to call or write her. I don't just date sixteen-year-olds." (Actually, she was still 14.) Pencils wiggled feverishly as he chatted with actresses Nancy Sinatra and Tina Louise. "I brought two lace shirts and a telegram greeting from my dad," said Sinatra. "I brought myself," said Louise (far right), later famous as Ginger, the ravishing movie star, on TV's *Gilligan's Island.* (When reporters in Germany told Priscilla about all of this, she "felt suddenly sick," but Elvis did phone her three weeks later.) He had much more than his love life to think about. In less than three weeks, he would receive $125,000 to appear on the *The Frank Sinatra Timex Show*. He was petrified. His only live performance in the Army had occurred when dancing girls at a Paris nightclub had pulled him onstage. "For the frst time in fifteen months, I was in front of an audience," he said. "Then it flew all over me, boy—sudden fear. I reckon when I get in front of those cameras I'm going to shake even more than I did before."

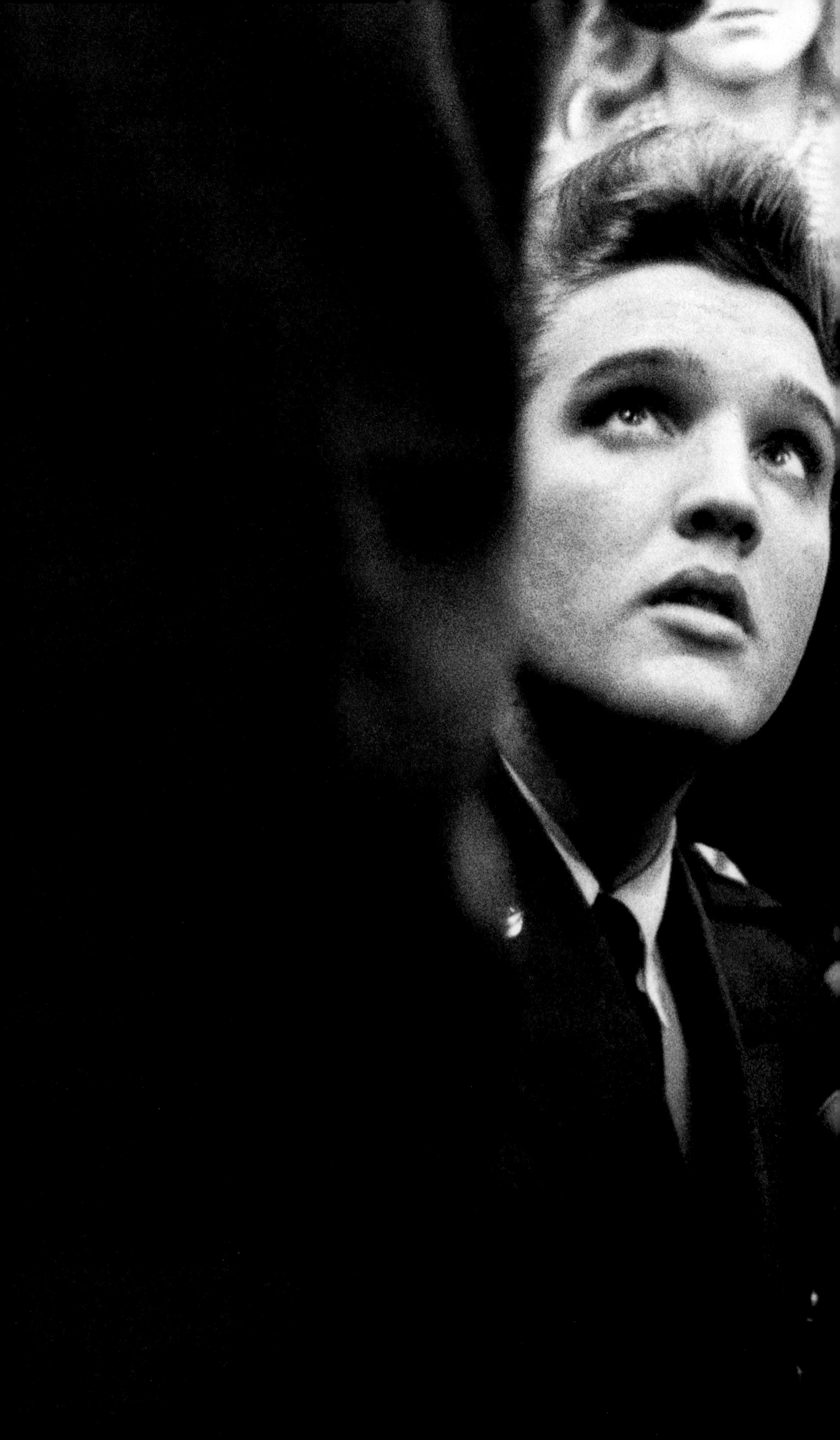

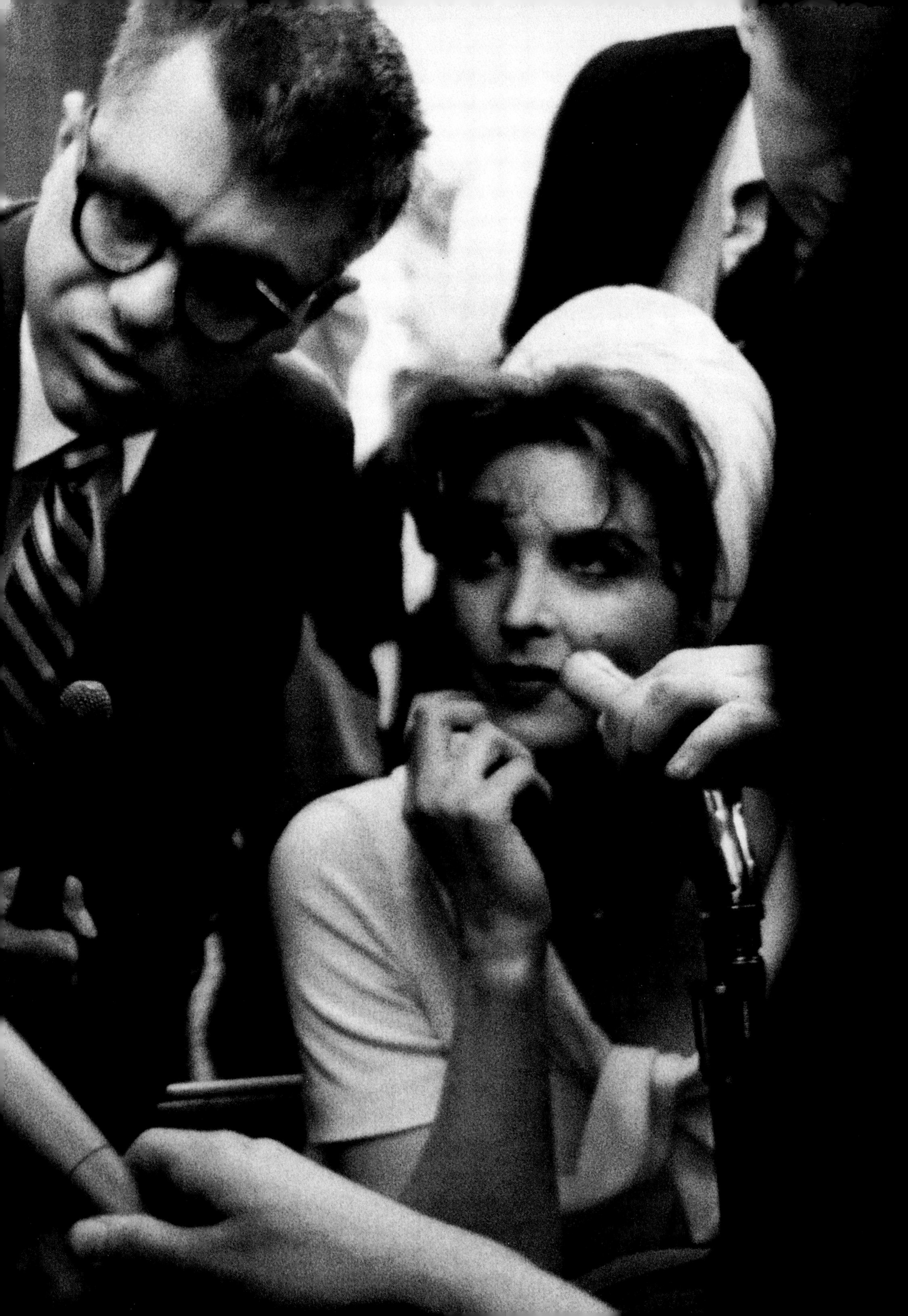

ALBERT FENN

THE SINATRA SHOW WENT FINE: THE CHAIRMAN OF THE BOARD SANG "LOVE ME TENDER" AND ELVIS SANG "WITCHCRAFT." HE WAS STILL ON TOP, BUT ADJUSTING TO HIS NEW LIFE WAS HARD. HE BURNED WITH ANGER OVER HIS FATHER'S MARRIAGE TO DEE STANLEY, DECLINING TO ATTEND THE WEDDING. HE DID HIS BEST TO WELCOME DEE TO GRACELAND WITH HER SONS ("I'VE ALWAYS WANTED A LITTLE BROTHER, AND NOW I HAVE THREE"), BUT WHEN SHE DID A LITTLE REDECORATING WITHOUT HIS PERMISSION, HE TORE DOWN THE CURTAINS IN A FURY. HIS ENERGY WAS NOW FOCUSED ON HOLLYWOOD. "MORE THAN ANYTHING, I WANT TO BE AN ACTOR," HE SAID. "THE KIND THAT STAYS AROUND FOR A LONG TIME." HIS PRODUCER, HAL WALLIS, CLAIMED TO REGARD HIM AS A "GENIUS" BUT, IN HIS OWN WORDS, "DECIDED TO TAKE ADVANTAGE OF THE SITUATION" AND CAST ELVIS IN *G.I. BLUES,* A MINDLESS FLICK ABOUT A ROCK-AND-ROLL SOLDIER. "ONE LONGS TO GRIP [WALLIS] BY THE LAPELS," ELAINE DUNDY LATER WROTE IN *ELVIS AND GLADYS,* "SHAKE HIM, AND SNARL, 'SO *THIS* IS THE WAY YOU TREAT YOUR GENIUSES!'"

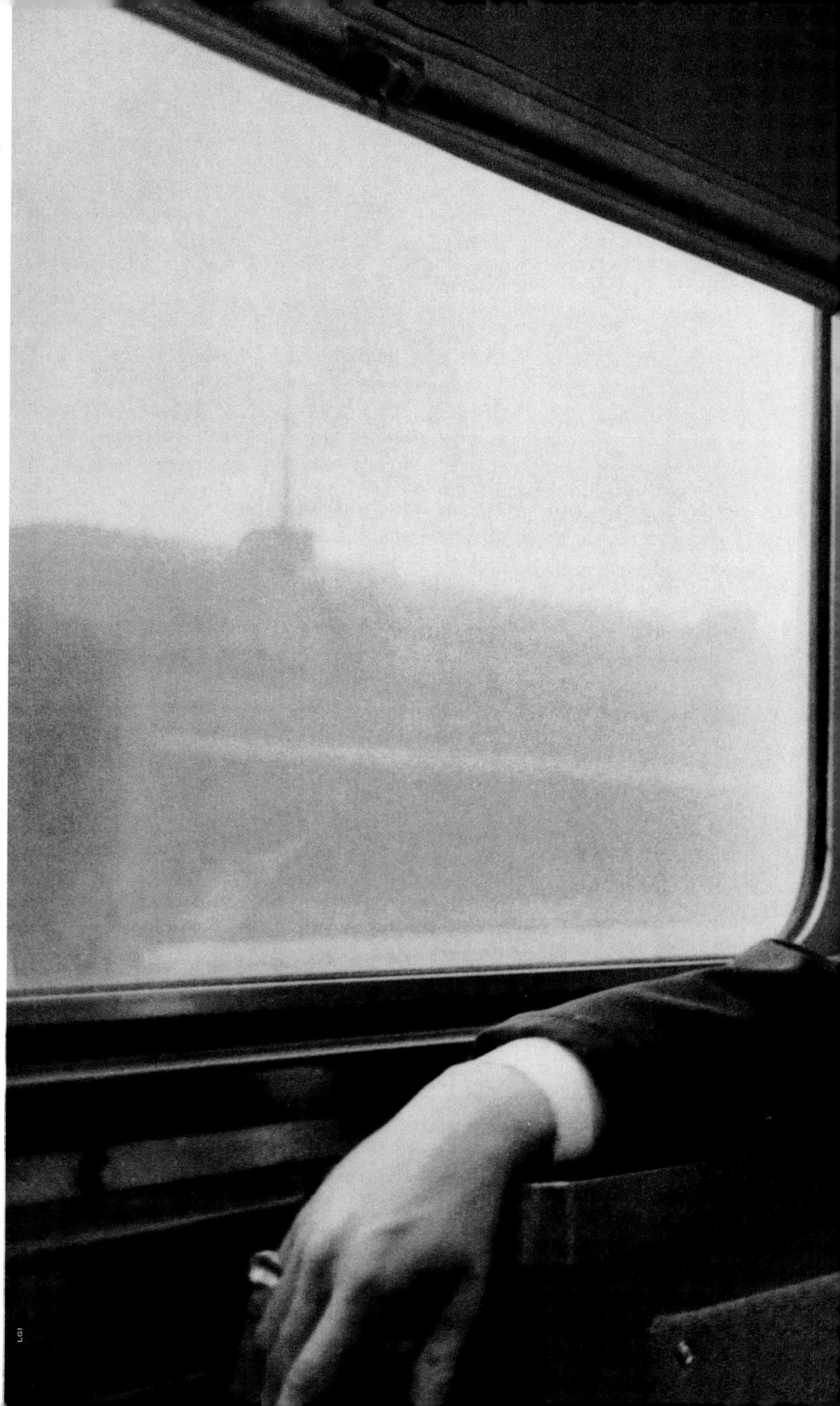

LGI

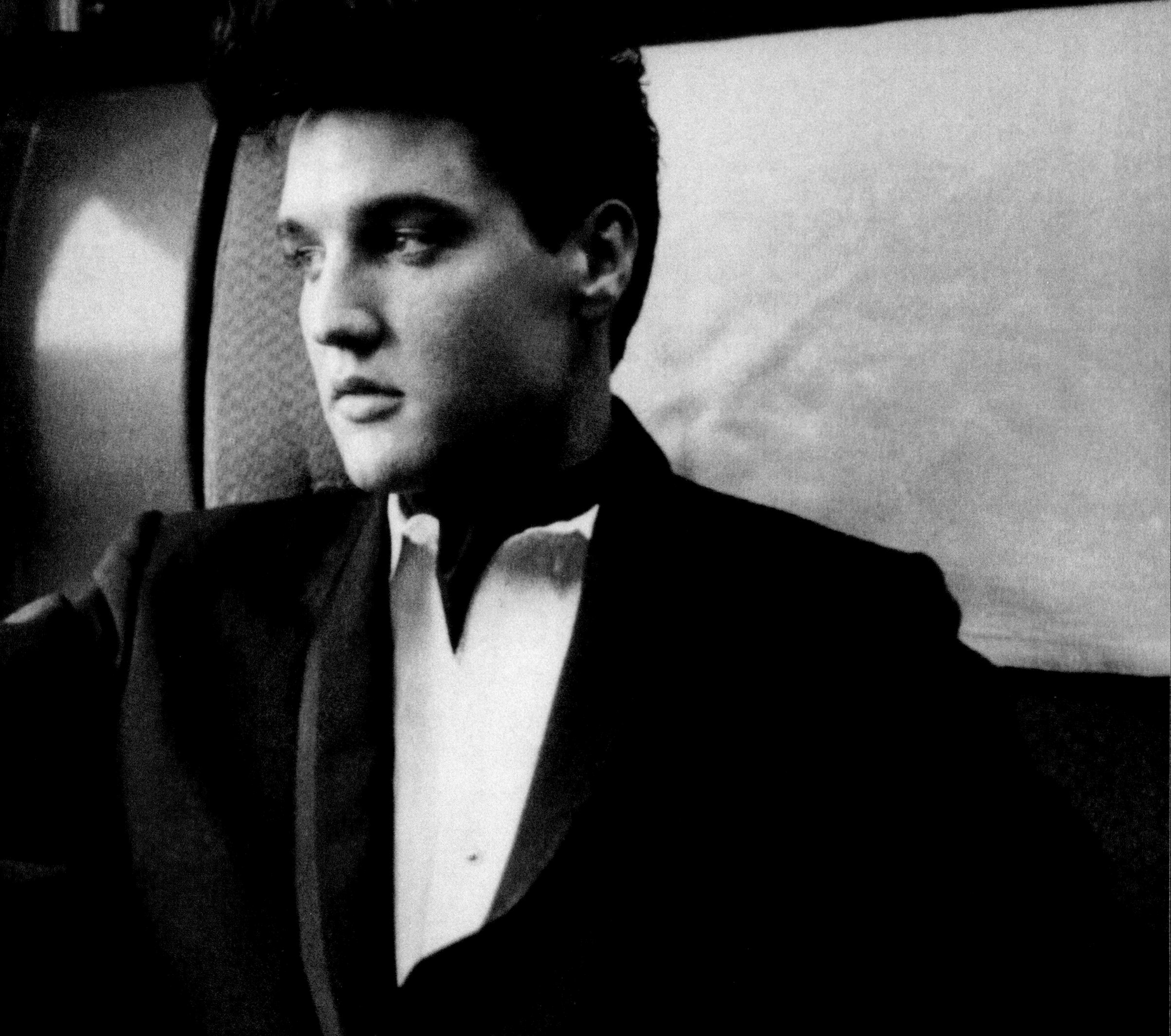

PRISONER OF HOLLYWOOD

IT WAS SO DAMNED AGGRAVATING. HE WAS GOING THROUGH STACKS OF DEMO RECORDS, CHOOSING SONGS FOR HIS NEXT MOVIE, BUT HE HATED THEM ALL. HE PLACED EACH ONE ON THE TURNTABLE, LISTENED TO A FEW BARS, THEN YANKED IT OFF IN DISGUST. FINALLY, HE FOUND ONE THAT DIDN'T SEEM AS BAD AS THE REST AND ASKED PRISCILLA TO LISTEN TO IT. "I DON'T REALLY LIKE IT," SHE SAID. HE EXPLODED WITH RAGE, HURLING A STACK OF RECORDS IN HER FACE. THEN, FLOODED WITH SHAME, HE TOOK HER IN HIS ARMS AND APOLOGIZED. IT WAS SO DAMNED AGGRAVATING.

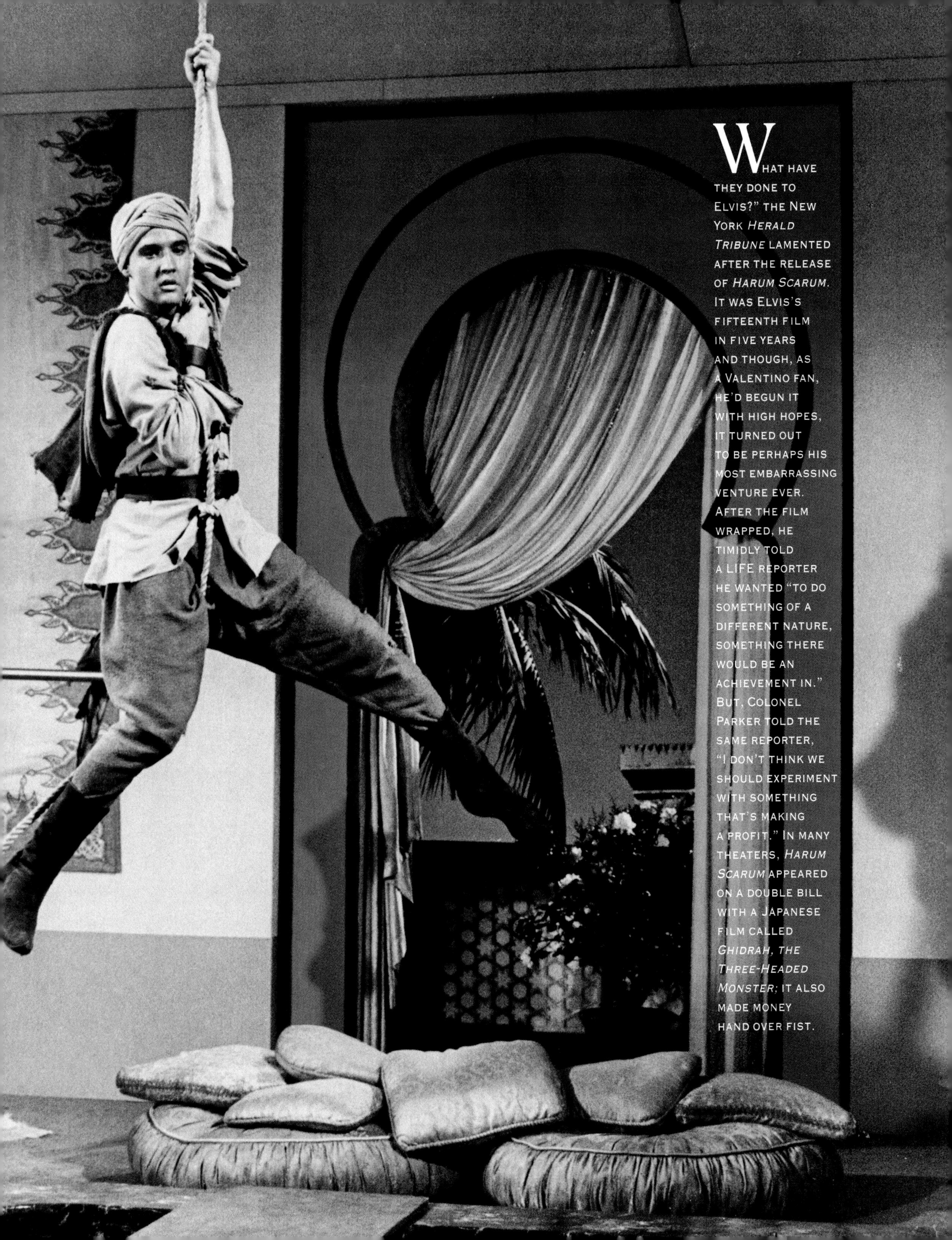

WHAT HAVE THEY DONE TO ELVIS?" THE NEW YORK *HERALD TRIBUNE* LAMENTED AFTER THE RELEASE OF *HARUM SCARUM*. IT WAS ELVIS'S FIFTEENTH FILM IN FIVE YEARS AND THOUGH, AS A VALENTINO FAN, HE'D BEGUN IT WITH HIGH HOPES, IT TURNED OUT TO BE PERHAPS HIS MOST EMBARRASSING VENTURE EVER. AFTER THE FILM WRAPPED, HE TIMIDLY TOLD A LIFE REPORTER HE WANTED "TO DO SOMETHING OF A DIFFERENT NATURE, SOMETHING THERE WOULD BE AN ACHIEVEMENT IN." BUT, COLONEL PARKER TOLD THE SAME REPORTER, "I DON'T THINK WE SHOULD EXPERIMENT WITH SOMETHING THAT'S MAKING A PROFIT." IN MANY THEATERS, *HARUM SCARUM* APPEARED ON A DOUBLE BILL WITH A JAPANESE FILM CALLED *GHIDRAH, THE THREE-HEADED MONSTER;* IT ALSO MADE MONEY HAND OVER FIST.

"THESE ARE PRESLEY PICTURES," AN MGM OFFICIAL TOLD *TIME* IN 1965. "THEY DON'T NEED TITLES. THEY COULD BE NUMBERED. THEY WOULD STILL SELL." IN FACT, THEY GROSSED MORE THAN $150 MILLION AT THE BOX OFFICE AND, EXCEPT FOR THE COST OF ELVIS HIMSELF, WERE RELATIVELY INEXPENSIVE TO PRODUCE. *HARUM SCARUM*, FOR INSTANCE, WAS SHOT IN 18 DAYS AND USED COSTUMES FROM *KISMET* AND A SET FROM CECIL B. DEMILLE'S *KING OF KINGS*. ELVIS MADE 31 MOVIES IN ALL (EXCLUDING DOCUMENTARIES), 27 OF THEM BETWEEN 1960 AND 1969. PICTURED HERE IS A POSTER OR LOBBY CARD FROM EACH ONE.

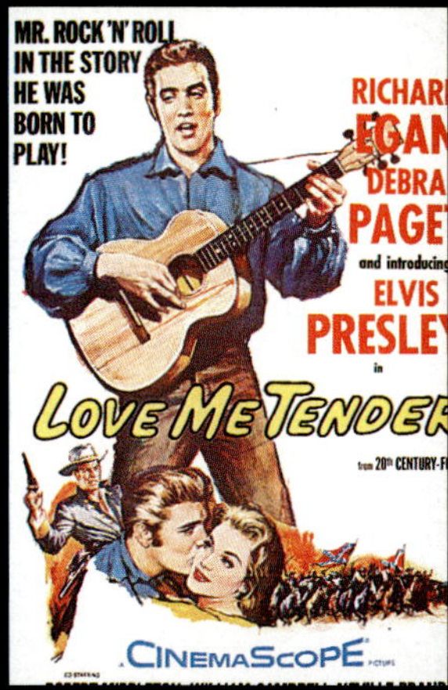

1956

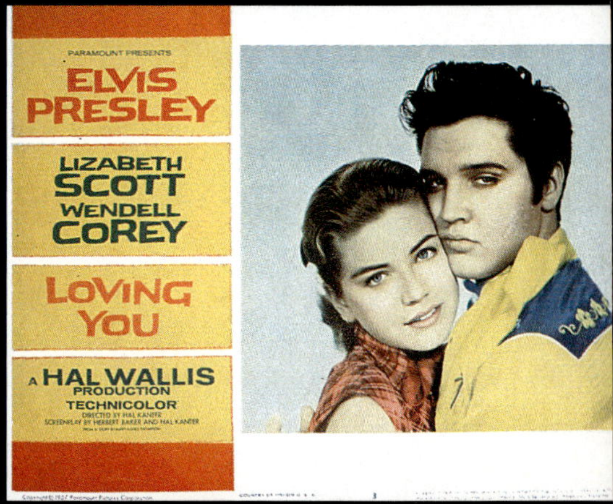

1957

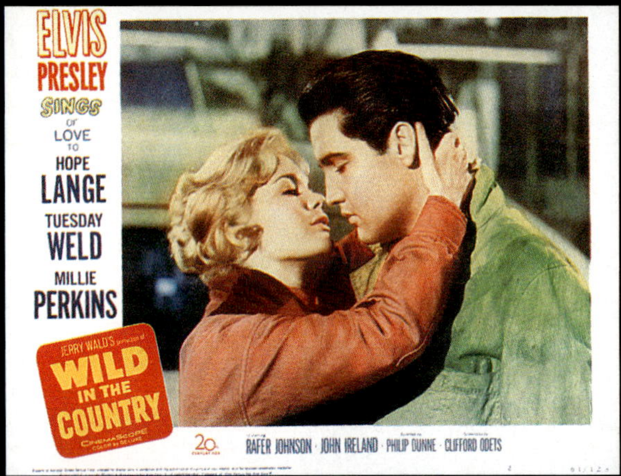

1961

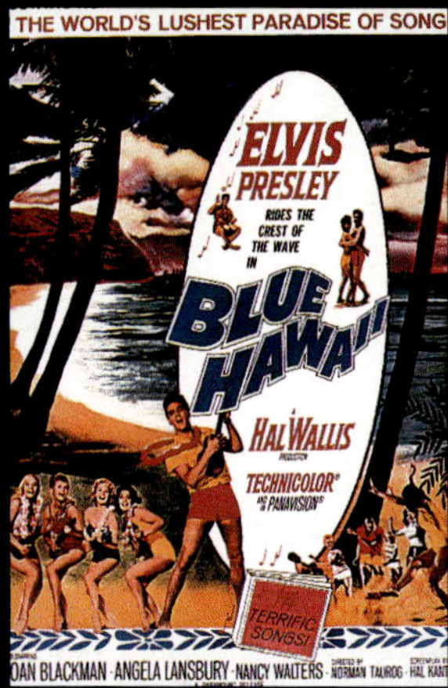

1961

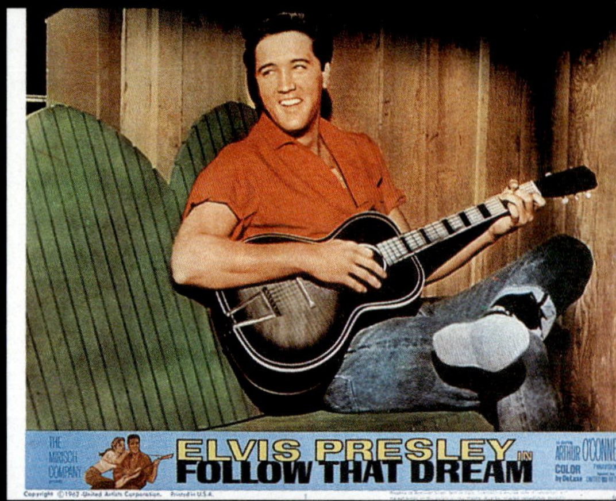

1962

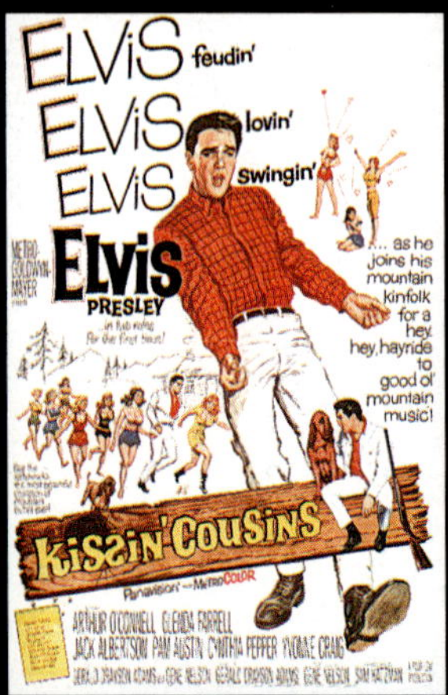

1964

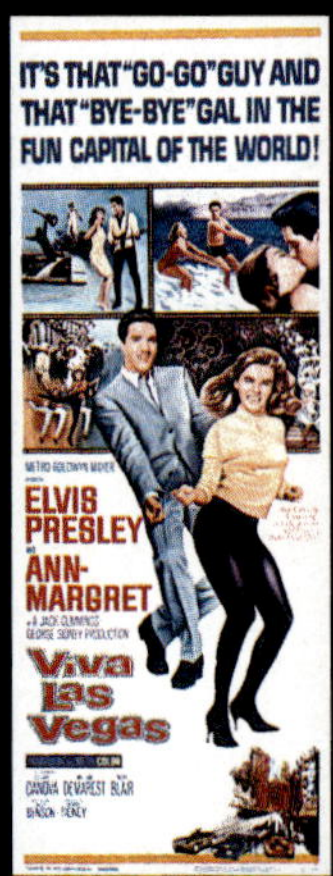

1964

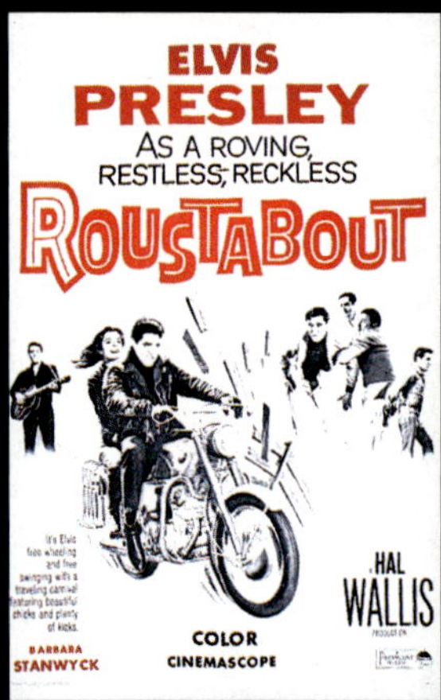

1964

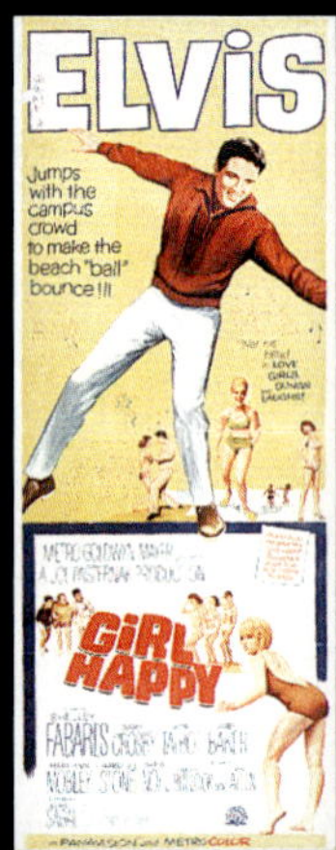

1965

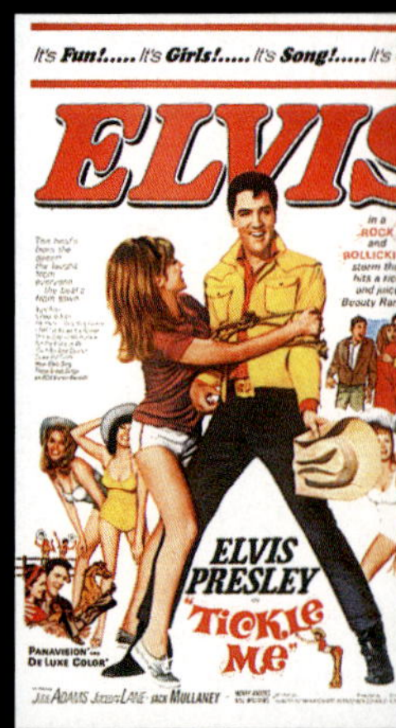

1965

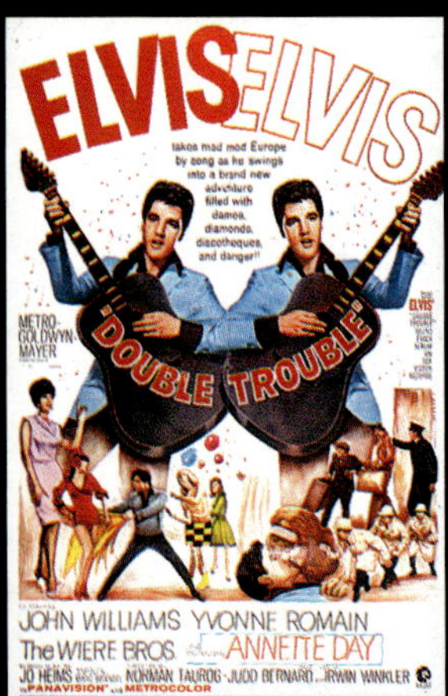

1967

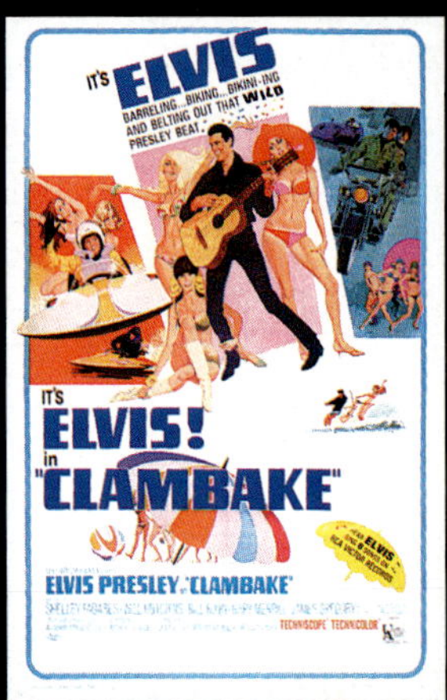

1967

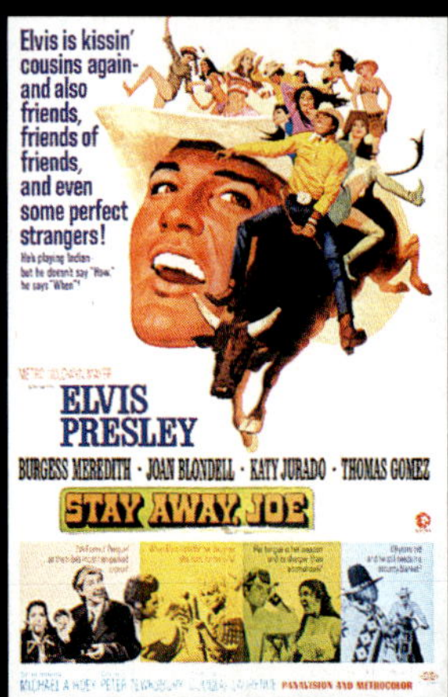

1968

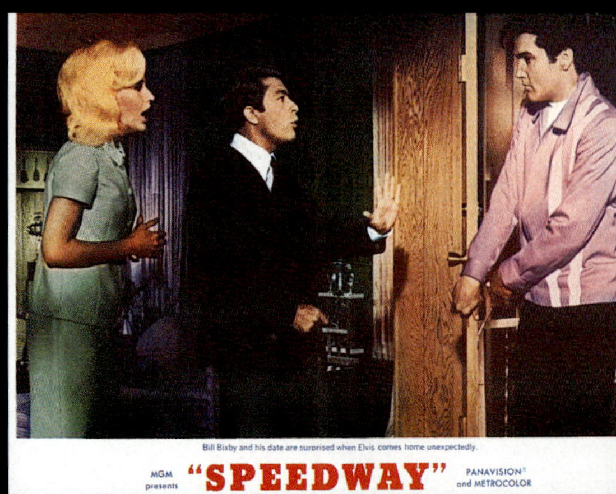

1968

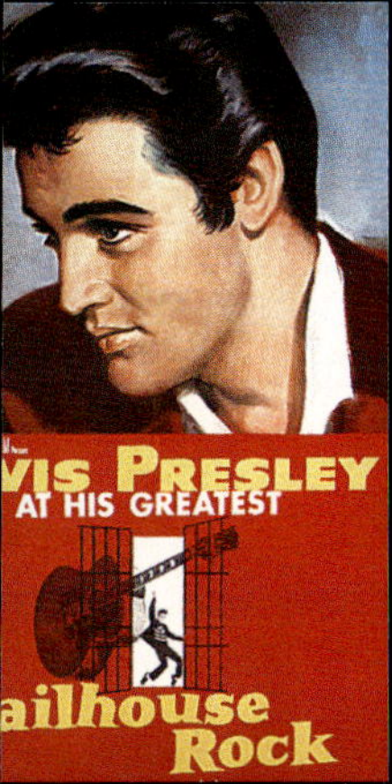

1957

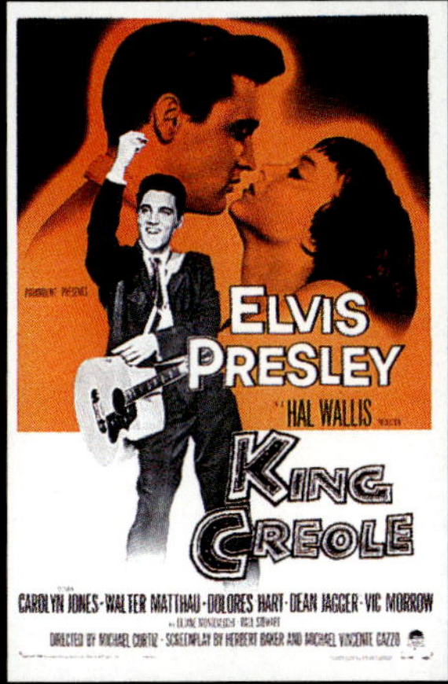

1958

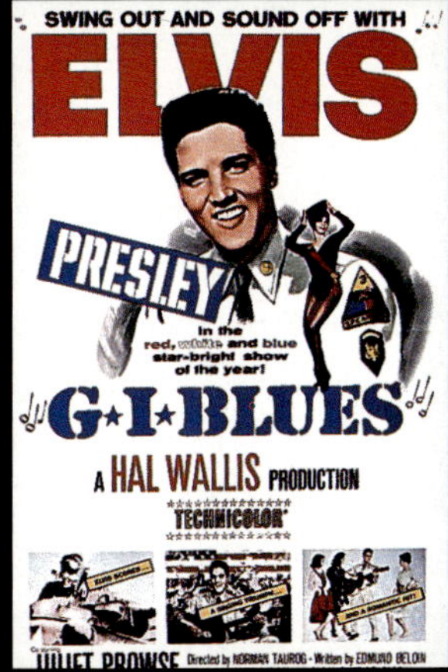

1960

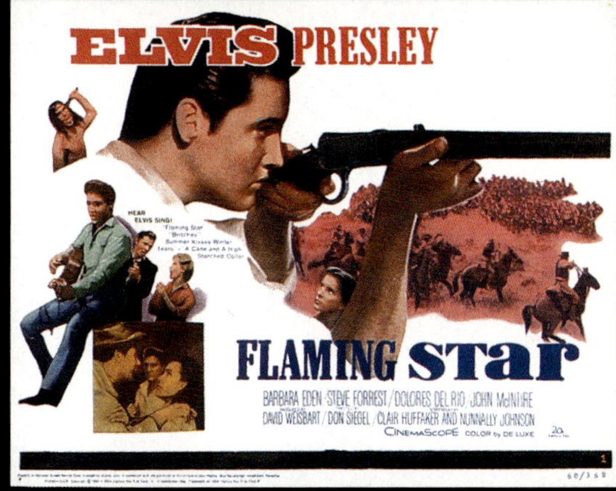

1960

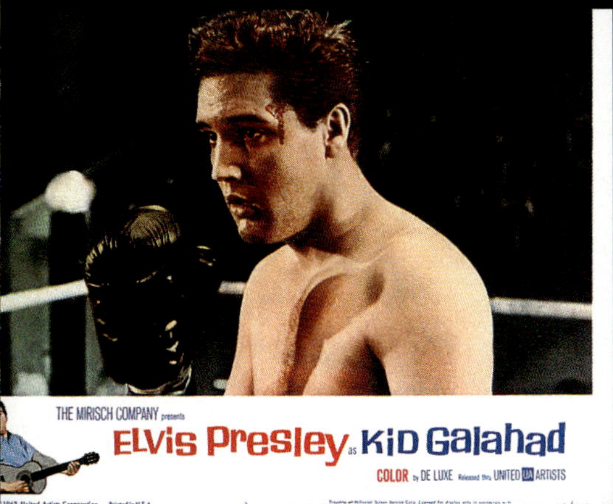

1962

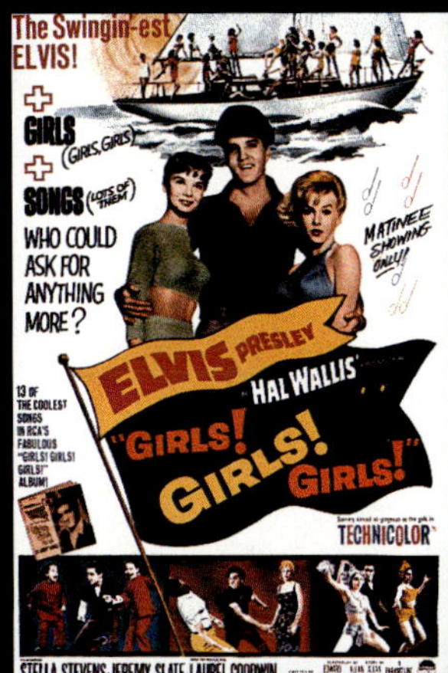

1962

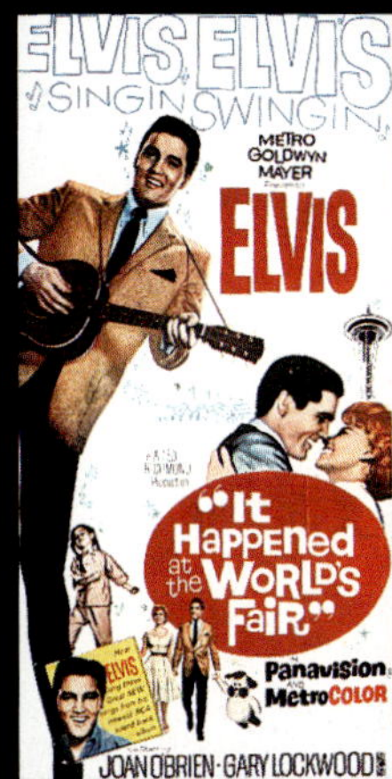

1963

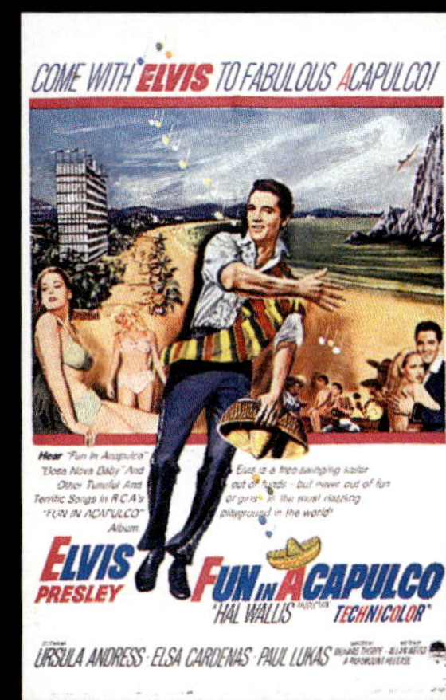

1963

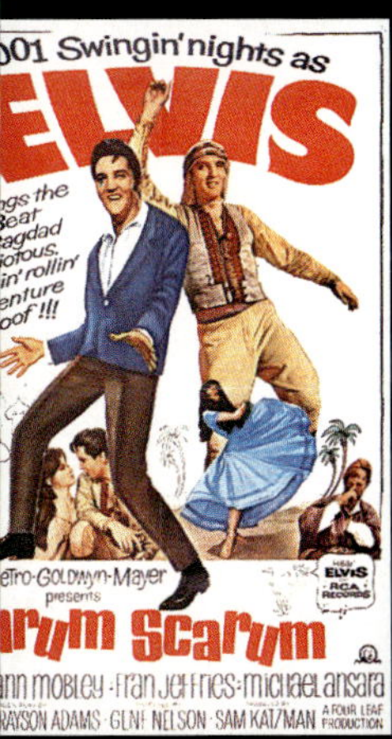

1965

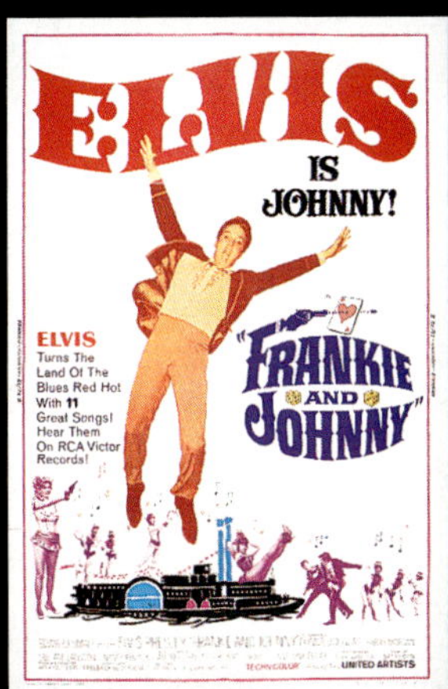

1966

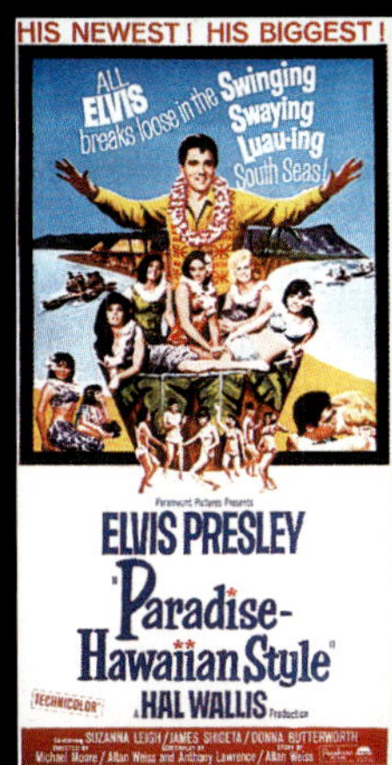

1966

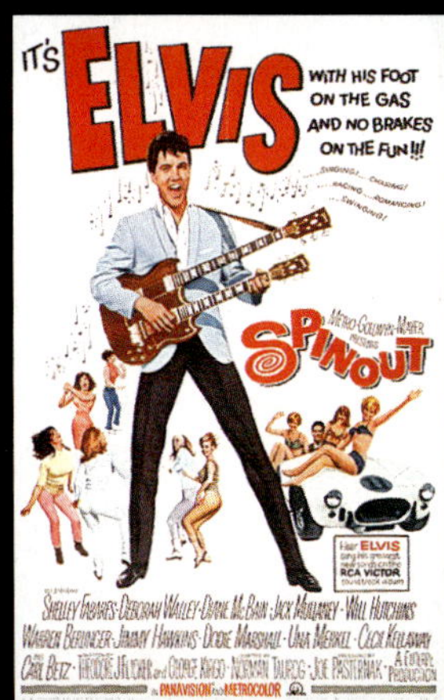

1966

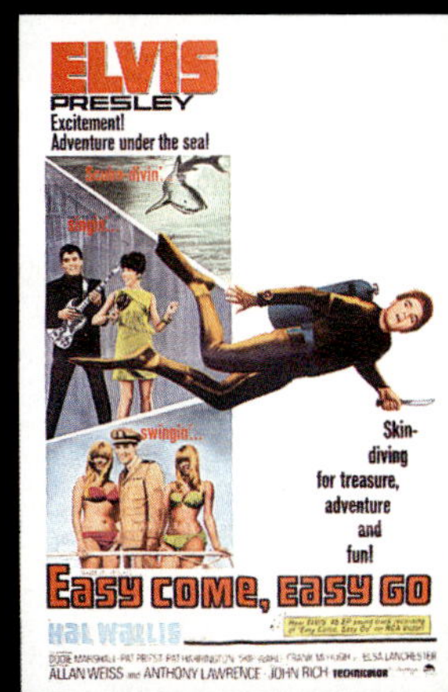

1967

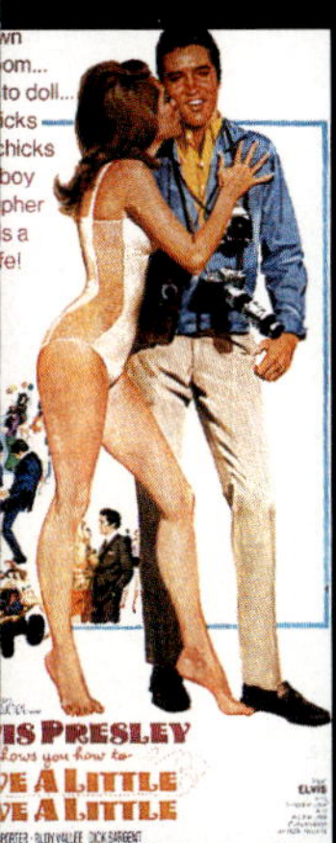
1968

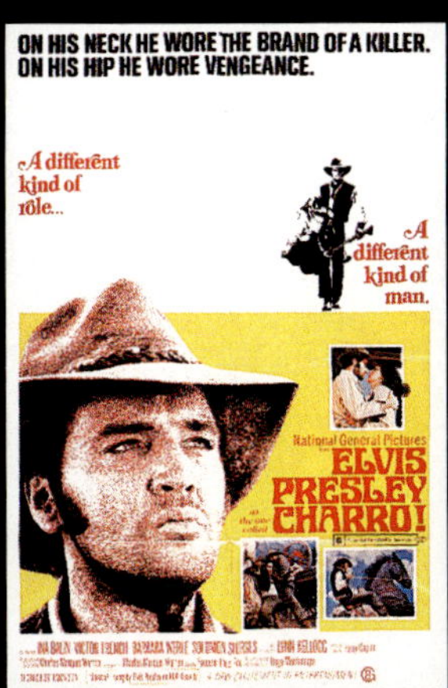

1969

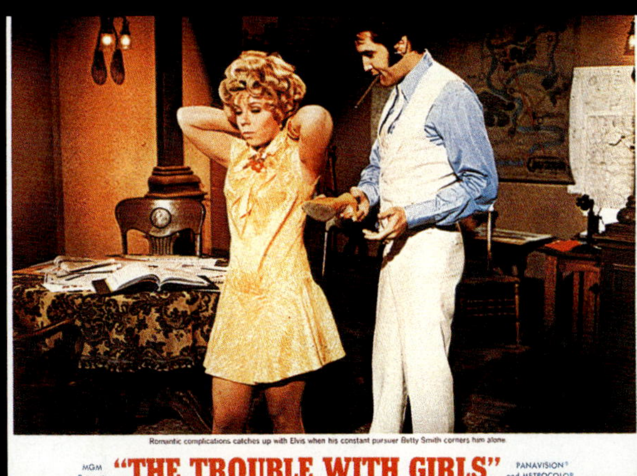

1969

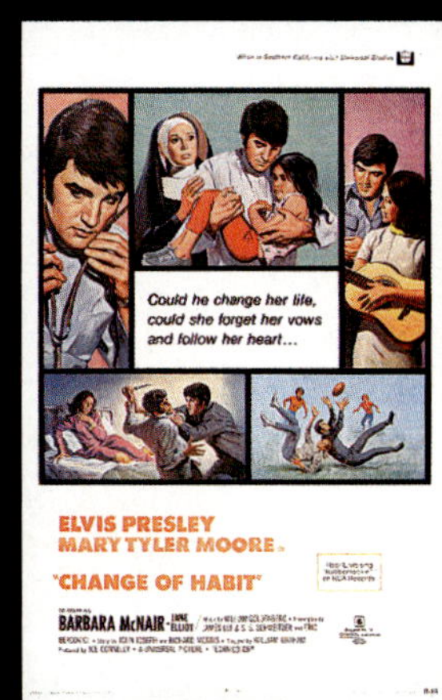

1969

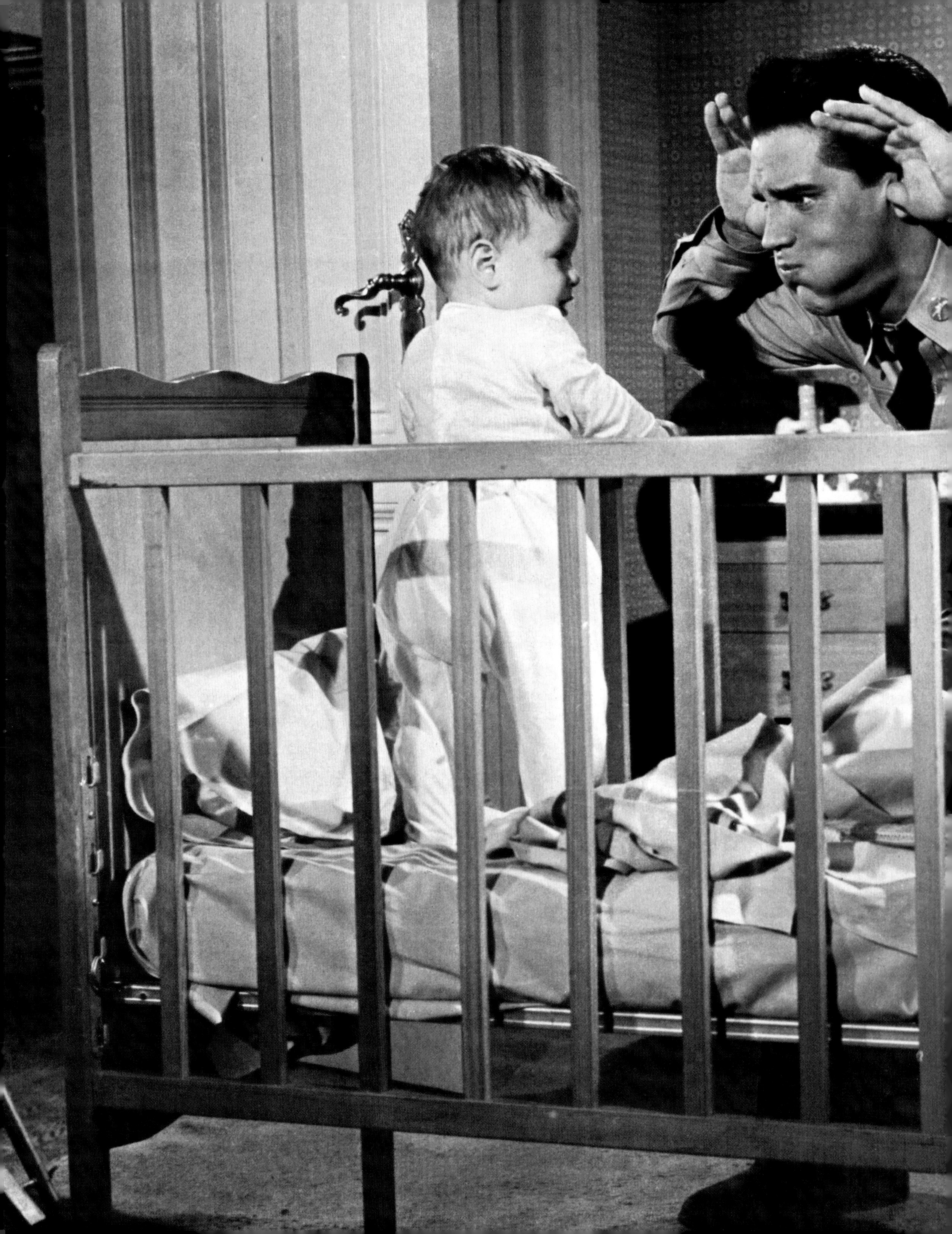

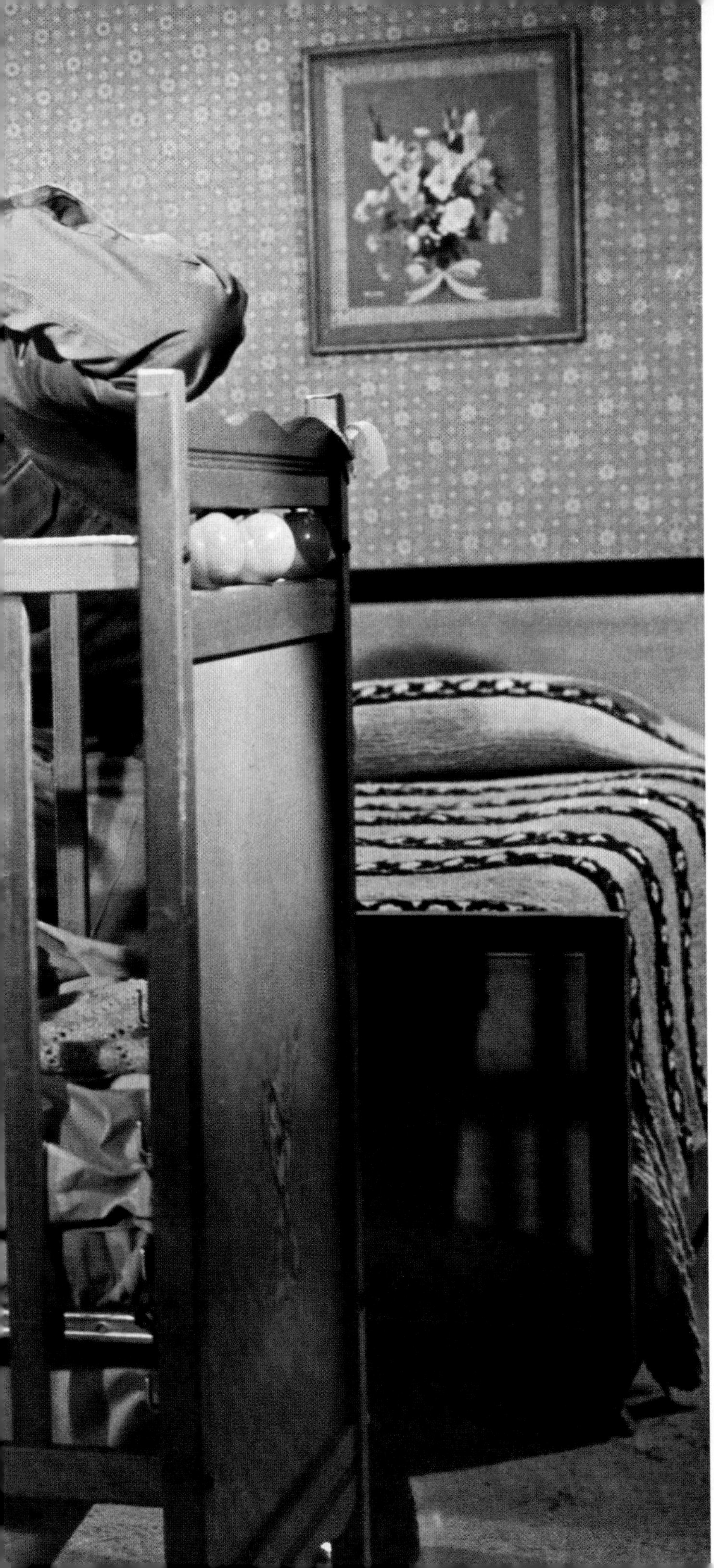

"He would be a dream to direct," said George Cukor, who had directed, among others, Tracy, Hepburn, Garland, Garbo, Bergman and Barrymore. "He can do *anything.*" The question is: Why didn't he? "The main reason was his inability to stand up to the Colonel," wrote Priscilla, and most of Elvis's friends and associates agreed. "He wouldn't stand up because the Colonel was a great businessman," said Red West, who worked on 27 of Elvis's films (including *G.I. Blues*, left). "No one in Elvis's family had a head for business, and he was afraid of making a wrong move—it was torture for him." It is important to note that Parker often bragged of his ability to "snow" people, and veteran producer Steve Binder was struck by his "strange, hypnotic, total control over Elvis." The late Philip Dunne, who directed *Wild in the Country,* added bluntly: "What I had against Parker was that he was a tasteless man who had power and used it."

"THE CRITICS CAN SAY WHATEVER THEY WANT," SAID MOVIE SONGWRITER BEN WEISMAN. "THE BOTTOM LINE IS: THE PUBLIC LOVED HIS MOVIES!" INDEED, DESPITE THEIR POOR QUALITY, THERE WAS ALWAYS SOMETHING TO LOVE: GOOFY HUMOR, CAMPY SEXINESS, EVEN THE REASSURING PREDICTABILITY THESE STILLS REFLECT.

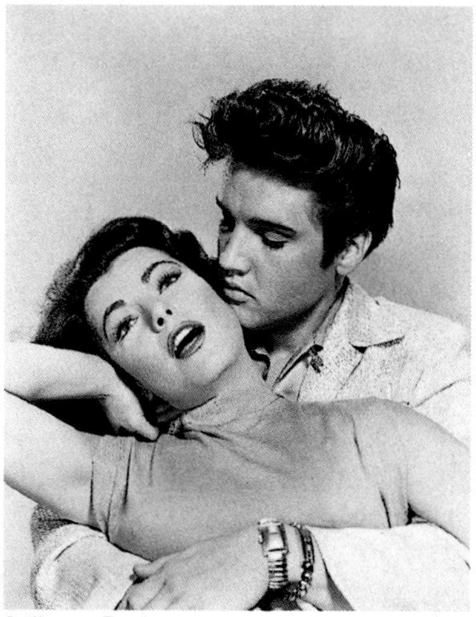
Jailhouse Rock

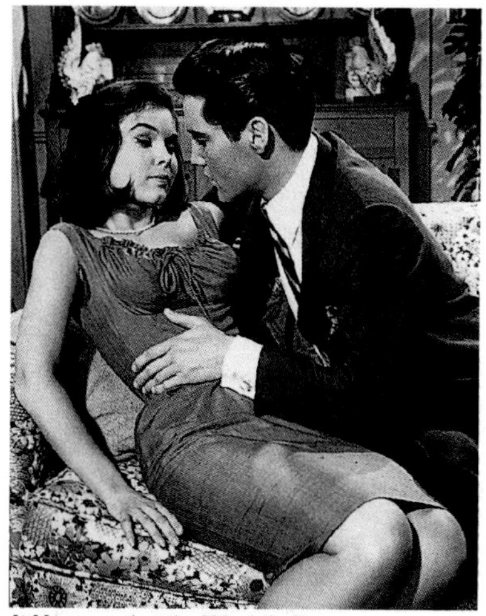
It Happened at the World's Fair

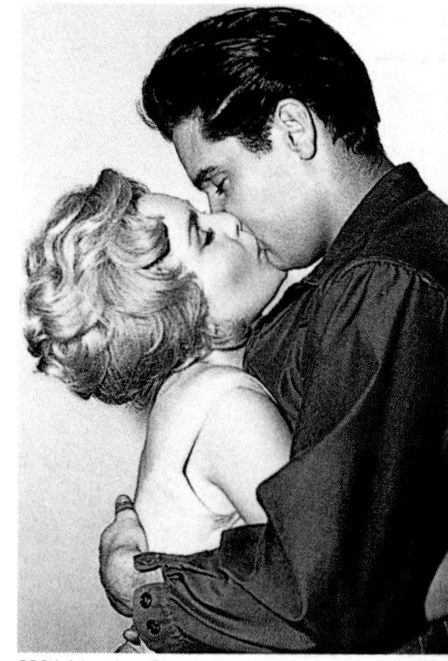
Wild in the Country

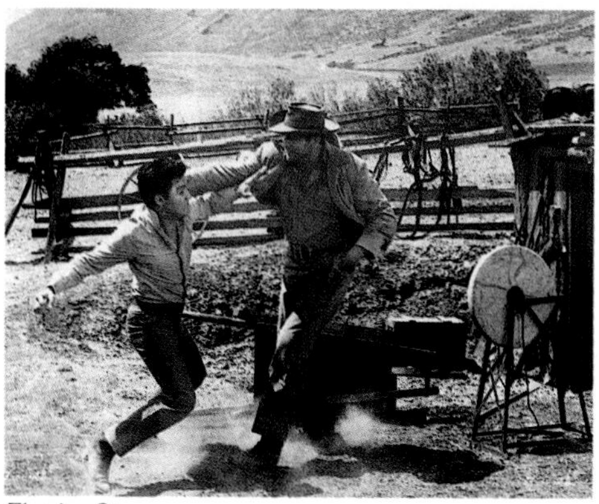
Flaming Star

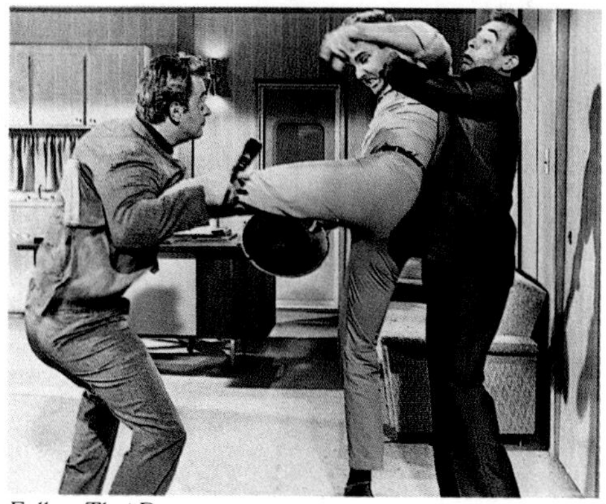
Follow That Dream

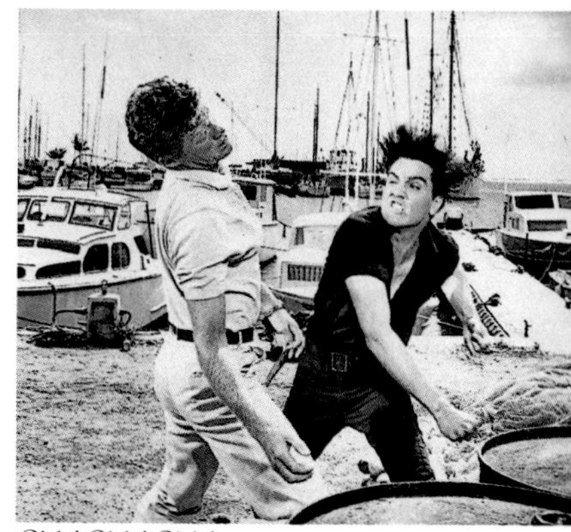
Girls! Girls! Girls!

"I FEEL LIKE A GODDAMN IDIOT BREAKING INTO SONG WHEN I'M TALKING TO SOME CHICK ON A TRAIN," HE COMPLAINED TO PRISCILLA IN 1960. LITTLE DID HE KNOW THAT, SEVEN YEARS LATER, HIS ROLE IN *STAY AWAY, JOE* WOULD REQUIRE HIM TO SING TO A BULL NAMED DOMINIC.

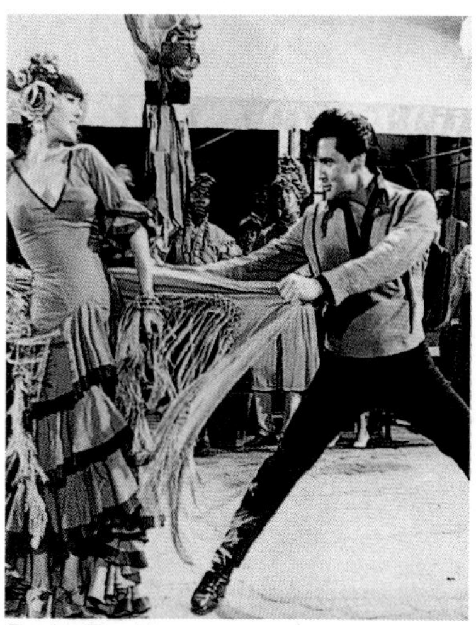
Double Trouble

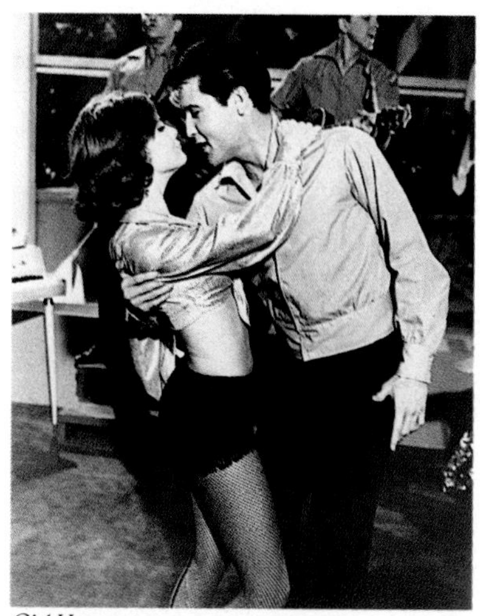
Girl Happy

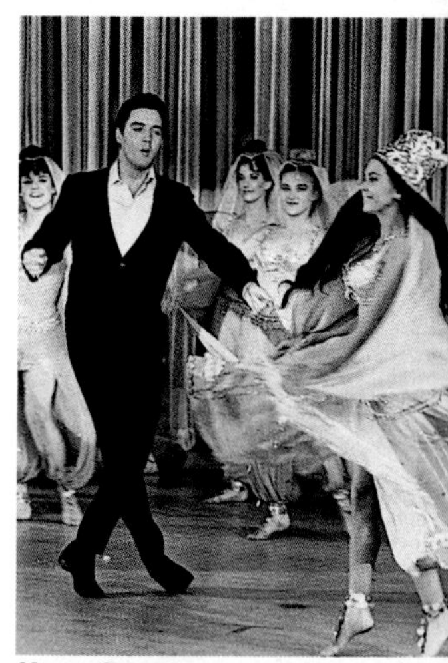
Harum Scarum

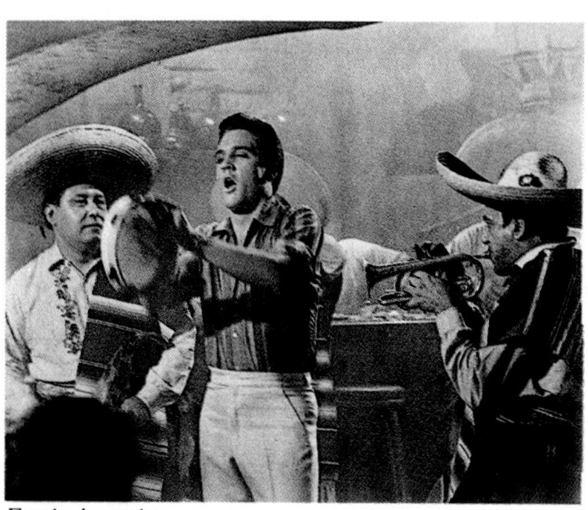
Fun in Acapulco

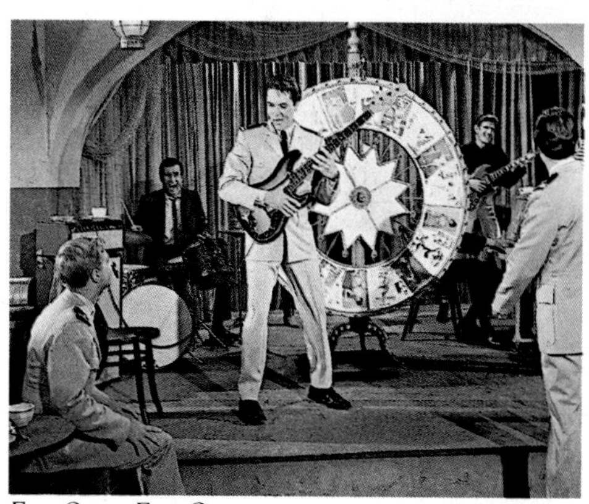
Easy Come, Easy Go

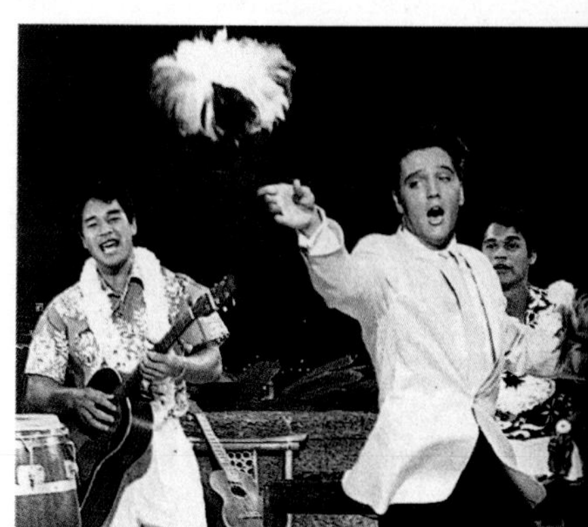
Blue Hawaii

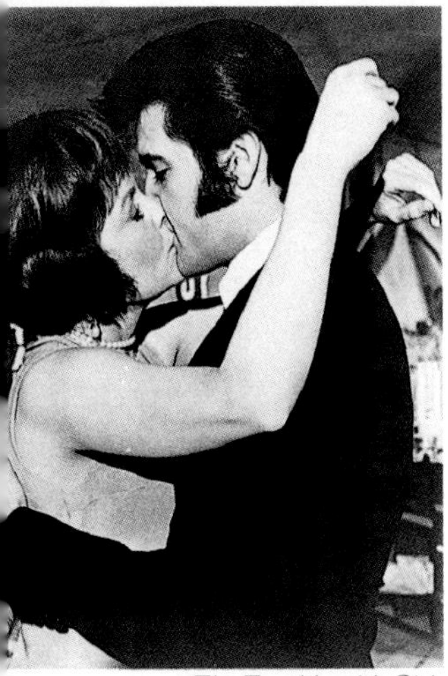

The Trouble with Girls

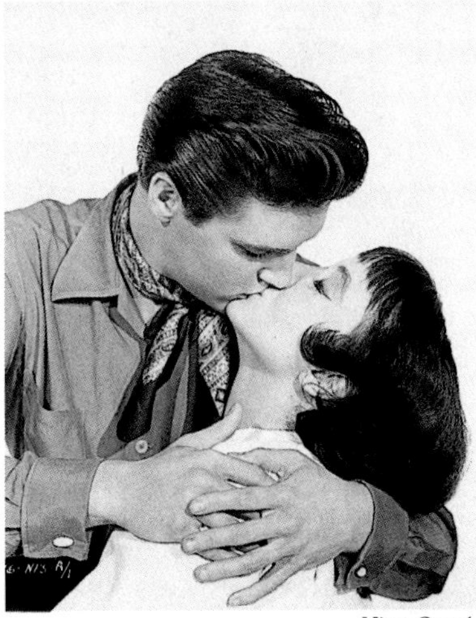

King Creole

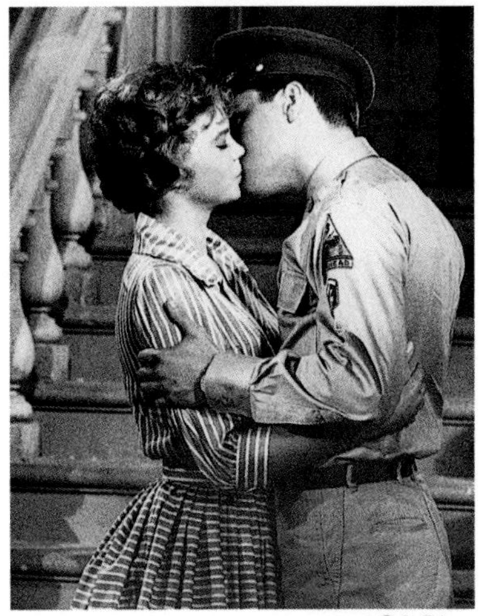

G.I. Blues

MUSIC WAS THE BIGGEST CASUALTY OF ELVIS'S FILM CAREER. HE LABORED THROUGH SUCH GROANERS AS "QUEENIE WAHINE'S PAPAYA," "YOGA IS AS YOGA DOES" AND "(THERE'S) NO ROOM TO RHUMBA IN A SPORTS CAR." "TERRIBLE STUFF!" SHUDDERED SCOTTY MOORE. "BUT ELVIS DID EVERY SONG TO THE VERY BEST OF HIS ABILITY."

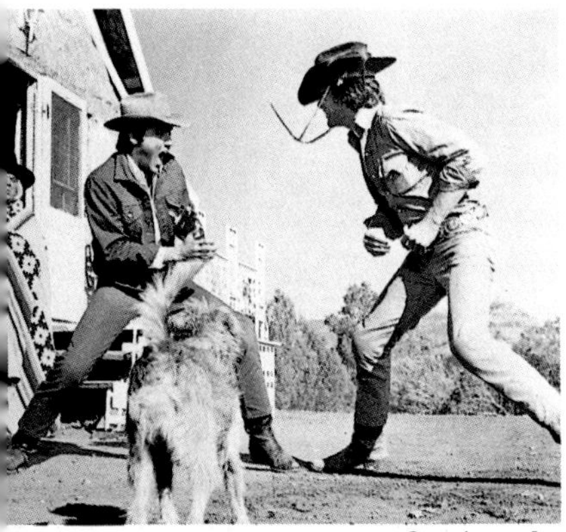

Stay Away, Joe

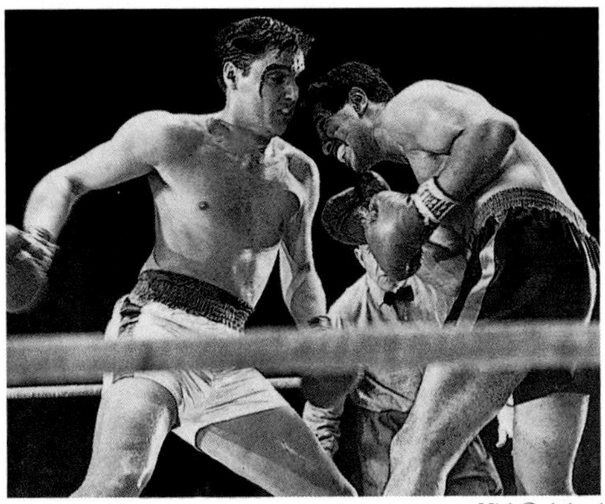

Kid Galahad

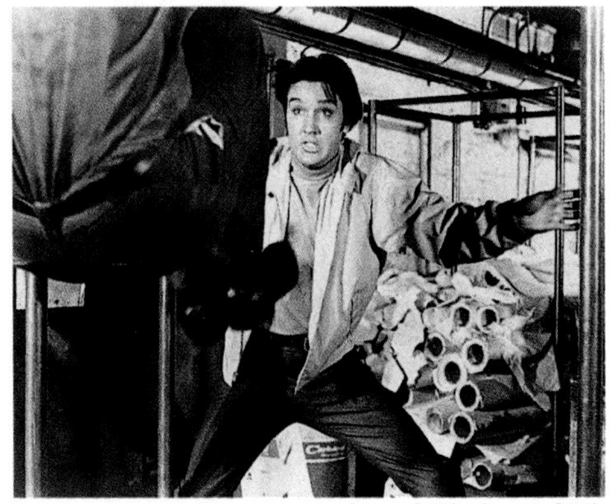

Live a Little, Love a Little

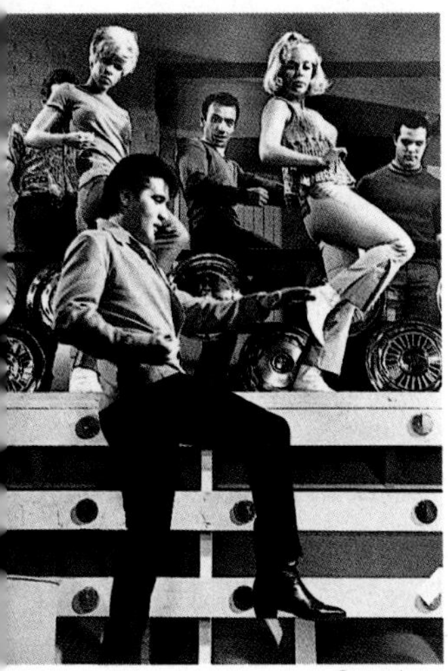

Speedway

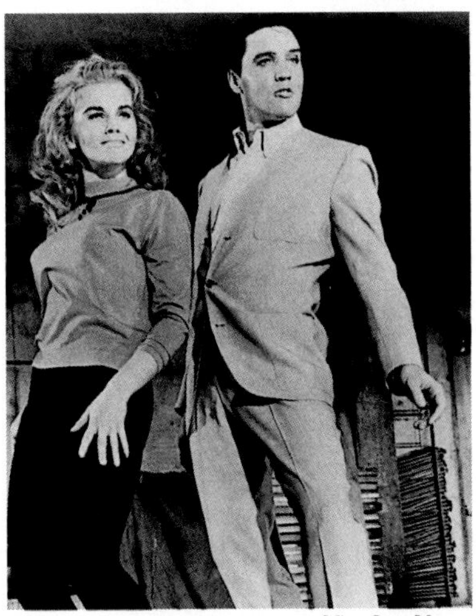

Viva Las Vegas

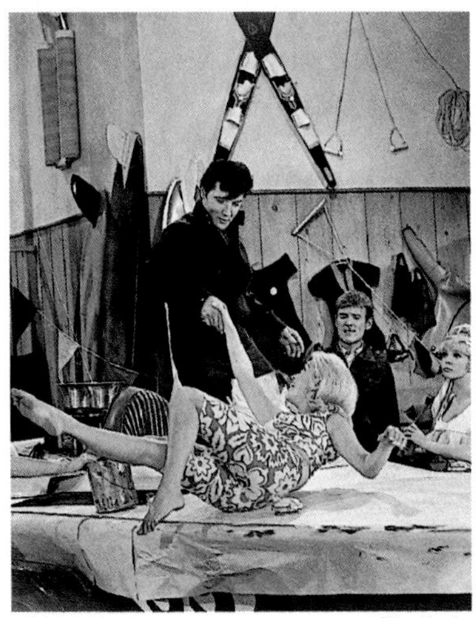

Clambake

FINALLY, IN 1969, HE WENT PUBLIC, ADMITTING TO BRITISH JOURNALIST RAY CONNOLLY THAT HE WAS "ASHAMED" OF SOME OF HIS MOVIES AND THAT HE'D "BEEN EXTREMELY UNHAPPY WITH THAT SIDE OF MY CAREER FOR SOME TIME. . . . FROM NOW ON," HE VOWED, "I'M GOING TO PLAY SERIOUS PARTS." BUT HE NEVER ACTED AGAIN.

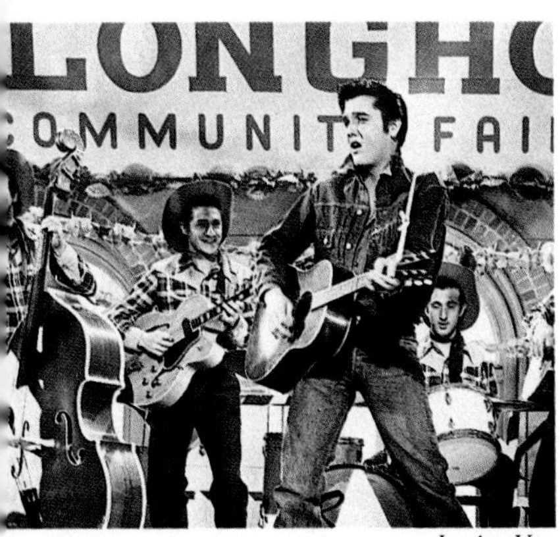

Loving You

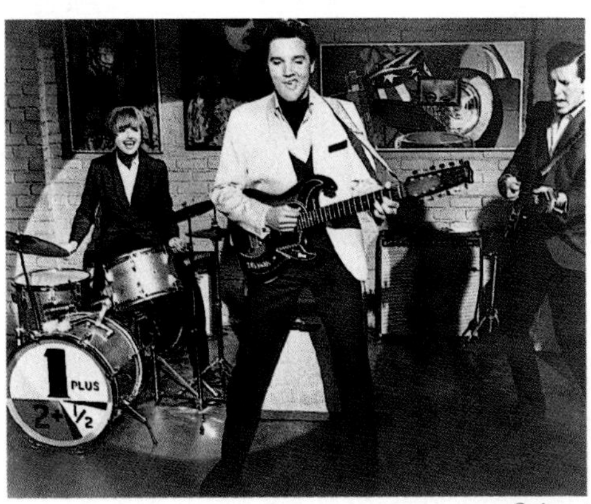

Spinout

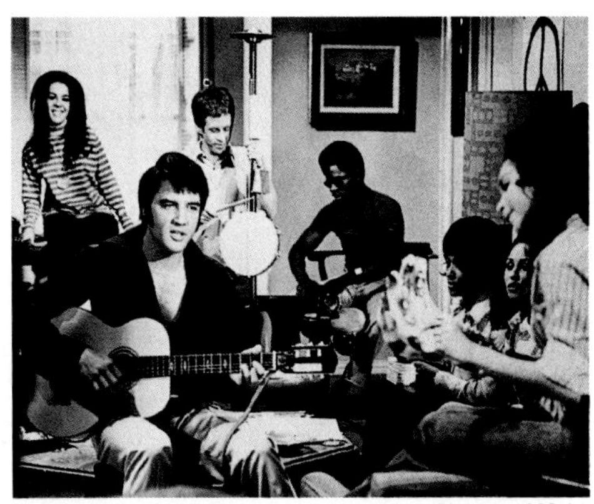

Change of Habit

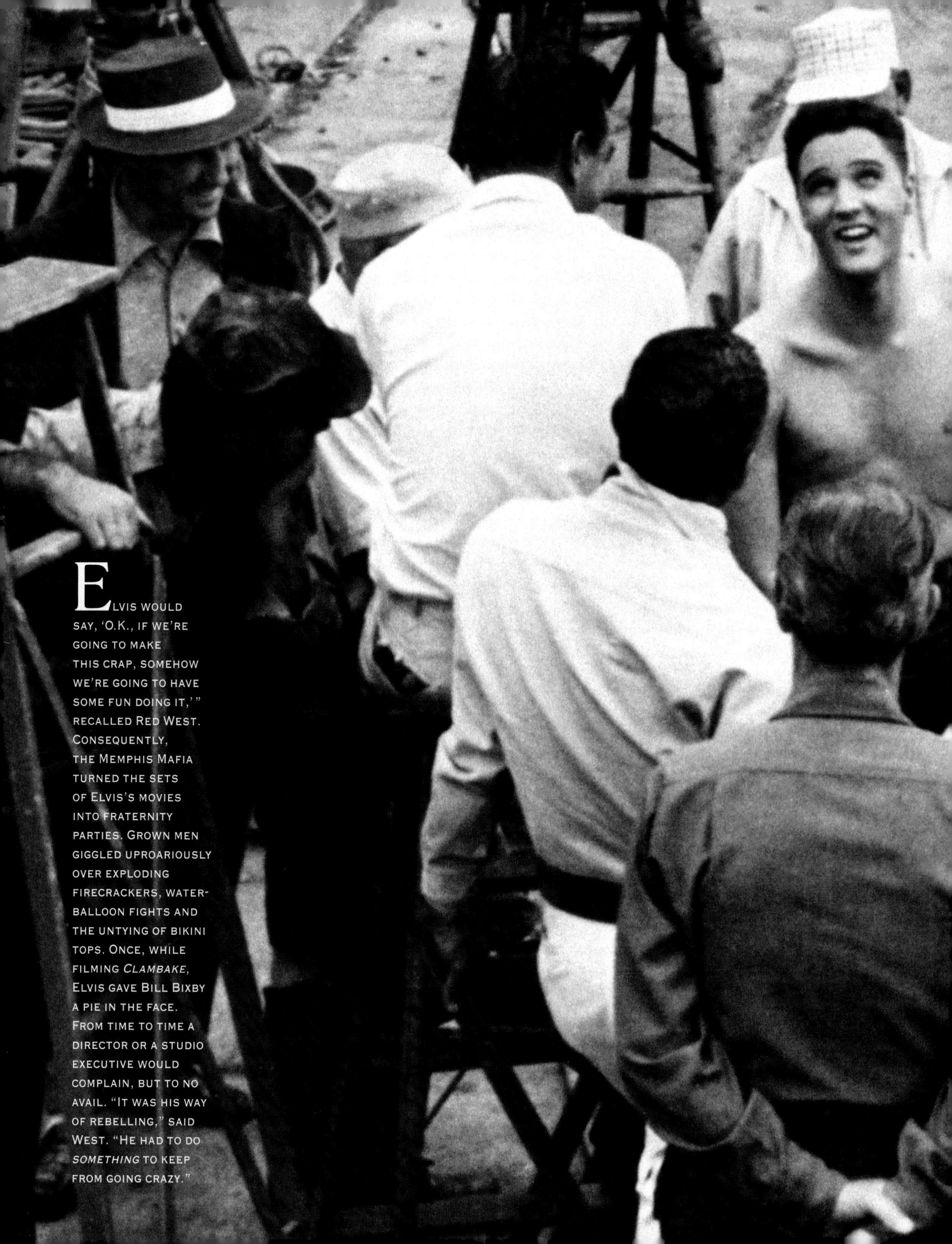

Elvis would say, 'O.K., if we're going to make this crap, somehow we're going to have some fun doing it,'" recalled Red West. Consequently, the Memphis Mafia turned the sets of Elvis's movies into fraternity parties. Grown men giggled uproariously over exploding firecrackers, water-balloon fights and the untying of bikini tops. Once, while filming *Clambake*, Elvis gave Bill Bixby a pie in the face. From time to time a director or a studio executive would complain, but to no avail. "It was his way of rebelling," said West. "He had to do *something* to keep from going crazy."

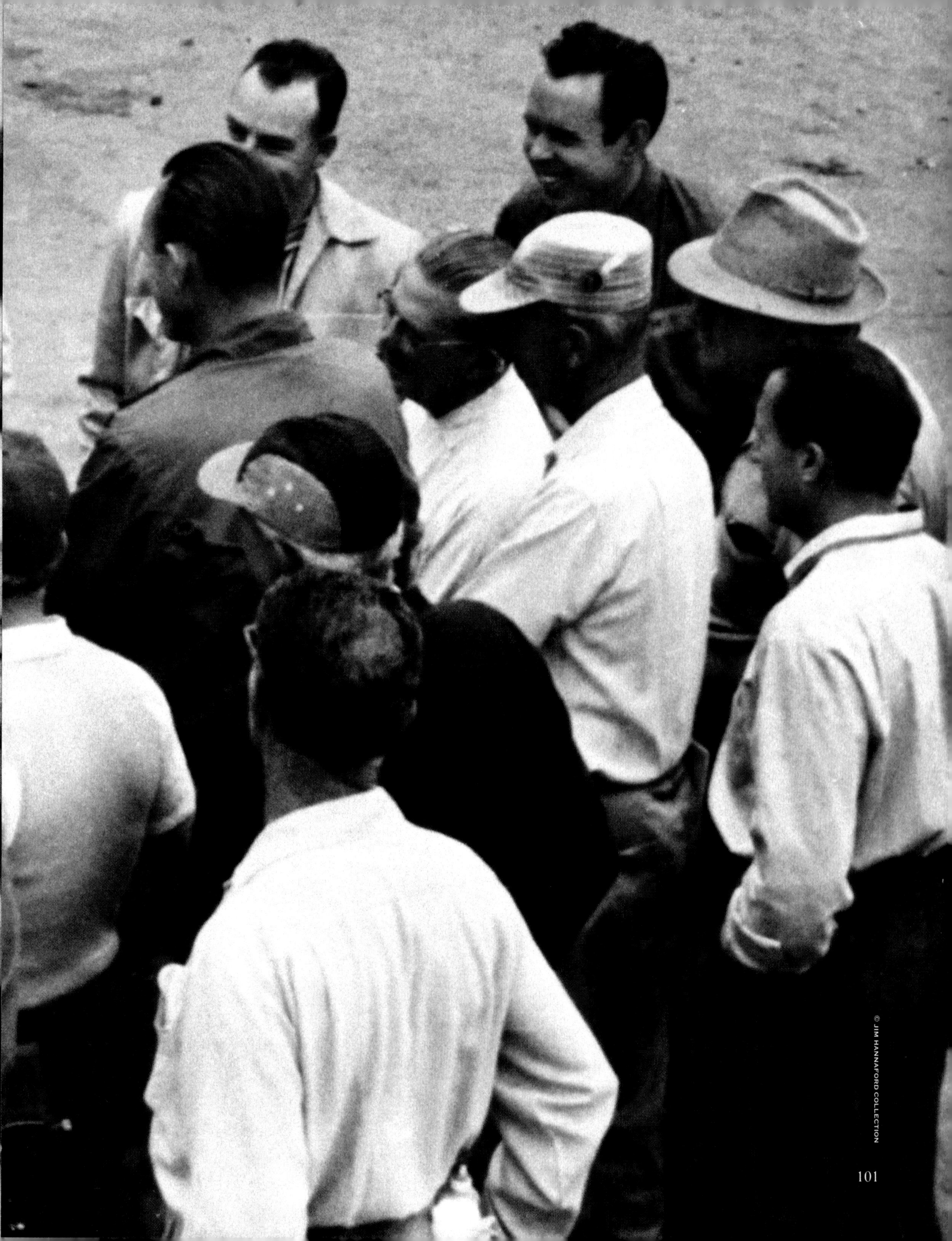

© JIM HANNAFORD COLLECTION

FOR FIVE YEARS, WHILE HER MAN PLAYED HOLLYWOOD CASANOVA, PRISCILLA BEAULIEU TRAINED TO BE MRS. ELVIS. FROM THE TIME SHE MOVED INTO GRACELAND AT THE AGE OF 17, ELVIS EXPECTED HER TO BE ONE PART SERVANT, ONE PART SEX KITTEN, AND ONE PART NAIVE SCHOOLGIRL, OBLIVIOUS TO HIS WOMANIZING. BUT SHE STUCK IT OUT, AND ON MAY 1, 1967, THE KING, WEARING A DARK PAISLEY TUX, WED HIS QUEEN. "SHE WAS ABSOLUTELY PETRIFIED," SAID NEVADA SUPREME COURT JUDGE DAVID ZENOFF, WHO MARRIED THEM. AND ELVIS "WAS SO NERVOUS HE WAS ALMOST BAWLING."

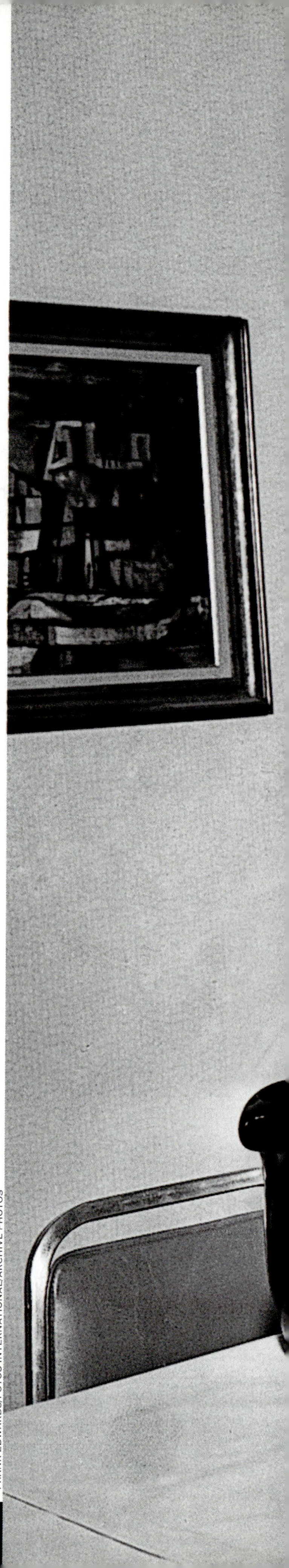

FRANK EDWARDS/FOTOS INTERNATIONAL/ARCHIVE PHOTOS

As filming begins on *Viva Las Vegas,* Elvis begins a torrid affair with costar Ann-Margret. ("She's the female you," one friend tells him.) The film turns out to be one of Elvis's best, largely because of the magnetism between the stars. After his death, many of Elvis's friends will insist that it was she whom Elvis wanted to wed—and should have.

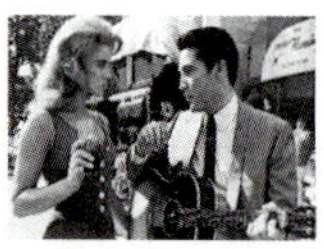

JULY 1963

Elvis meets his mop-topped rivals when the Beatles stop by his Bel-Air, Calif., digs for a chat and a bit of a sing. Paul McCartney is amazed by Elvis's remote-control TV switch: "He was the first guy I ever saw who had one of those."

AUGUST 1965

Elvis purchases the Circle G Ranch near Walls, Miss., for about $300,000. For a while he and the Memphis Mafia enjoy dressing up like cowboys and riding the range, but before the end of the year, he will grow bored with the place.

FEBRUARY 1967

A car is set ablaze on the Graceland grounds, and the following day Elvis beats up a yardman, Troy Ivy. The public begins to get the sense that all is not right in the Kingdom.

SEPTEMBER 1967

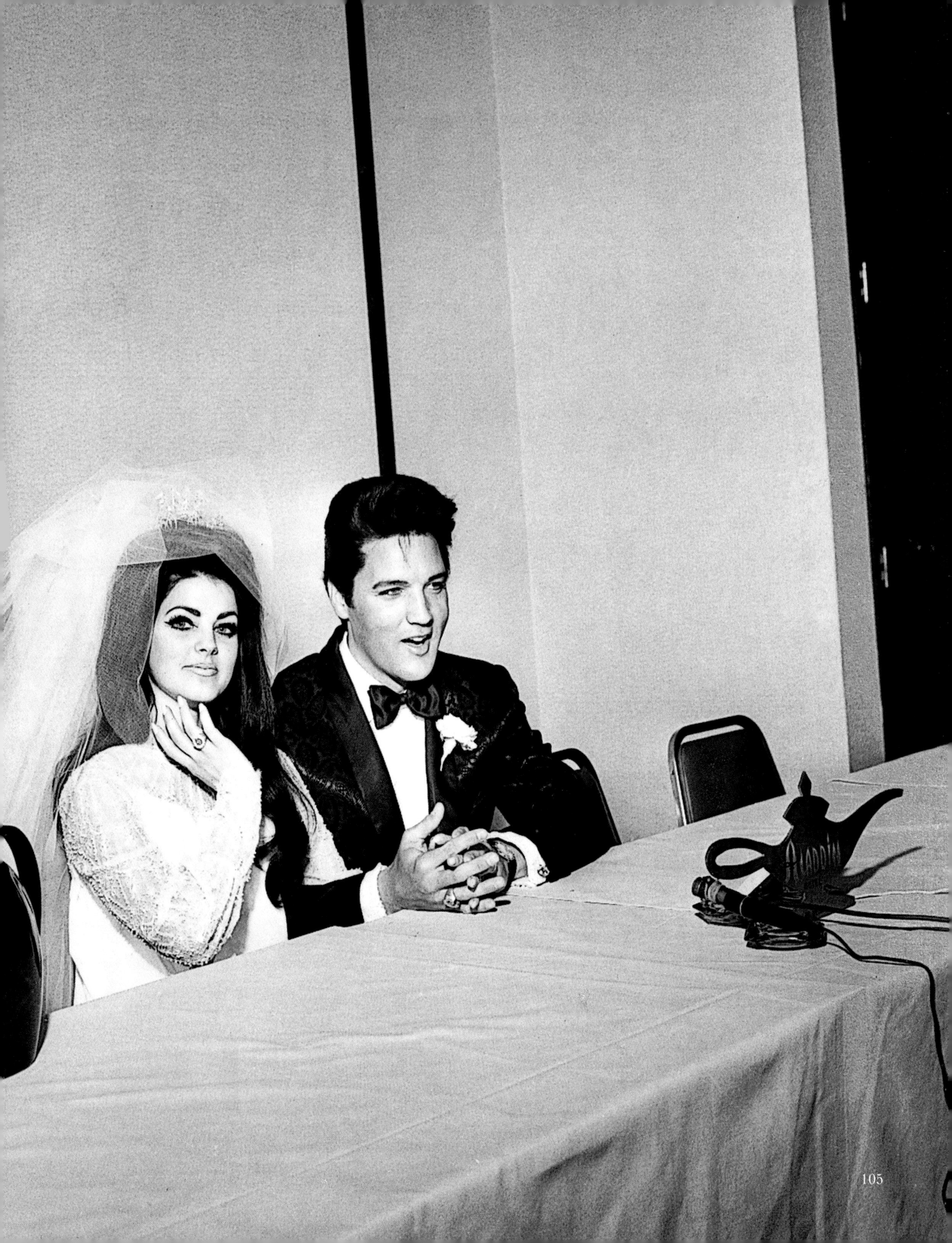
Aladdin

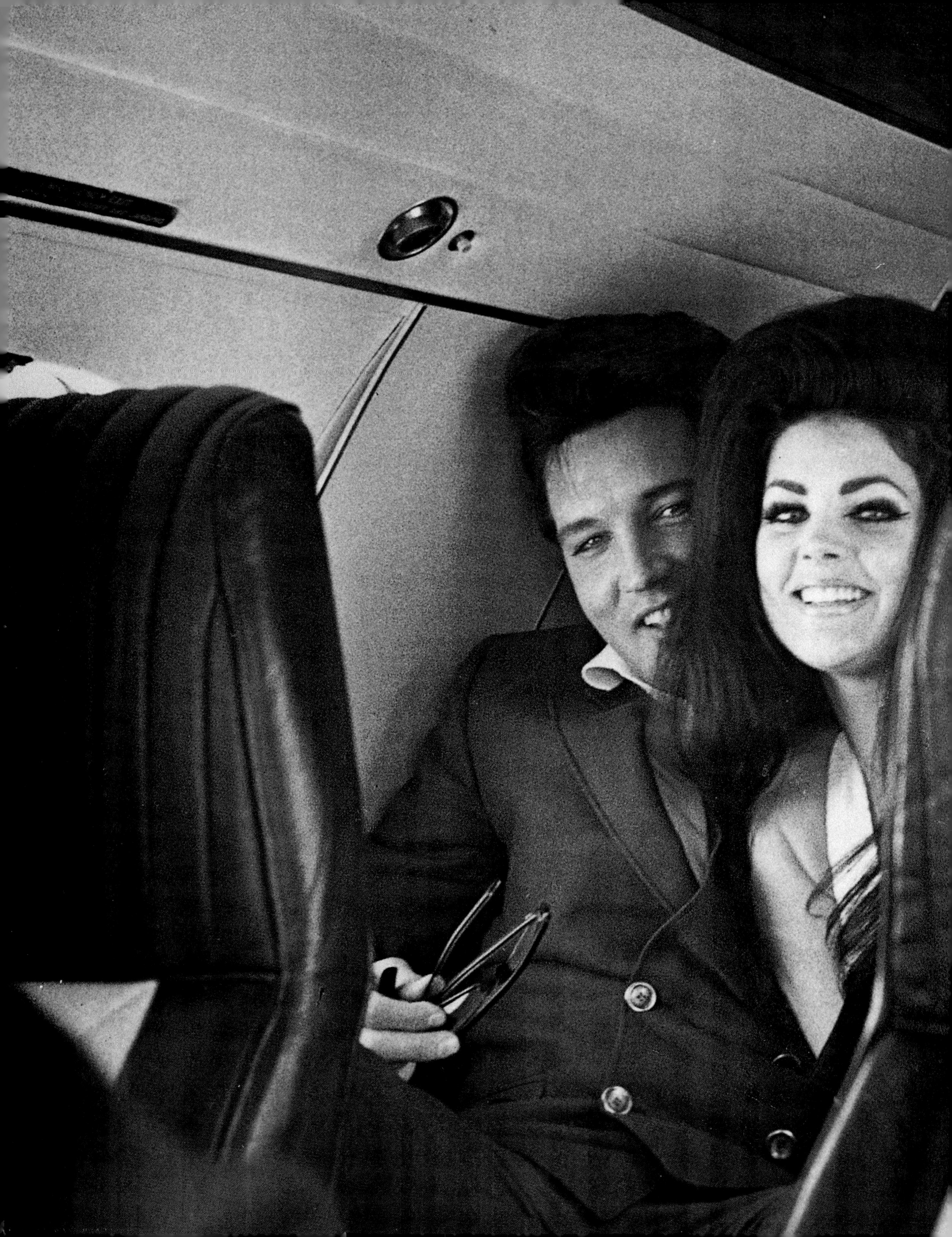

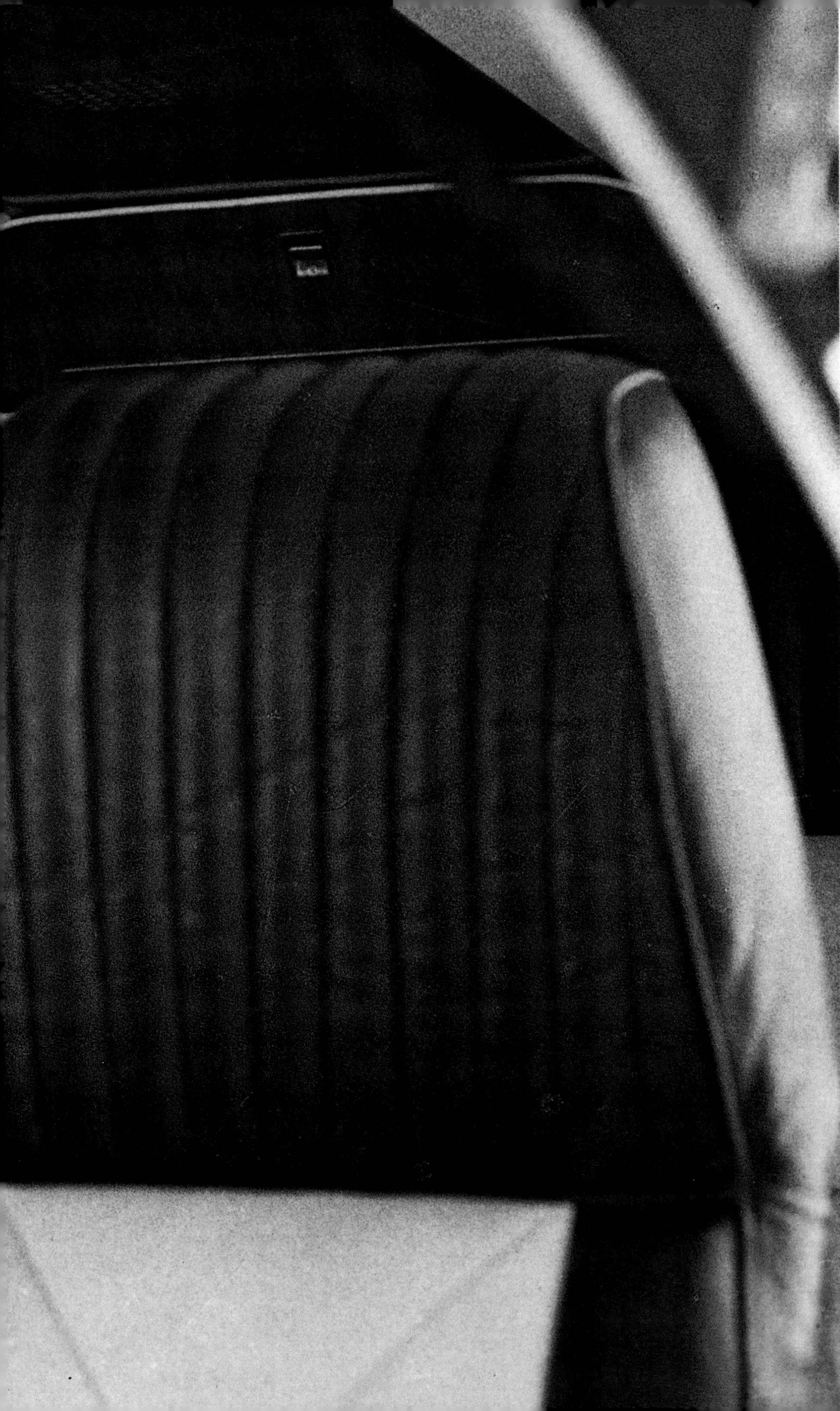

ELVIS HAD LITTLE TO SMILE ABOUT IN THE MONTHS BEFORE WINGING HIS WAY TO PALM SPRINGS WITH HIS BRIDE. HE HAD NOT APPEARED IN CONCERT SINCE MARCH OF 1961, AND HIS CAREER WAS AT AN ALL-TIME LOW. TO MAKE MATTERS WORSE, JUST AS HE WAS TO BEGIN FILMING *CLAMBAKE* (ABOUT TWO MONTHS BEFORE THIS PICTURE WAS TAKEN), HE HAD TRIPPED ON AN ELECTRICAL CORD, WHACKED HIS HEAD ON A BATHTUB AND SUFFERED A CONCUSSION. IT WAS WONDERFUL TO FORGET ALL THIS FOR A WHILE. AFTER THE HONEYMOON HE TOOK PRISCILLA TO HIS RANCH IN MISSISSIPPI, WHERE THEY STAYED IN A TRAILER. THEN, NINE MONTHS TO THE DAY AFTER THEIR MARRIAGE, SHE GAVE BIRTH TO THEIR FIRST AND ONLY CHILD, LISA MARIE.

BETTMANN/UPI

ON A SUMMER DAY IN 1968 HE STOOD IN FRONT OF AN UNOPEN BAR ON L.A.'S SUNSET STRIP. STEVE BINDER WAS RIGHT: HE WAS UNRECOGNIZABLE; PEOPLE WERE PASSING BY WITHOUT GIVING HIM A SECOND LOOK. THE NBC PRODUCER HAD DARED ELVIS TO SHOW HIMSELF IN PUBLIC, AND THERE WAS NO GETTING AROUND IT, ELVIS WAS AS COLD AS WEEK-OLD CORN BREAD. SOMETHING HAD TO BE DONE.

BACK COMING

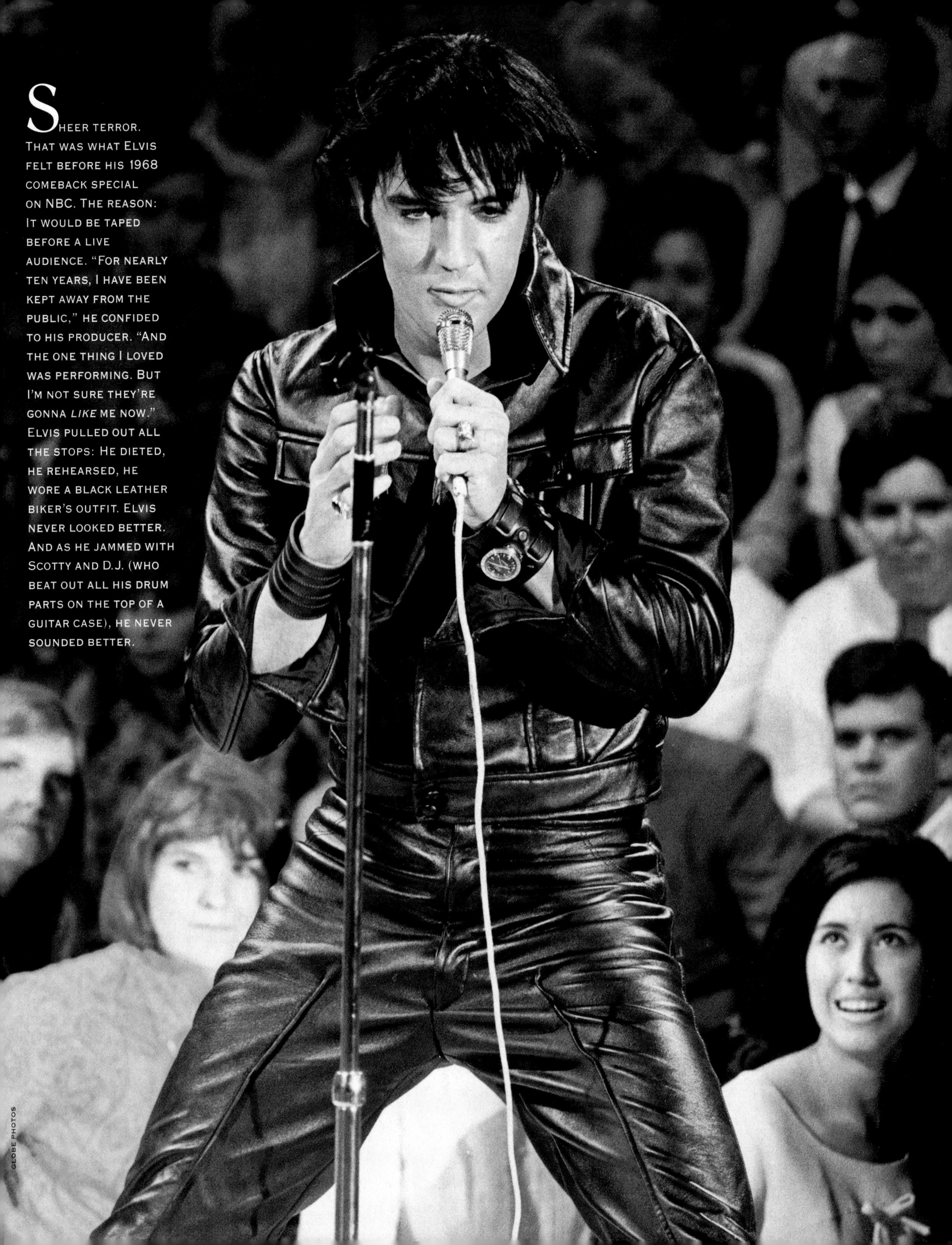

Sheer terror. That was what Elvis felt before his 1968 comeback special on NBC. The reason: It would be taped before a live audience. "For nearly ten years, I have been kept away from the public," he confided to his producer. "And the one thing I loved was performing. But I'm not sure they're gonna *like* me now." Elvis pulled out all the stops: He dieted, he rehearsed, he wore a black leather biker's outfit. Elvis never looked better. And as he jammed with Scotty and D.J. (who beat out all his drum parts on the top of a guitar case), he never sounded better.

GLOBE PHOTOS

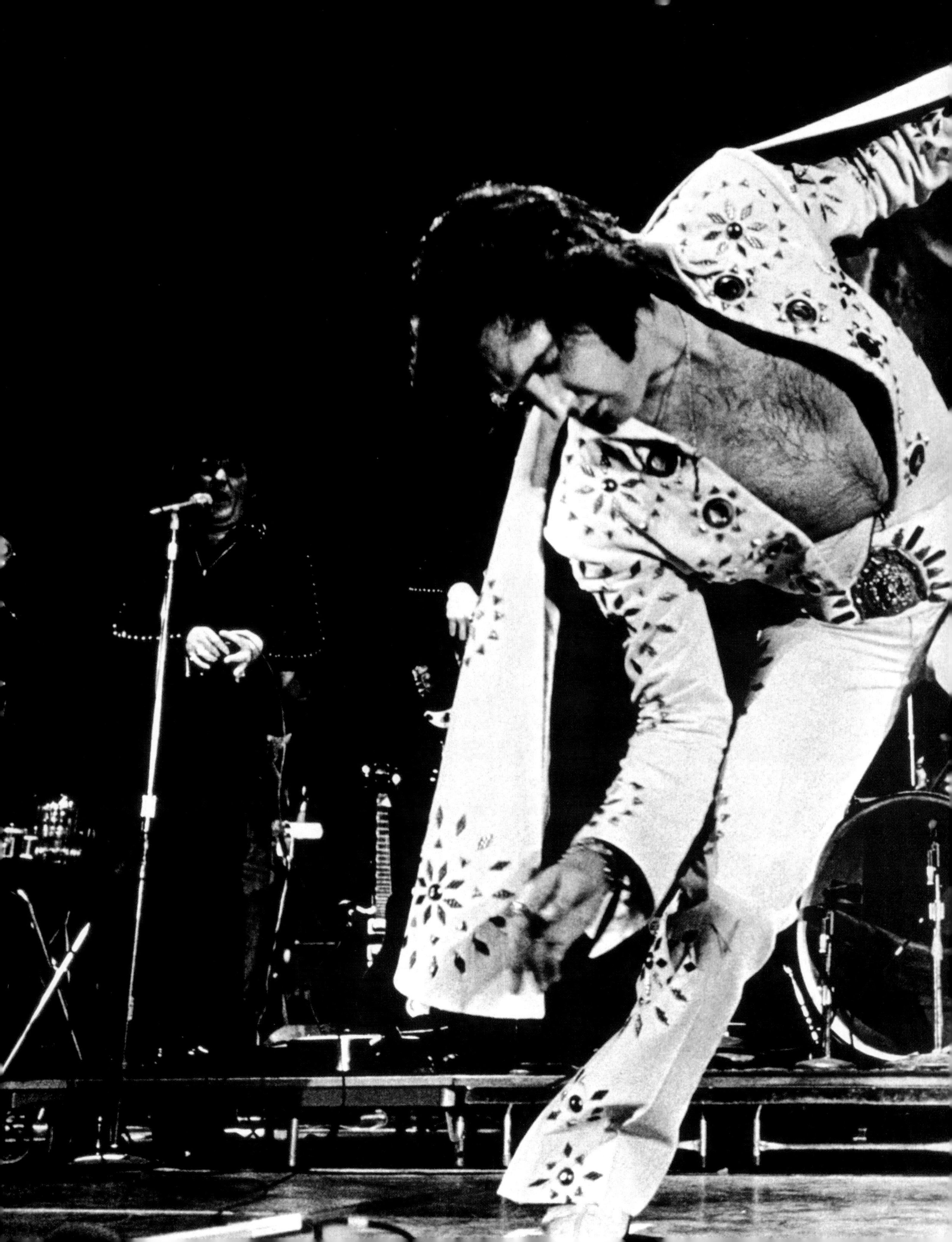

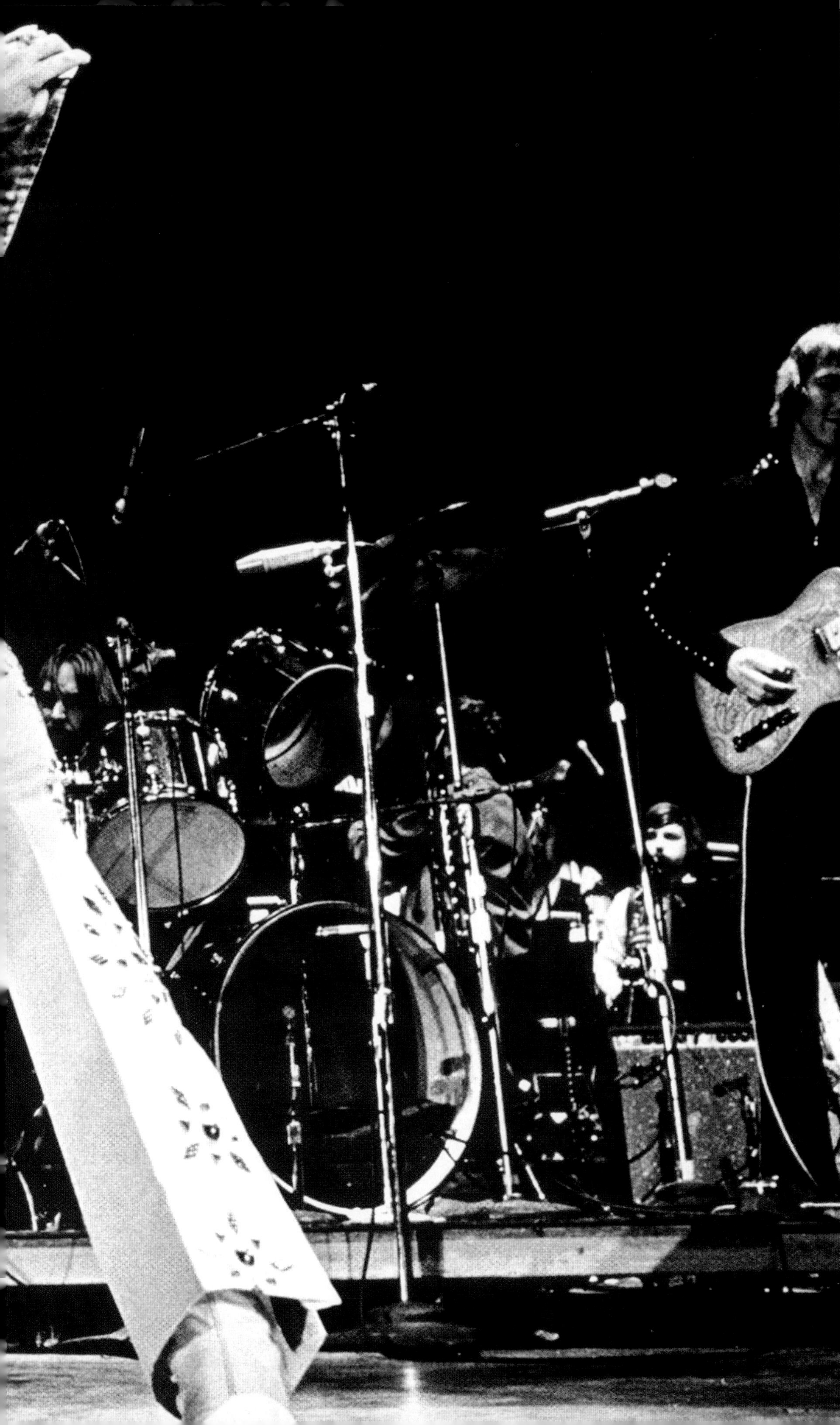

I'VE GOT TO GET BACK IN FRONT OF THE PUBLIC," AN ELATED ELVIS TOLD COLONEL PARKER AFTER THE COMEBACK SPECIAL. ON JULY 31, 1969, HE PLAYED HIS FIRST LIVE DATE IN ALMOST A DECADE. THE AUDIENCE AT THE INTERNATIONAL HOTEL IN LAS VEGAS INCLUDED CARY GRANT, FATS DOMINO, HENRY MANCINI AND SAMMY DAVIS JR. *ROLLING STONE* CALLED HIS PERFORMANCE "SUPERNATURAL." FOR THE REST OF HIS LIFE, HE TRIED TO SURPASS IT (AS AT RIGHT, CIRCA 1972).

MOTION PICTURE & TV PHOTO ARCHIVE

ATTENDING AN ELVIS CONCERT IN THE '70S WAS LIKE ROLLING THE DICE IN A VEGAS CASINO: ANYTHING FROM A JACKPOT TO A CRAP-OUT WAS POSSIBLE. HIS JUMPSUITS WERE SPECTACULAR (RIGHT)—BUT IF HIS WEIGHT WAS OUT OF CONTROL, HE WAS LIABLE TO BUST HIS SEAMS, AS HE DID ONE NIGHT IN PONTIAC, MICH., BEFORE 62,000 ASTONISHED FANS. HIS TCB (TAKIN' CARE OF BUSINESS) BAND WAS ALMOST ALWAYS SPLENDID—BUT IF HE HAD GOBBLED TOO MANY DRUGS BEFORE COMING ONSTAGE, HE WAS LIABLE TO FORGET HIS LYRICS OR BURST INTO FITS OF GIGGLING. HE WAS WALKING A TIGHTROPE. IN RETROSPECT, IT IS INCREDIBLE THAT HE WAS ABLE TO KEEP HIS BALANCE AS LONG AS HE DID.

DECEMBER 1970

Elvis writes President Nixon a rambling letter, requesting a visit and a federal narc's badge. He says he wants to fight "drug abuse and communist brainwashing techniques." Elvis gets his meeting—and his badge—but subsequently turns down Nixon's invitation to play the White House.

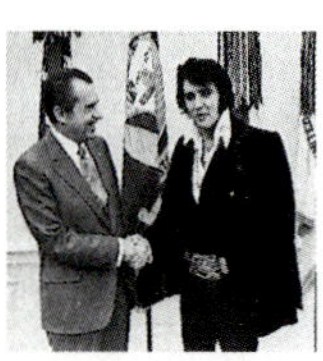

JANUARY 1973

A live performance at the Honolulu International Center is beamed to television audiences in 36 countries around the world. As many as 1.5 billion people will tune in. When it's all over, Elvis—who had dropped 20 pounds for the show—is so exhausted, he sleeps for 24 hours.

AUGUST 1974

Elvis holds discussions with Barbra Streisand at the Las Vegas Hilton on the possibility of costarring with her in *A Star Is Born.* Elvis wants desperately to do it, but the Colonel later turns thumbs down.

APRIL 1975

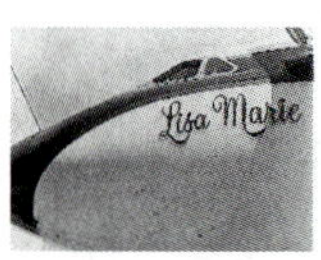

He purchases a Convair 880 jet for $250,000, names it the *Lisa Marie,* then spends $750,000 customizing it with a purple carpet, queen-size bed and gold bathroom fixtures.

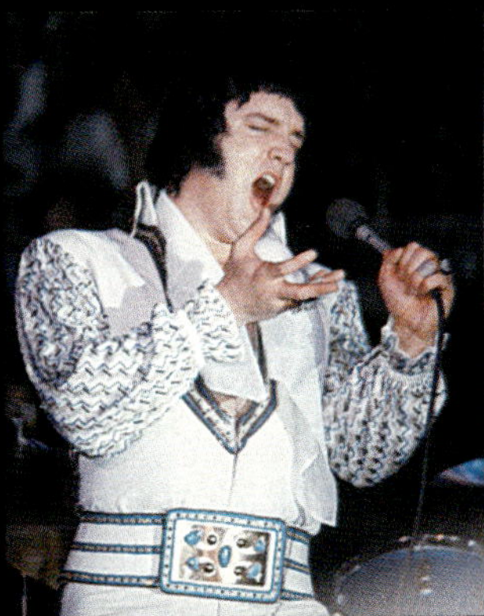
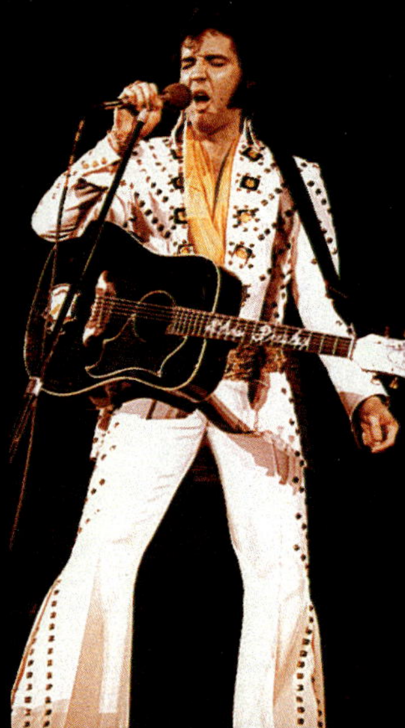
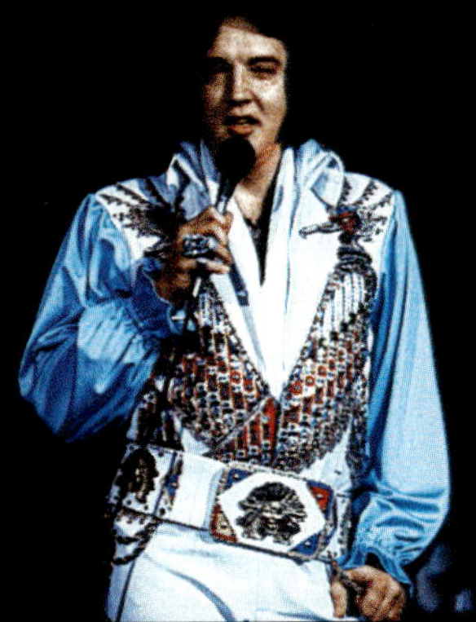
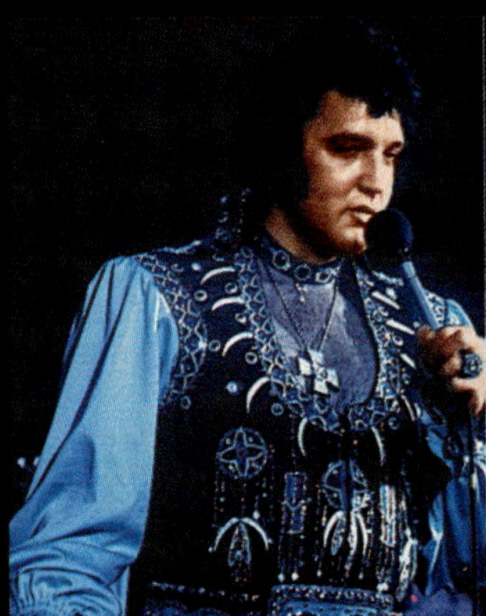
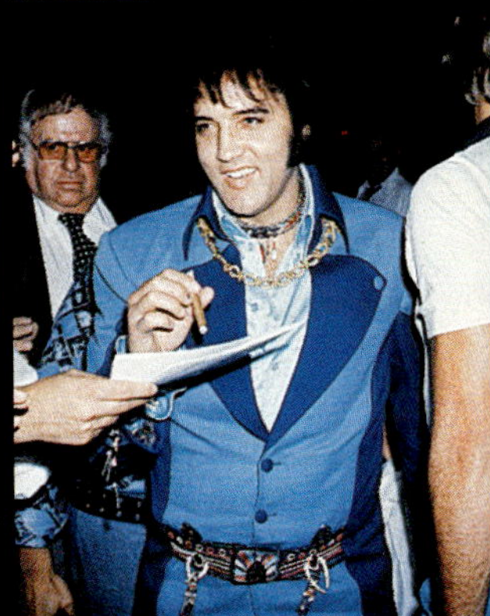
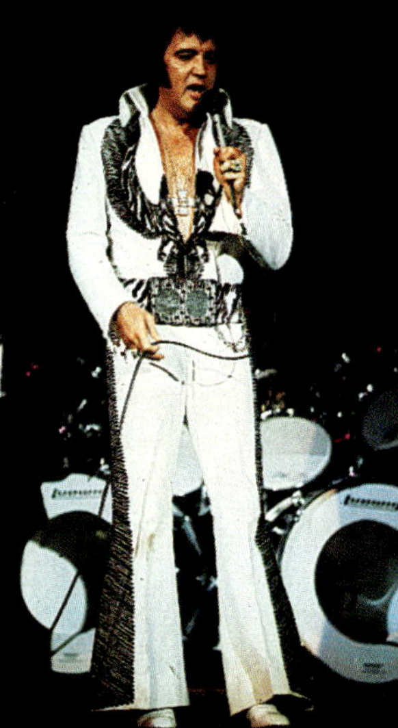
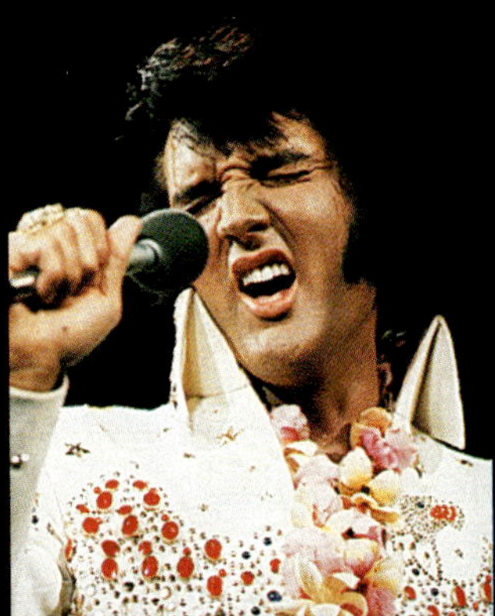
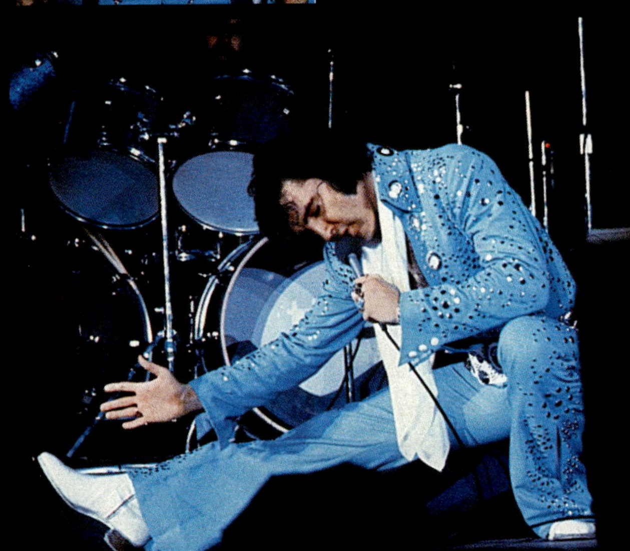
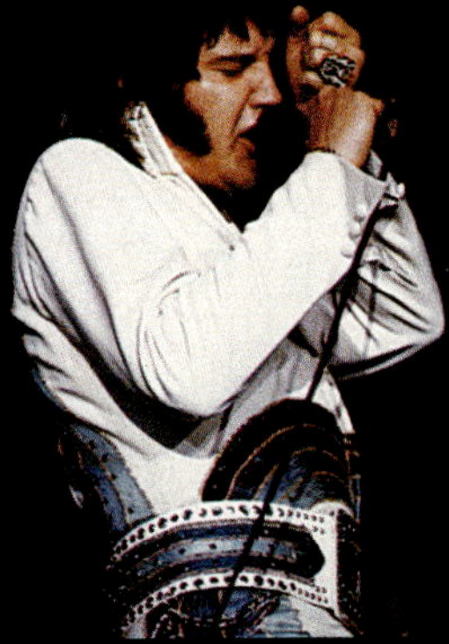

ELVIS'S LAST HOPE FOR SURVIVAL LAY WITH HIS FAMILY, WHOM HE TRULY LOVED. BUT DRUGS AND HIS PHILANDERING DROVE PRISCILLA AWAY FROM HIM, AND DRUGS AND WORK KEPT HIM FROM GIVING LISA MARIE THE ATTENTION SHE DESERVED. ALTHOUGH THIS 1971 PORTRAIT FOUND THE FAMILY IN A RARE OPTIMISTIC MOOD—ELVIS WAS BACK ON TOP AND PRISCILLA WILLING TO MAKE ANOTHER GO OF IT—THEY SEPARATED THE FOLLOWING YEAR.

APRIL 1976

A group of investors, including his physician George "Dr. Nick" Nichopoulos and longtime Memphis Mafioso "Diamond" Joe Esposito, convince Elvis to invest in a scheme to build racquetball courts. The following year, they will wind up suing him over this faltering venture—though Esposito will remain his employee and Dr. Nick his doctor until Elvis's death.

NOVEMBER 1976

Jerry Lee Lewis, with whom Elvis had so enjoyed jamming at Sun Studios 20 years before, is arrested in the wee hours of the morning in front of Graceland's gates. "The Killer," as Lewis calls himself, is drunk, disorderly and armed with a .38 derringer. "I was really rockin' that night," he will later laugh.

DECEMBER 1976

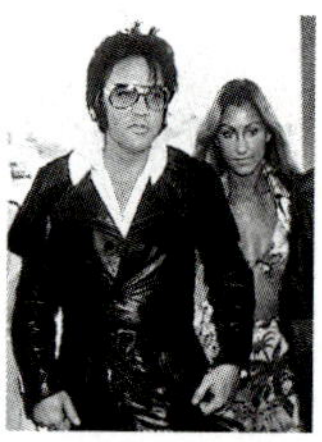

After nearly five years as his lover, Linda Thompson moves out of Graceland. She is tired of "baby-sitting" Elvis, she says, and worried that he is killing himself.

AUGUST 1977

Furious at being abruptly fired after years of faithful service, Memphis Mafia members Dave Hebler and Red and Sonny West publish *Elvis: What Happened?*, which details their former boss's drug use, sex life and obsession with guns. Elvis sees the book in galleys and wails: "My life is over. I'm a dead man."

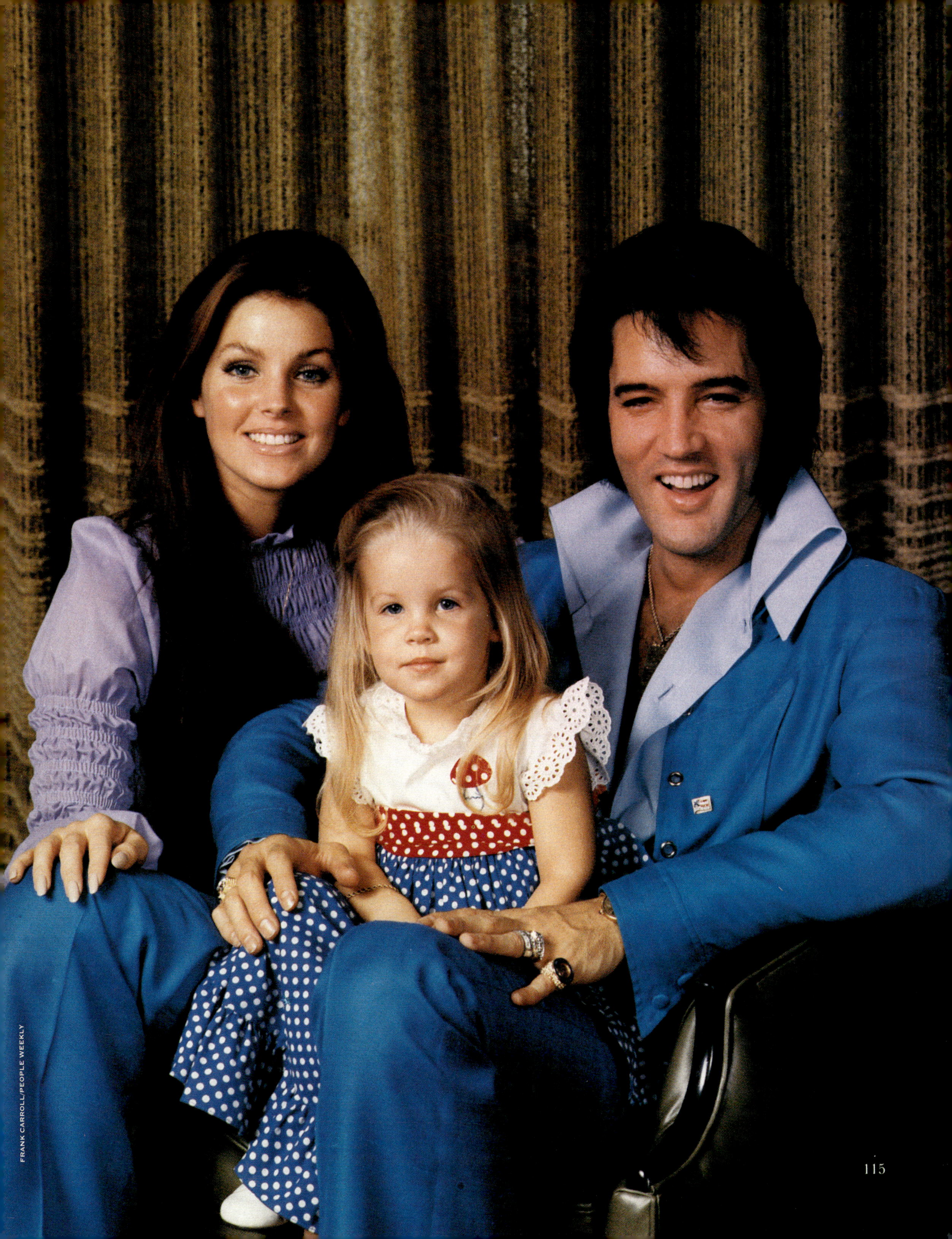

FRANK CARROLL/PEOPLE WEEKLY

He was so very sick and it was so very obvious. He would stuff himself to the gills with corn bread and buttermilk or sausage and biscuits, and then, after his weight ballooned, he would starve himself for days. He would prepare for performances by taking inhuman doses of uppers, then unwind with equally outsize doses of downers. From time to time, he would check into a hospital, but as soon as he came out he would embark on a new series of engagements as though he were in the very pink of health. The beginning of the end came in the form of a grueling five-month tour of 50 cities. His skin was pasty, bloated and drizzled with sweat. His eyelids drooped, and his voice was hoarse and crackling. There were nights when he literally struggled to keep his feet. His fans, steadfast, loyal and true, cheered him nonetheless. But the King of Rock and Roll deserved a more noble finale.

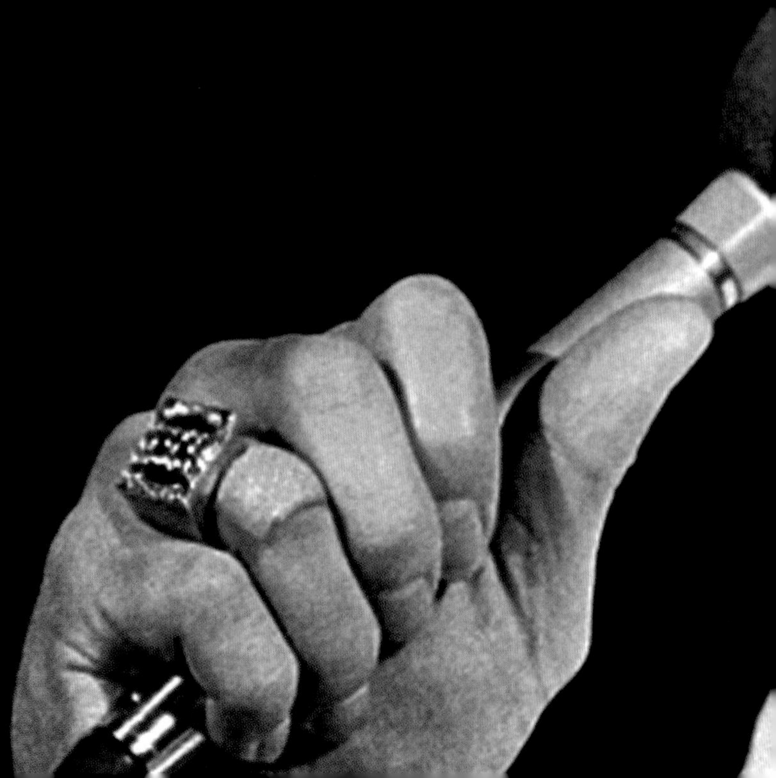

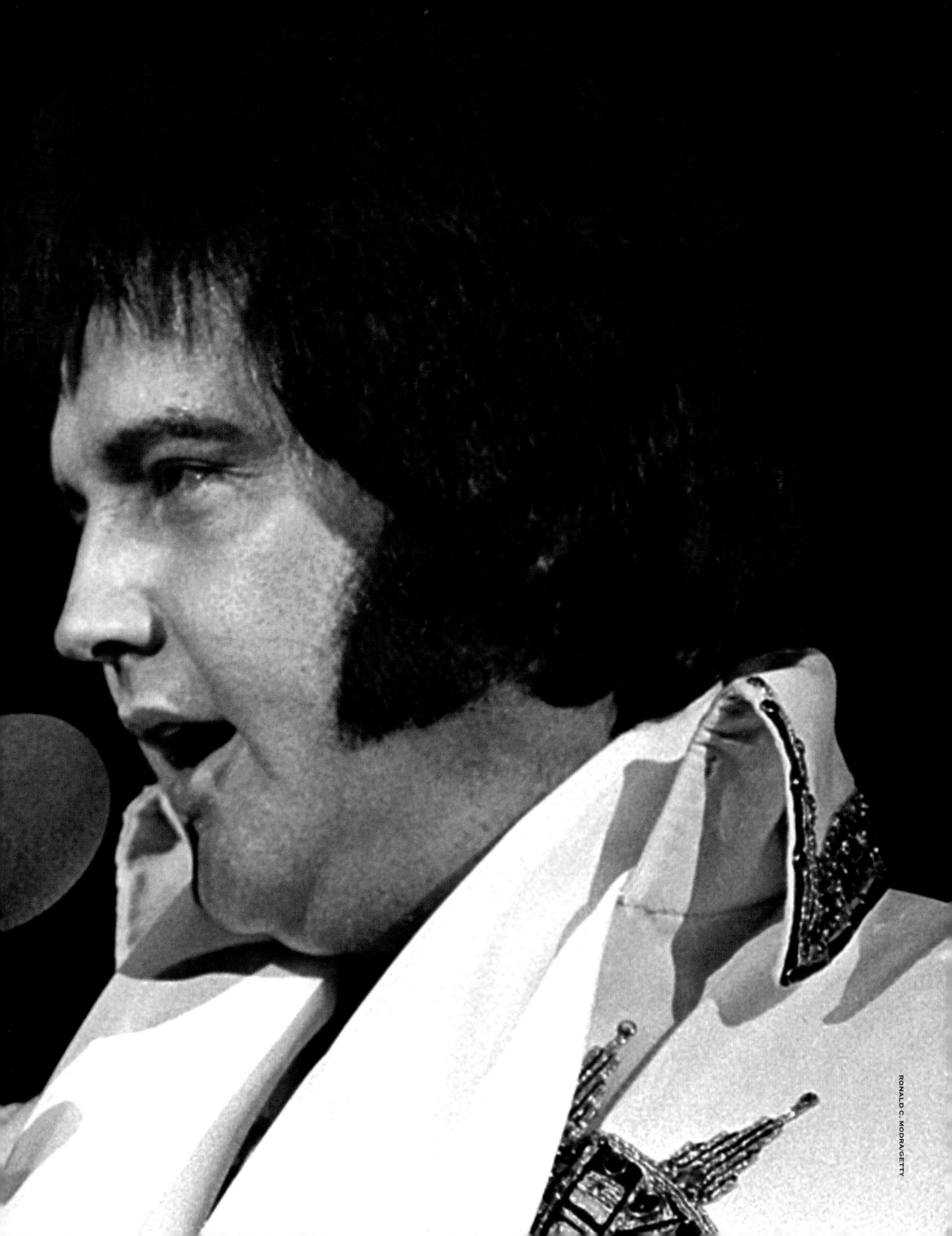

RONALD C. MODRA/GETTY

HE WAS SAID TO BE SUFFERING FROM GLAUCOMA, HYPERTENSION, AN ENLARGED HEART, CLOGGED ARTERIES AND A TWISTED COLON. HE WAS PROBABLY TAKING PERCODAN (A NARCOTIC PAINKILLER), DEXEDRINE (A STIMULANT), AMYTAL (A BARBITURATE), QUAALUDE (A HYPNOTIC SEDATIVE), DILAUDID (ANOTHER PAINKILLER), BIPHETAMINE (AN AMPHETAMINE) AND THE DEVIL ONLY KNEW WHAT ELSE. STILL, WHEN THE END DID COME, IT WAS A SHOCK. "I WILL NEVER FORGET THE LOOKS OF TOTAL DISBELIEF ON THE FACES THAT LINED BOTH SIDES OF ELVIS PRESLEY BOULEVARD FOR THE FUNERAL PROCESSION," SAID SAM PHILLIPS. "IT SEEMED AS THOUGH EACH PERSON STOOD COMPLETELY ALONE."

1977

AUGUST 16

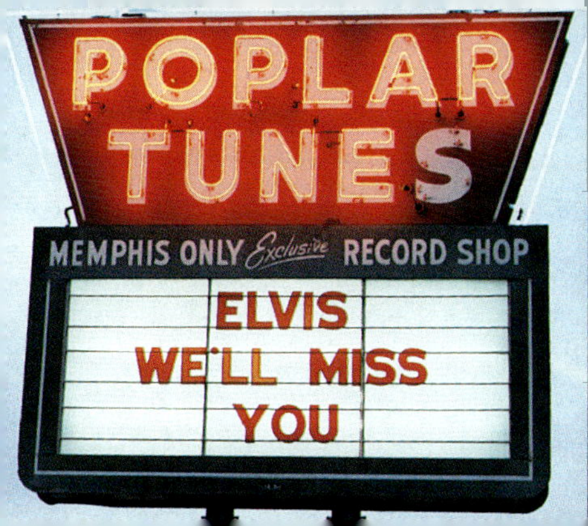

N REININGER/CONTAC

HOW MUCH IS HE MISSED? SHORTLY AFTER HIS DEATH, A FEMALE ELVIS IMPERSONATOR HAD PLASTIC SURGERY TO MAKE HER ACT MORE CONVINCING. SOME 15 YEARS LATER, A JAPANESE MAN PAID MORE THAN FIVE MILLION YEN FOR HIS ELVIS REGALIA AND CONDUCTED AN EXHAUSTIVE STUDY OF THE PRESLEY KI (JAPANESE FOR "SPIRIT") EN ROUTE TO WINNING THE SIXTH ANNUAL INTERNATIONAL ELVIS IMPERSONATORS CONTEST. BY THE BEGINNING OF 1995, TWO GROUPS OF SKYDIVING IMPERSONATORS, THE "FLYING ELVISES" AND THE "FLYING ELVI," WERE SUING EACH OTHER IN FEDERAL COURT. *THAT* IS HOW MUCH HE IS MISSED.

ELVIS LIVES

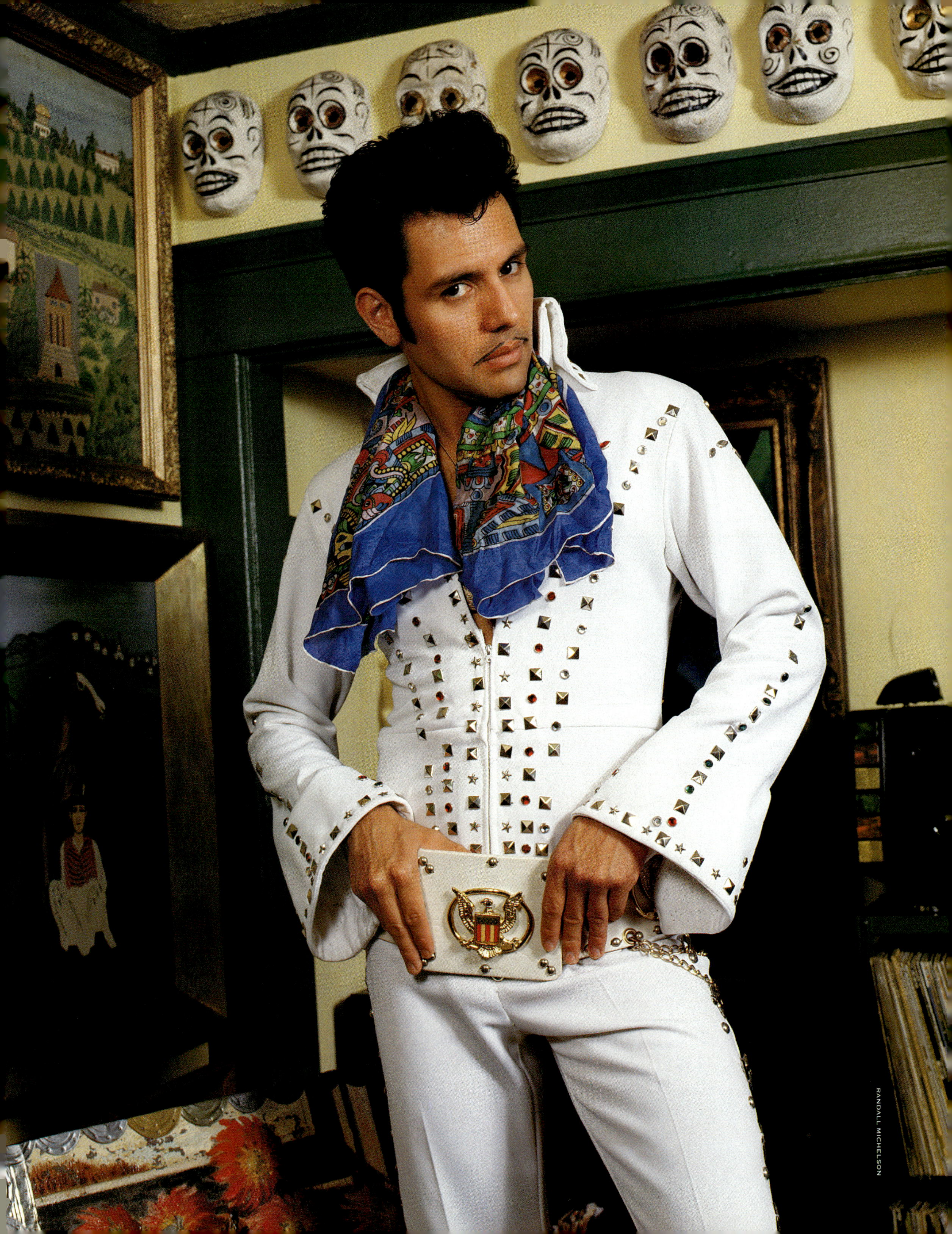

RANDALL MICHELSON

The merchandising of Elvis has continued unabated since his passing. Even the Richard Nixon Presidential Library in Yorba Linda, Calif., has gotten into the act, offering a $45 wristwatch decorated with a portrait of the former President shaking hands with the onetime King. At a recent Butterfield & Butterfield auction, a piece of broken tree limb from Graceland was sold for $747.50. But the market does seem to have settled down a bit since 1979, when Memphis dry cleaner William Res Carwile had Elvis's original crypt at Forest Hill Cemetery carved into 44,000 pieces (Elvis's body had been moved to Graceland, where it lies today) and offered them for sale at $80 a chunk.

(Previous Page) His name is El Vez and he is not, he says, so much an "Elvis impersonator" as an "Elvis interpreter." He refries Presley and serves him up *con salsa* with such fiery fare as "You Ain't Nothin' But a Chihuahua." Among Senor Vez's many costumes is a purple crushed velvet jumpsuit embroidered with an image of the Virgin of Guadalupe.

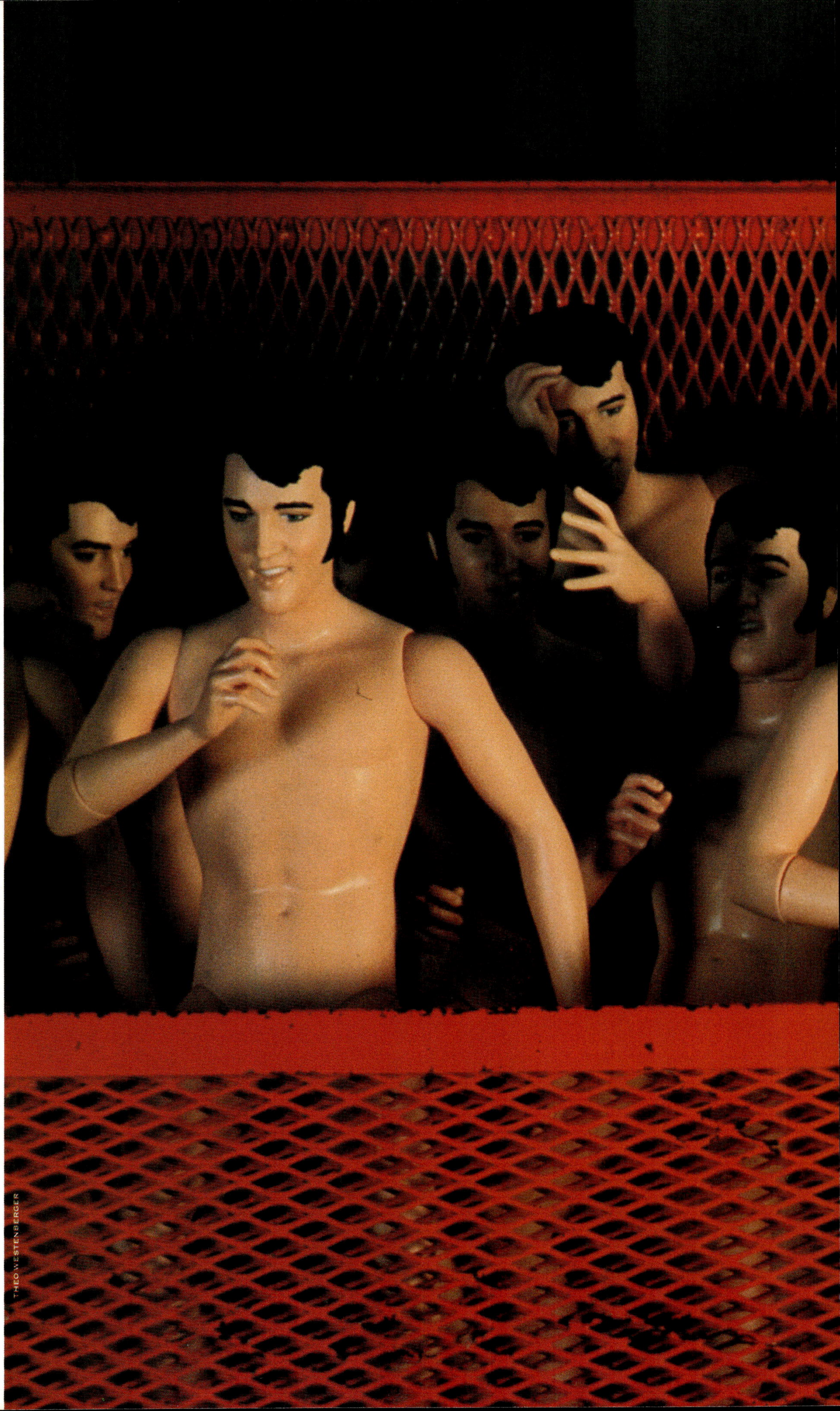

THEO WESTENBERGER

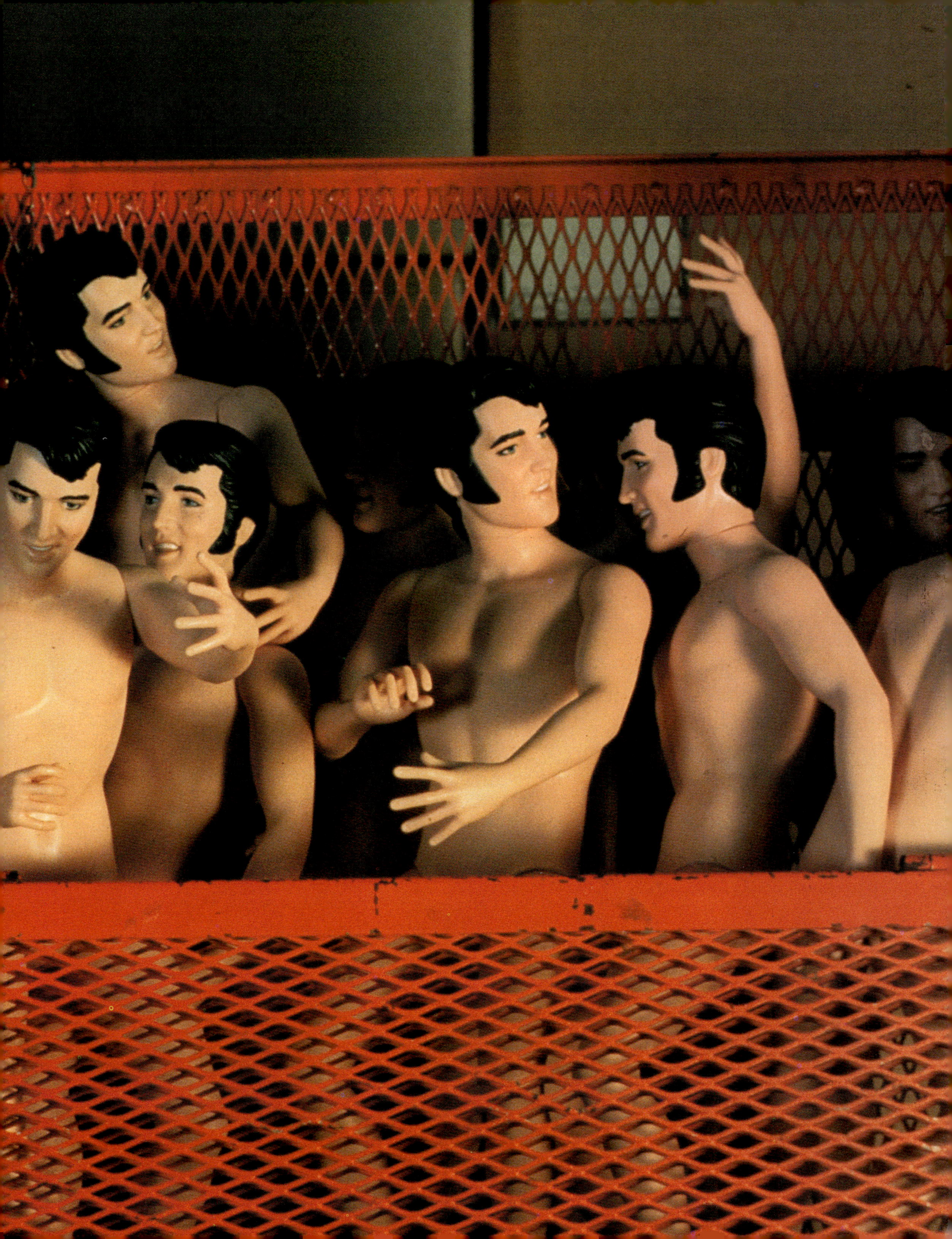

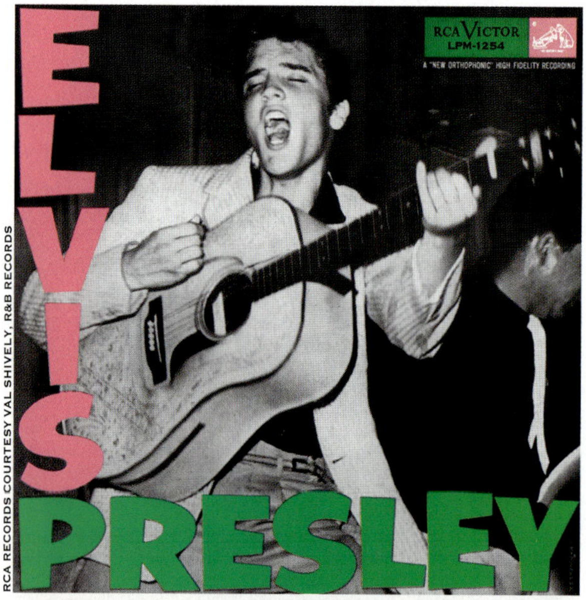

RCA Records courtesy Val Shively, R&B Records

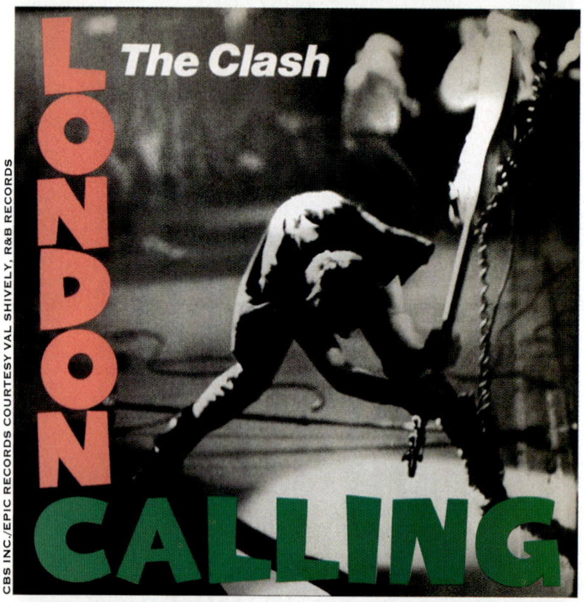

CBS Inc./Epic Records courtesy Val Shively, R&B Records

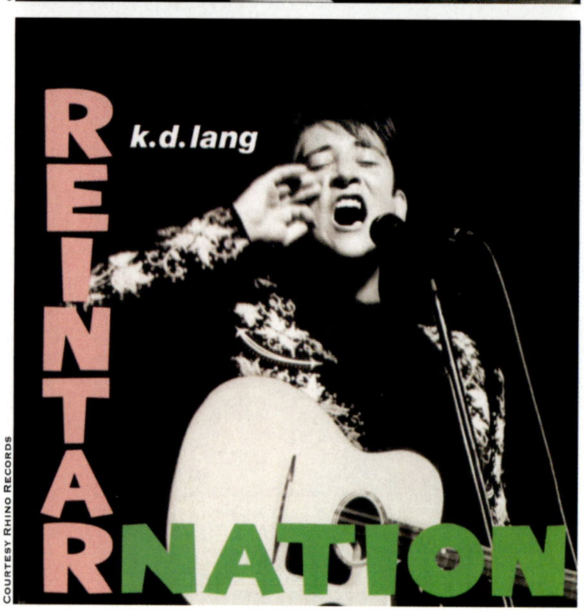

Courtesy Rhino Records

He is still everywhere in our global culture, every day—as an influence, as a commodity, as a figure to whom homage must be paid. There have been feature films and TV movies made about him. His music is available 24/7 via a satellite radio station broadcasting from—where else?—Graceland. The first Elvis postage stamp was issued by Grenada, of all countries, in 1978 to commemorate the first anniversary of his death; more than 50 countries, from Antigua to Zaire, have followed suit. When the U.S. planned its tribute in 1992, it ran an unprecedented contest allowing the public to choose between a rendering of a young Elvis or a "mature" one (usually called "The Fat Elvis Stamp"). Nearly 1.2 million ballots were cast, 75 percent of them for the youthful rocker, which remains the best-selling commemorative stamp of all time with over a half billion sold. The iconic cover of Elvis's first album has been sampled by many other artists, including The Clash (on 1979's punk classic *London Calling*) and k.d. lang (on her 2006 rockabilly reissue). It's good to align yourself with the king.

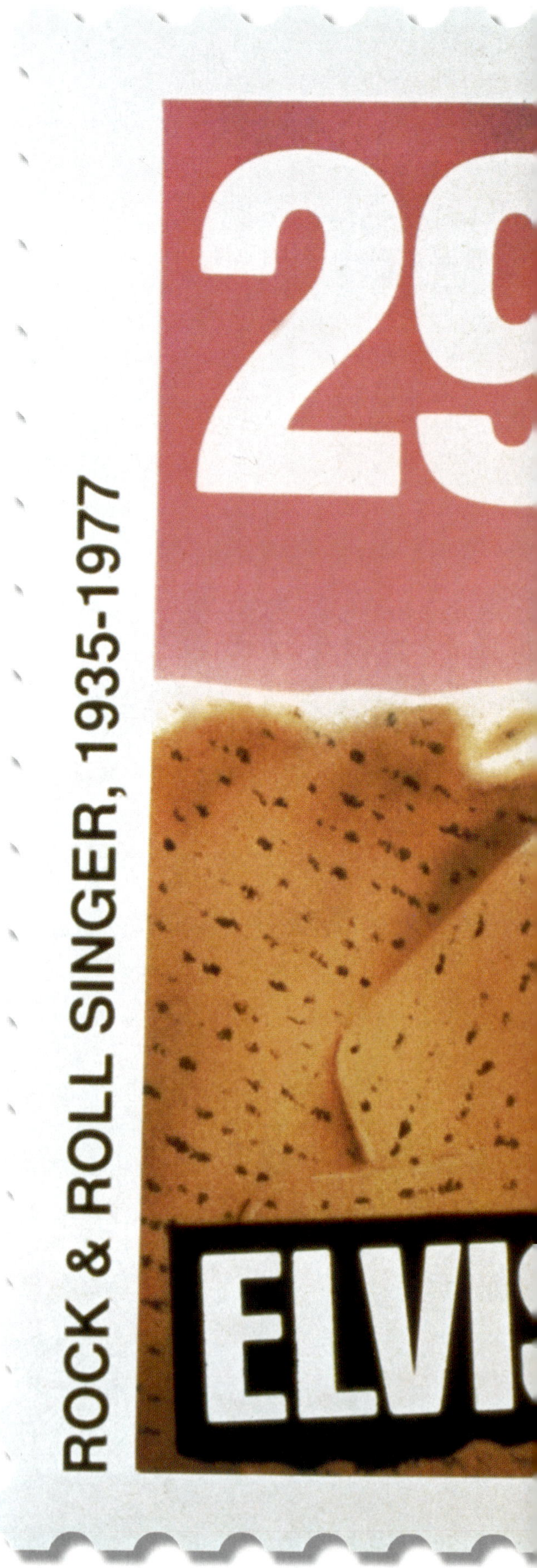

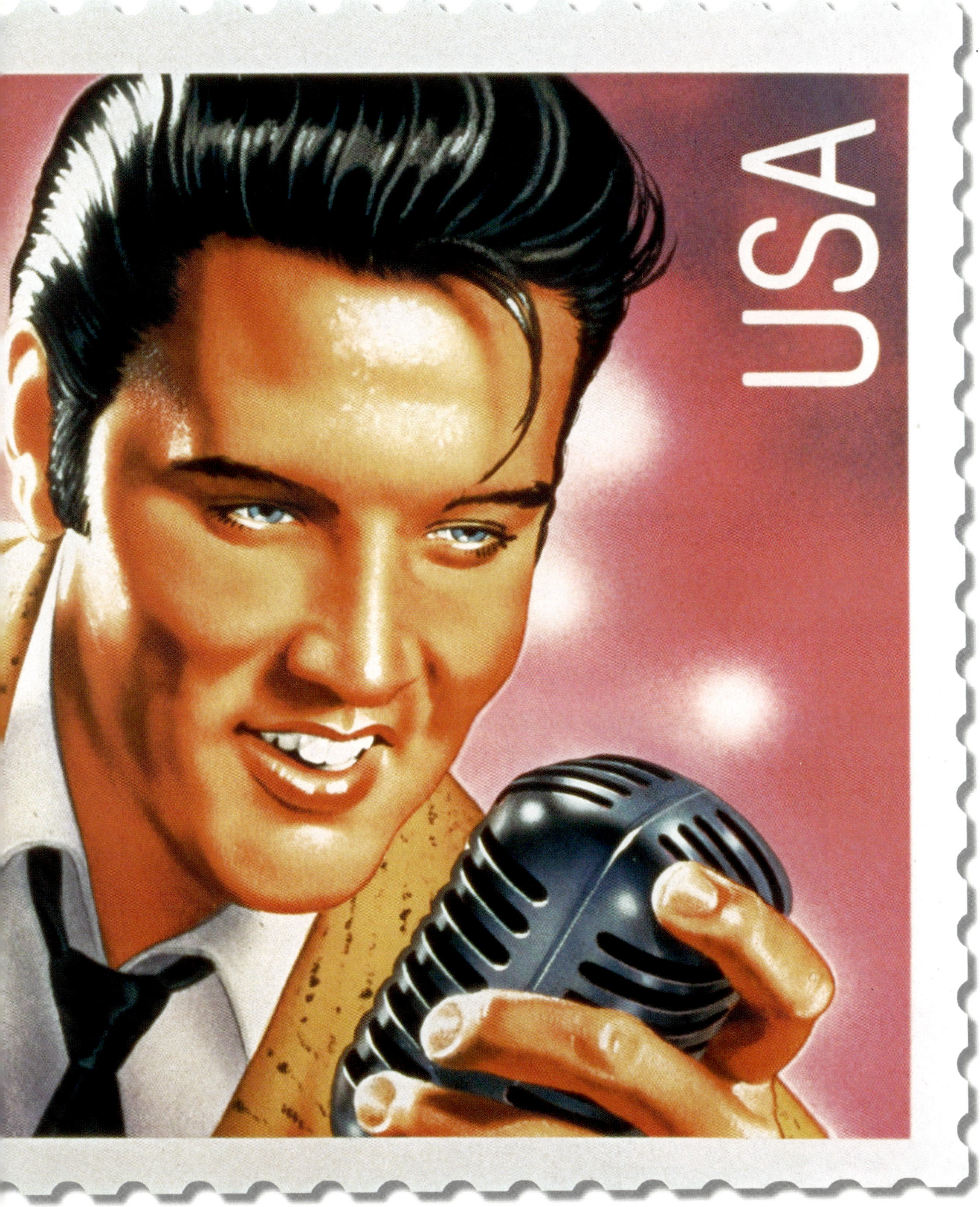

U.S. POSTAL SERVICE

Almost as soon as he was reported dead, people began swearing they'd seen Elvis walking among us, as alive as on the day he was born. He was first observed at Felpausch Food Center in Vicksburg, Mich.; then at a Burger King in Kalamazoo; then at a bar in Riverhead, N.Y.; then at a carnival in Denton, Tex.; and so on. In 1991 a Yankelovich poll found that approximately one out of six Americans believed Elvis might still be alive. Nonsense, said Mary Jenkins. She was a Graceland domestic for 26 years and she knew. According to Jenkins, not long after Elvis died, his spirit came to her in a dream and asked permission to drop by for a rest. "And I said, 'Well, you know you're *always* welcome.' And I fixed the room for him in the back of my house, and his spirit moved on in." Jenkins and the spirit of Elvis spent much time together before Jenkins herself passed away in 2000.

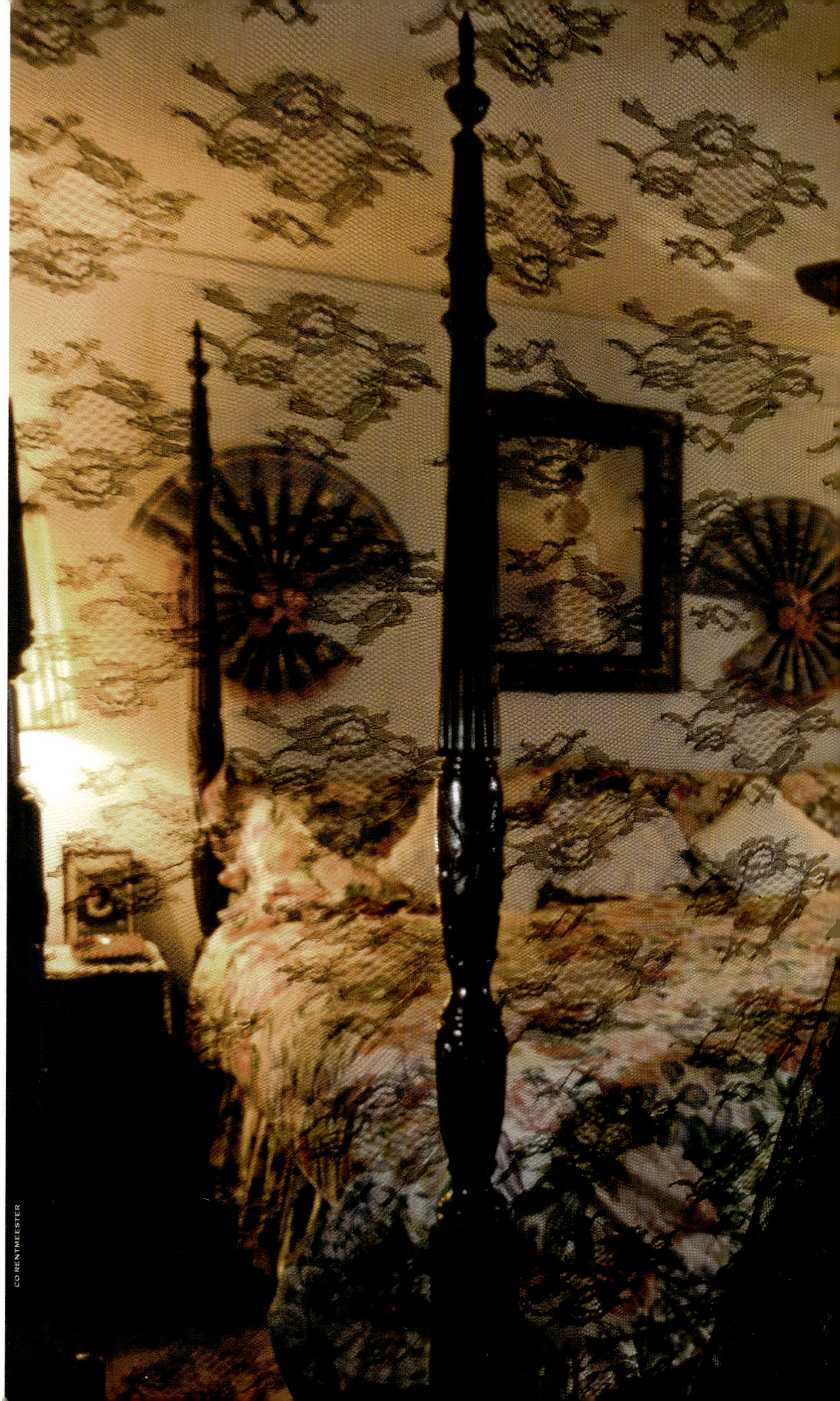

CO RENTMEESTER

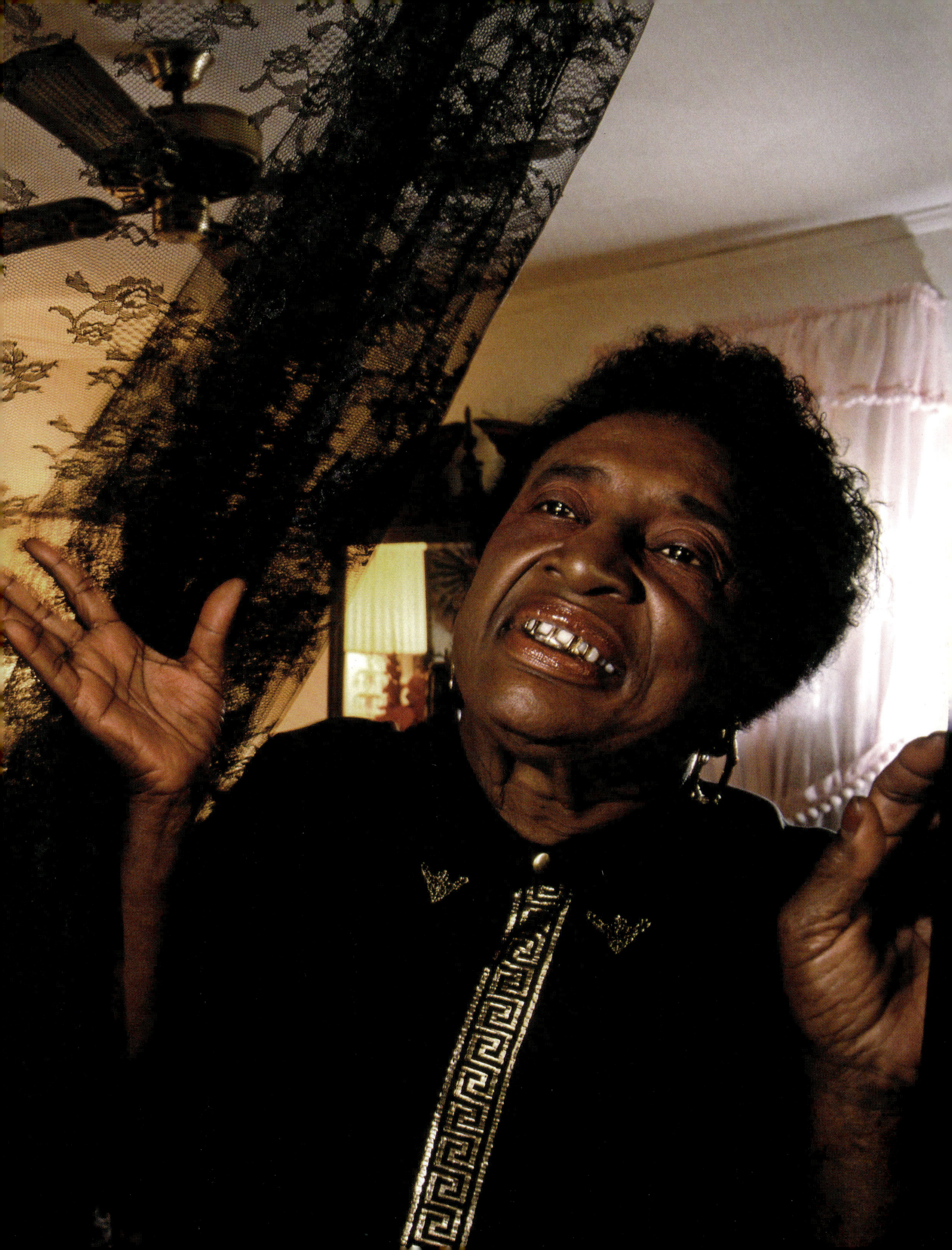

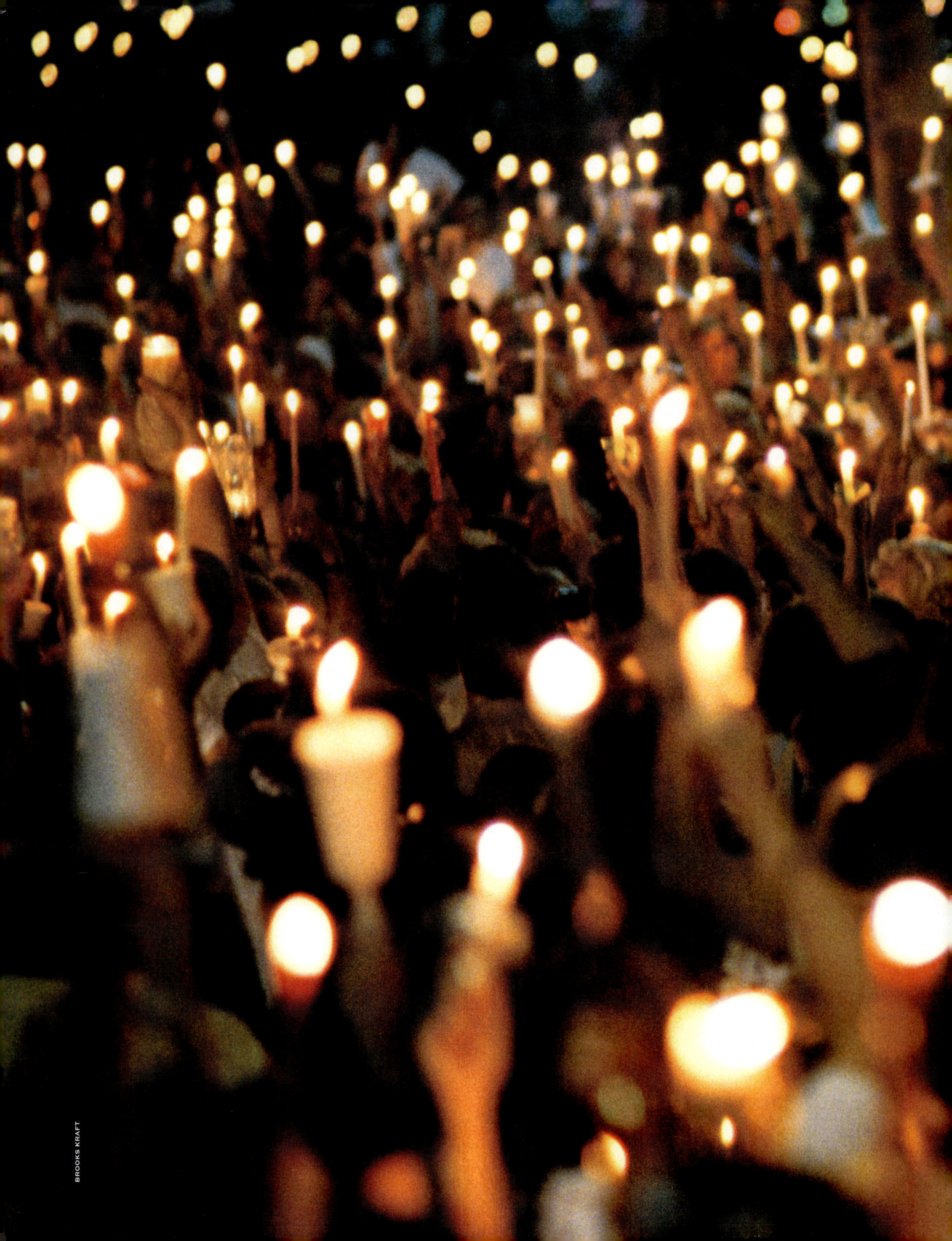

BROOKS KRAFT

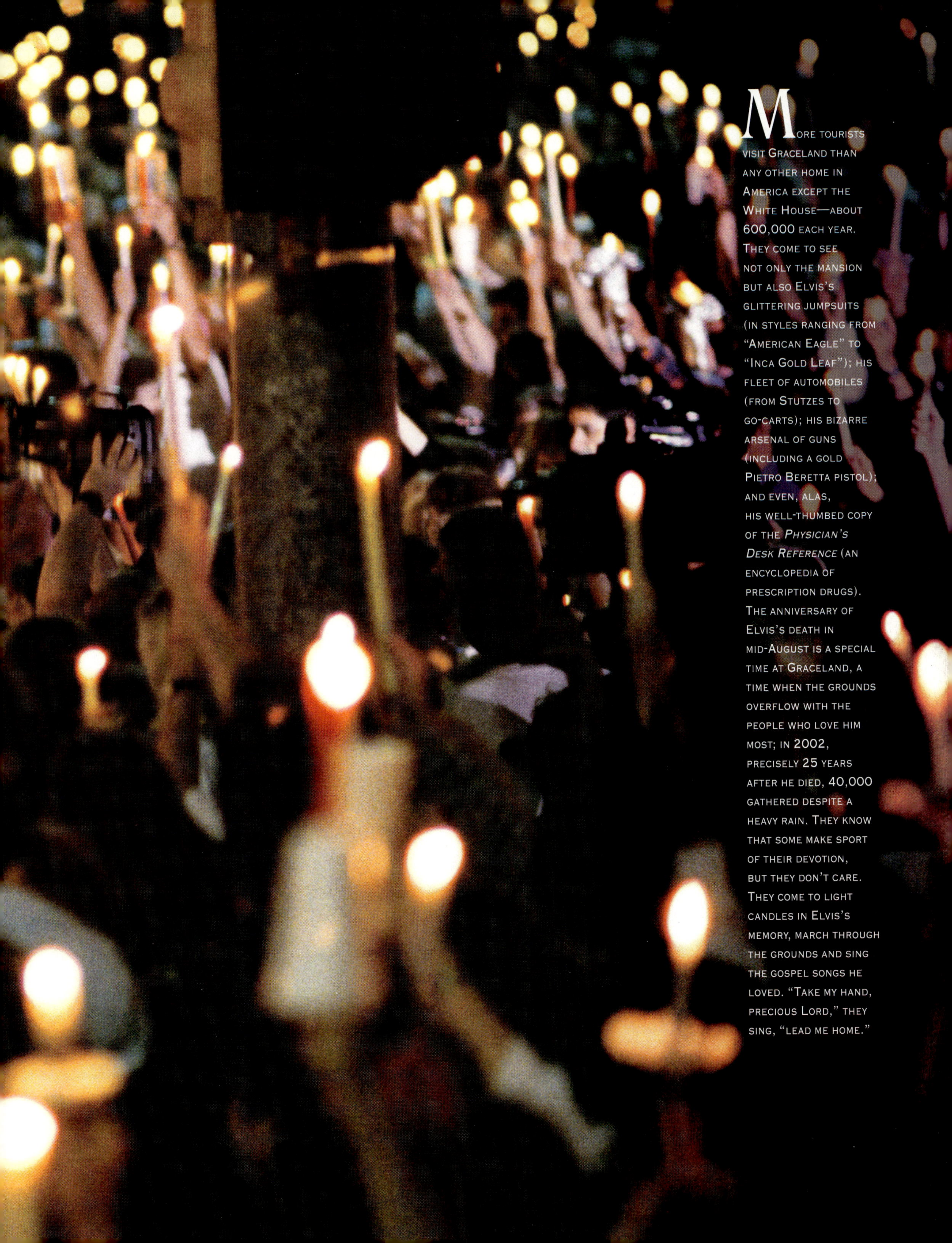

More tourists visit Graceland than any other home in America except the White House—about 600,000 each year. They come to see not only the mansion but also Elvis's glittering jumpsuits (in styles ranging from "American Eagle" to "Inca Gold Leaf"); his fleet of automobiles (from Stutzes to go-carts); his bizarre arsenal of guns (including a gold Pietro Beretta pistol); and even, alas, his well-thumbed copy of the *Physician's Desk Reference* (an encyclopedia of prescription drugs). The anniversary of Elvis's death in mid-August is a special time at Graceland, a time when the grounds overflow with the people who love him most; in 2002, precisely 25 years after he died, 40,000 gathered despite a heavy rain. They know that some make sport of their devotion, but they don't care. They come to light candles in Elvis's memory, march through the grounds and sing the gospel songs he loved. "Take my hand, precious Lord," they sing, "lead me home."

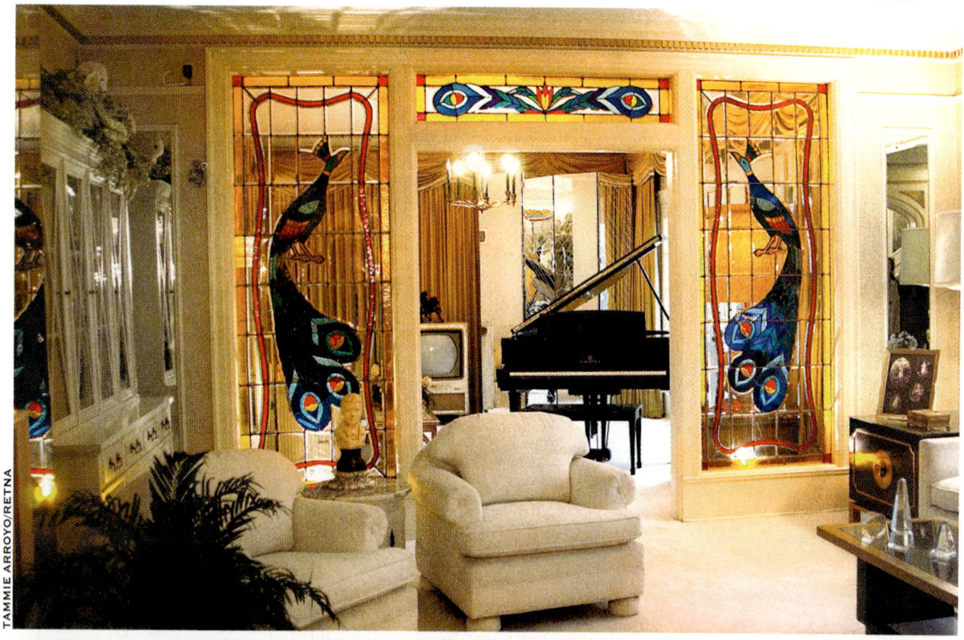

TAMMIE ARROYO/RETNA

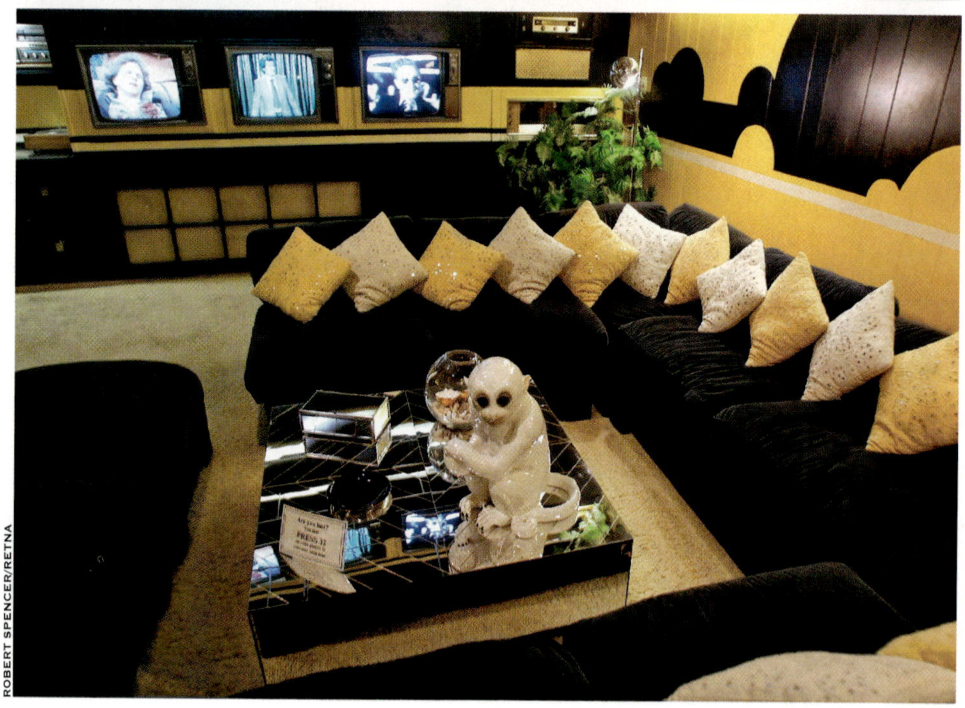

ROBERT SPENCER/RETNA

Over the years, the mansion was renovated many times, and grew from just over 10,000 square feet to 17,552. Elvis reveled in an Elvis kind of opulence. He had Graceland specially painted to glow at night; his Jungle Room sported an indoor waterfall; the TV Room (left, below) had three of Graceland's 16 sets mounted in a wall (Elvis would watch three sporting events at once, or sometimes the feed from surveillance cameras on his property). In the gold-curtained Music Room stood a piano, and just through a doorway flanked by stained-glass peacocks was the Living Room, where Elvis's funeral was held. Elvis and Gladys were first buried in Forest Hill Cemetery, but after a grave-robbing attempt, they were reinterred in Graceland's Meditation Garden (right), where they rest in peace along with Vernon and Minnie Mae. There's also a marker for Elvis's stillborn twin, Jesse.

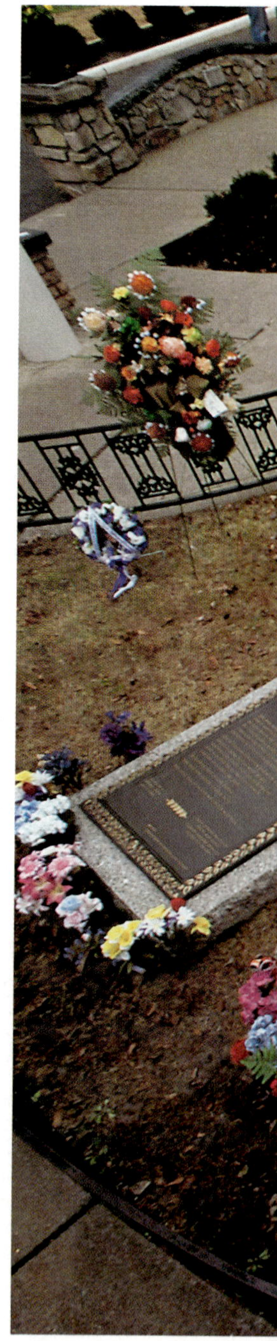

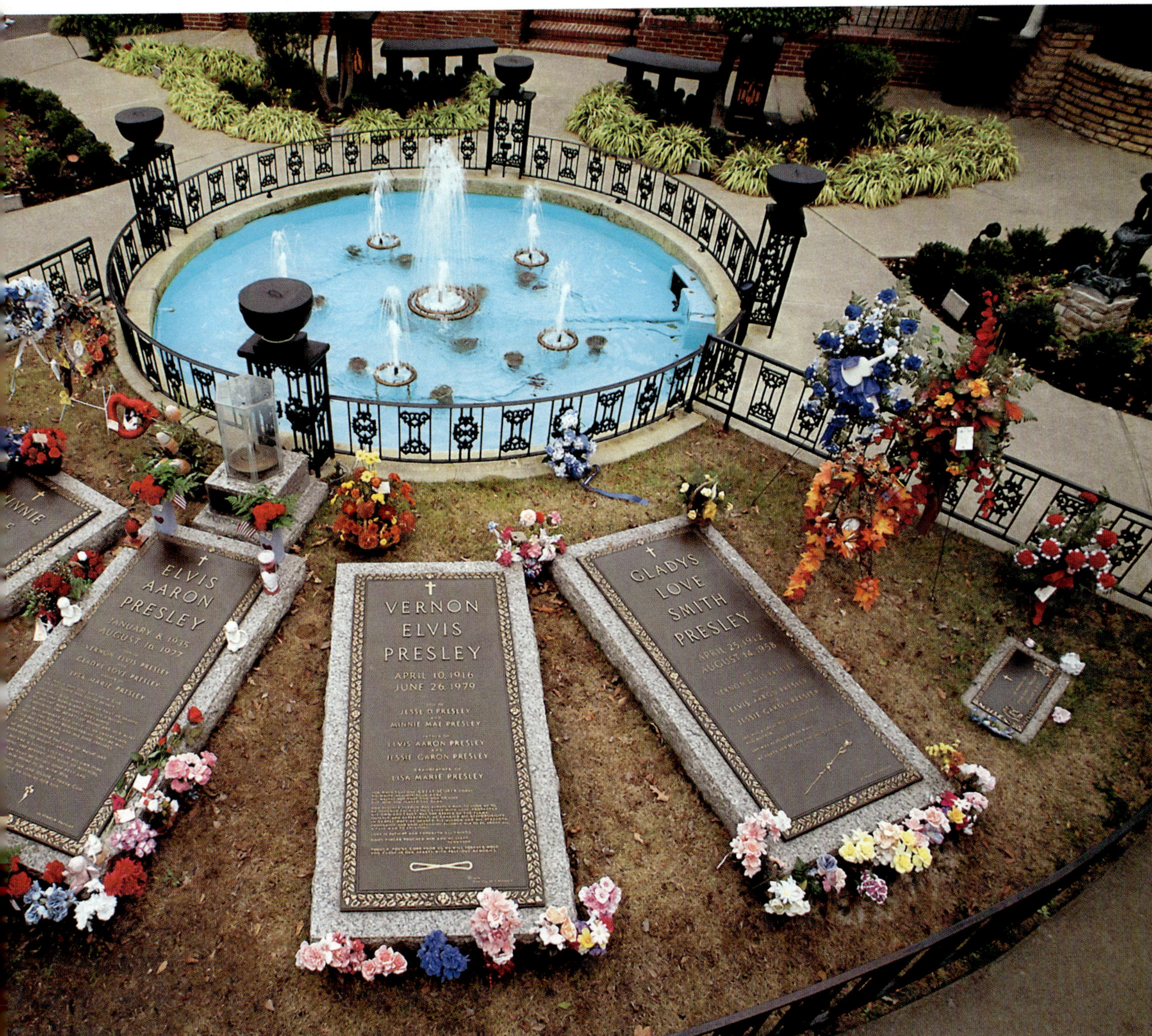
ELVIS
AARON
PRESLEY
VERNON
ELVIS
PRESLEY
APRIL 10, 1916
JUNE 26, 1979
JESSE D. PRESLEY
MINNIE MAE PRESLEY
ELVIS AARON PRESLEY
JESSIE GARON PRESLEY
LISA MARIE PRESLEY
GLADYS
LOVE
SMITH
PRESLEY

There is always, with historical figures and artifacts, buried treasure. Somewhere there's a rough draft of *Huck Finn* waiting to be unearthed, an early copy of the Declaration of Independence hidden in the back of a picture frame, another forgotten Marilyn Monroe photo shoot or Caruso recording lurking unseen and unheard—for now. The editors of *LIFE* wondered what pictures of the King of Rock and Roll might yet be hiding. It was worth the wondering. Enjoy!

ELVIS FOUND

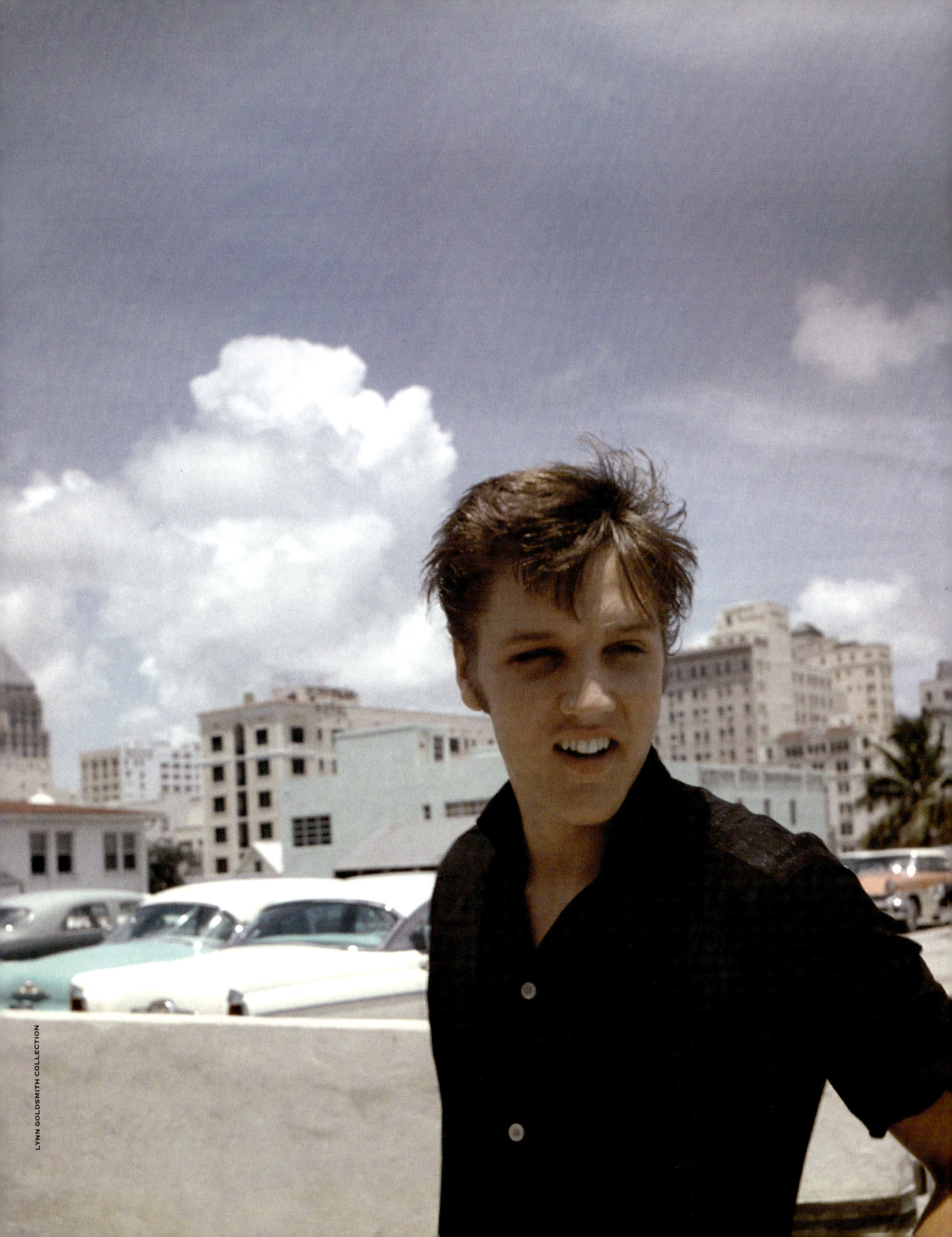

LYNN GOLDSMITH COLLECTION

The photographer Lynn Goldsmith was "nine when I saw him on *The Ed Sullivan Show*. Elvis was very important in my life from then on." Years later, having gained fame for her rock photographs, among others, she kept stumbling upon—and buying—obscure original pictures of Presley, like the ones at the far right and on the previous page. "I don't even know where they were taken, but they say something about Elvis and the times. The shot with his hair blowing: He looks 15, and doesn't have the full Elvis hair. It's such a cool, surprising shot." Less surprising perhaps is a photo of Elvis on a motorcycle (his love of Harleys is legend), which is from the archives at Graceland.

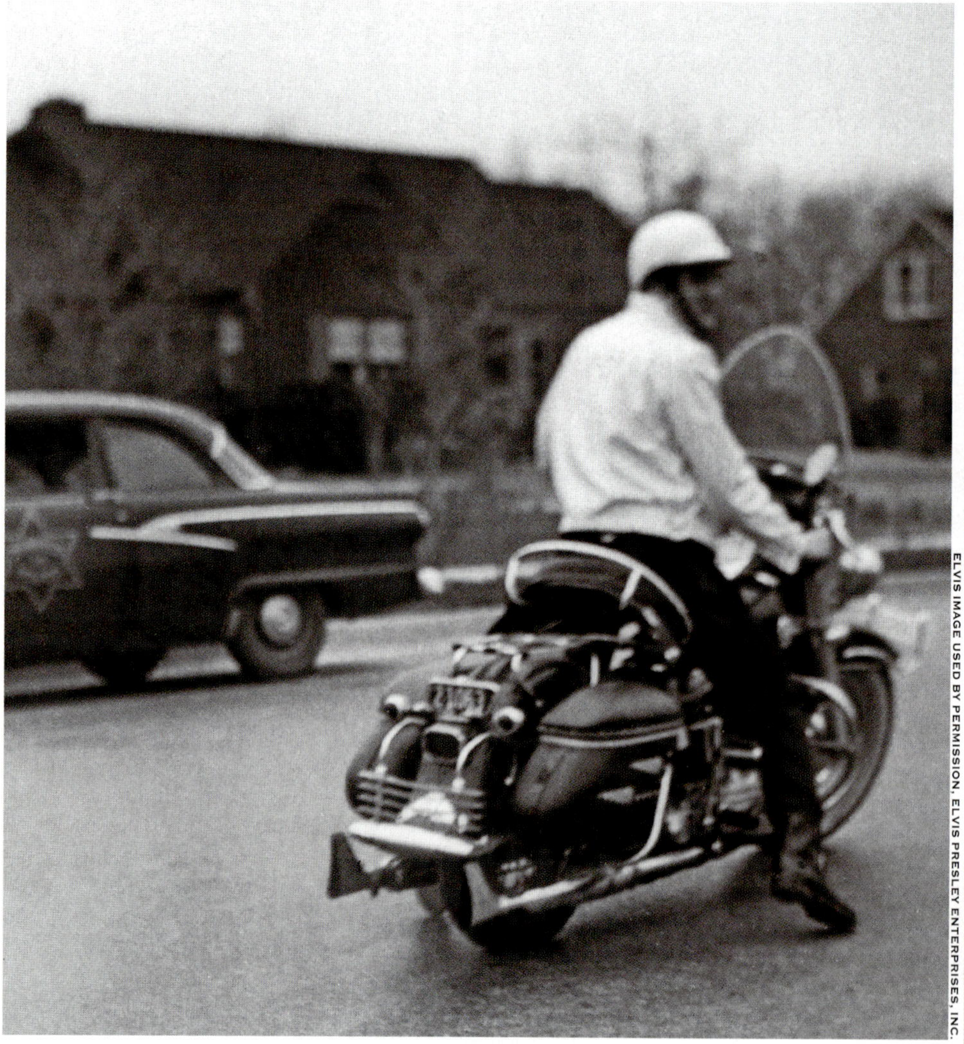

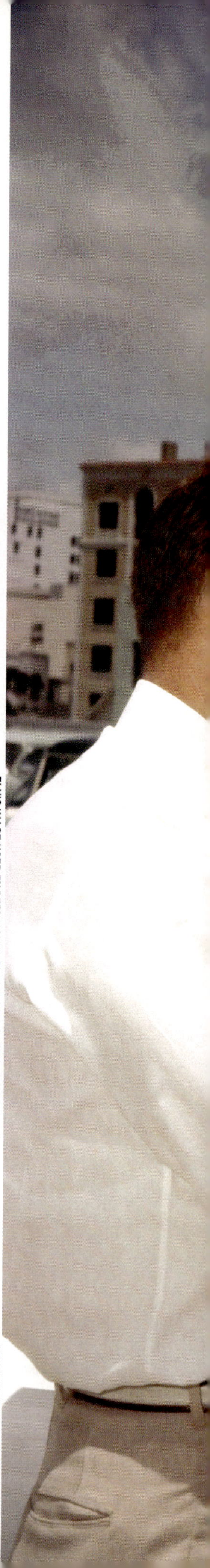

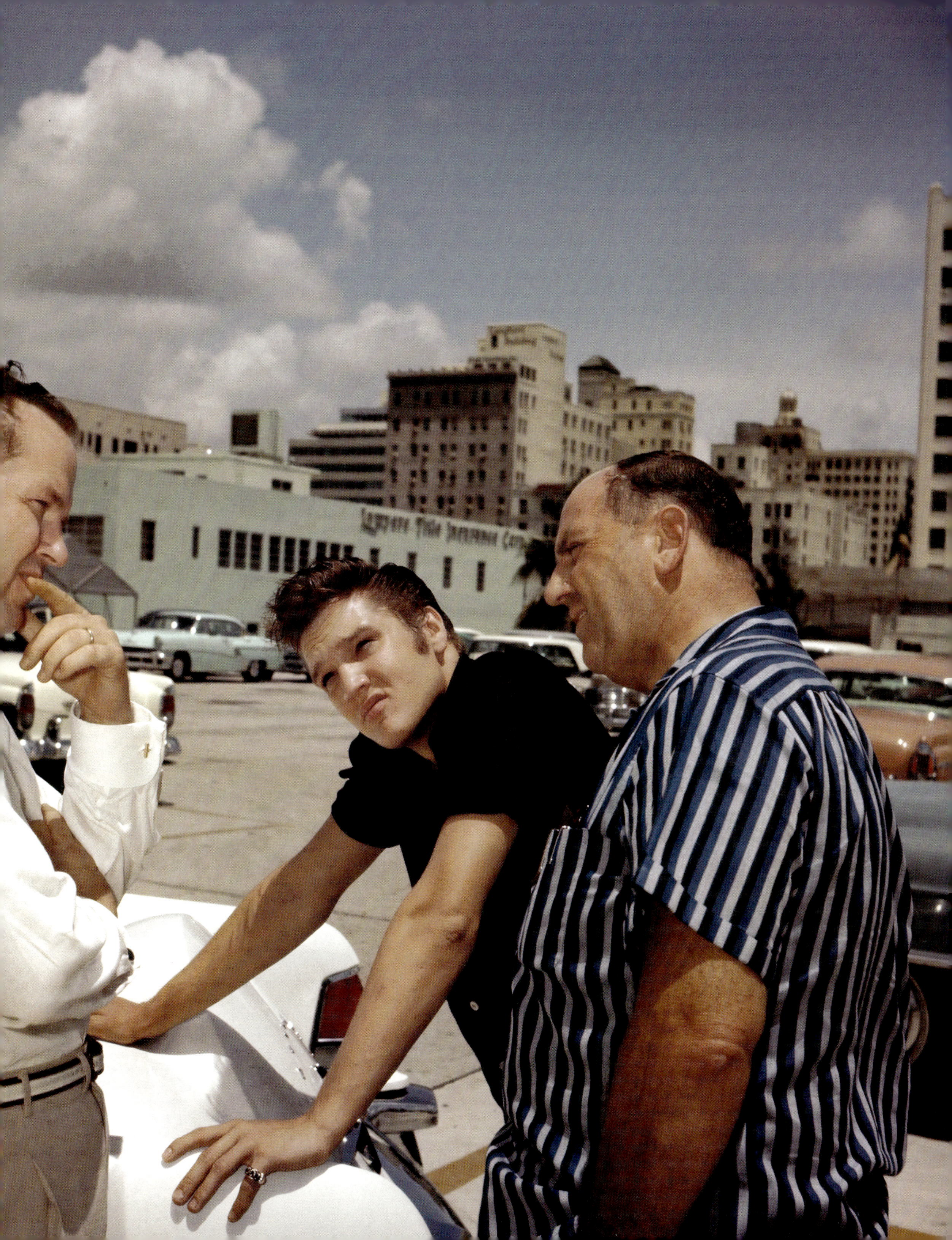

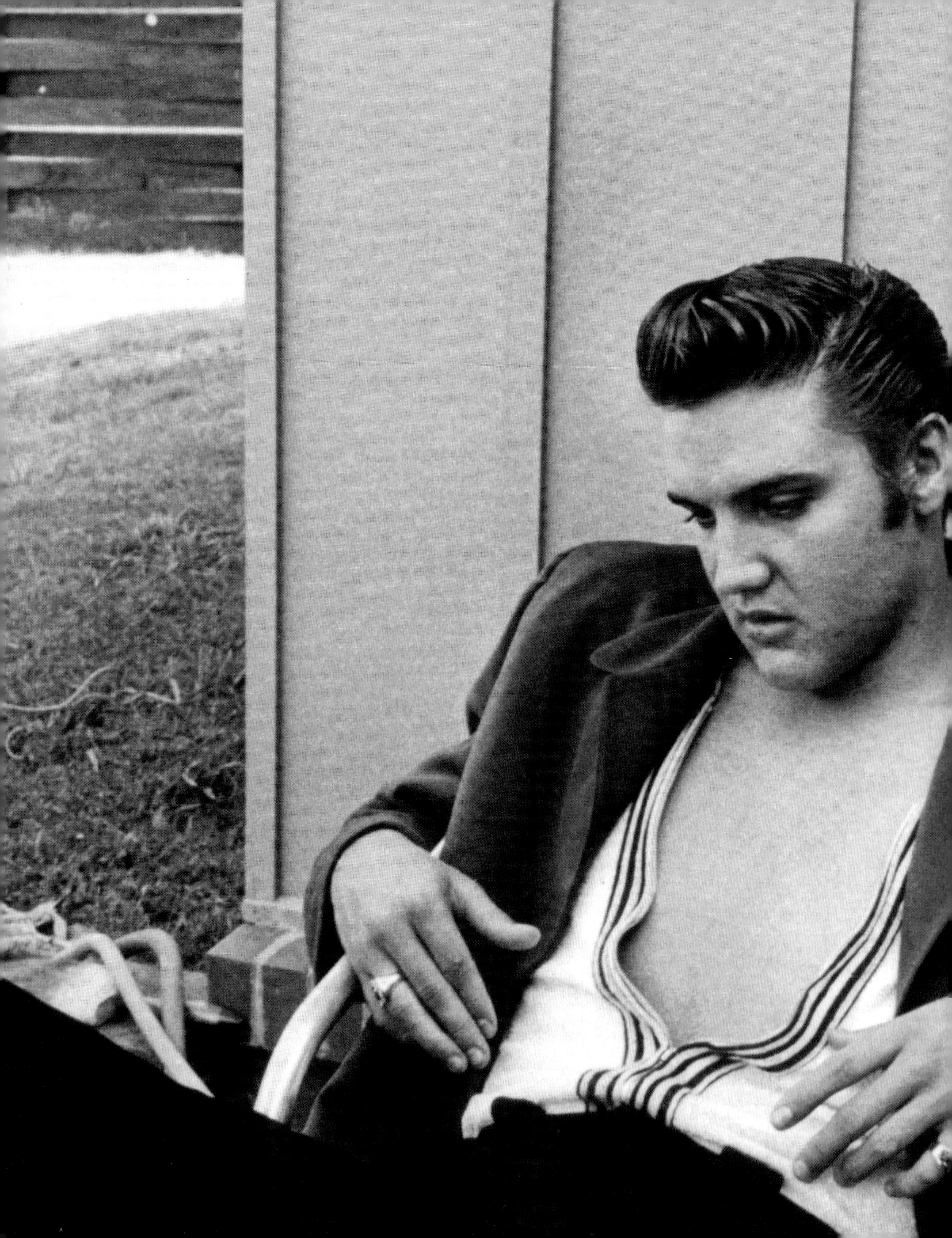

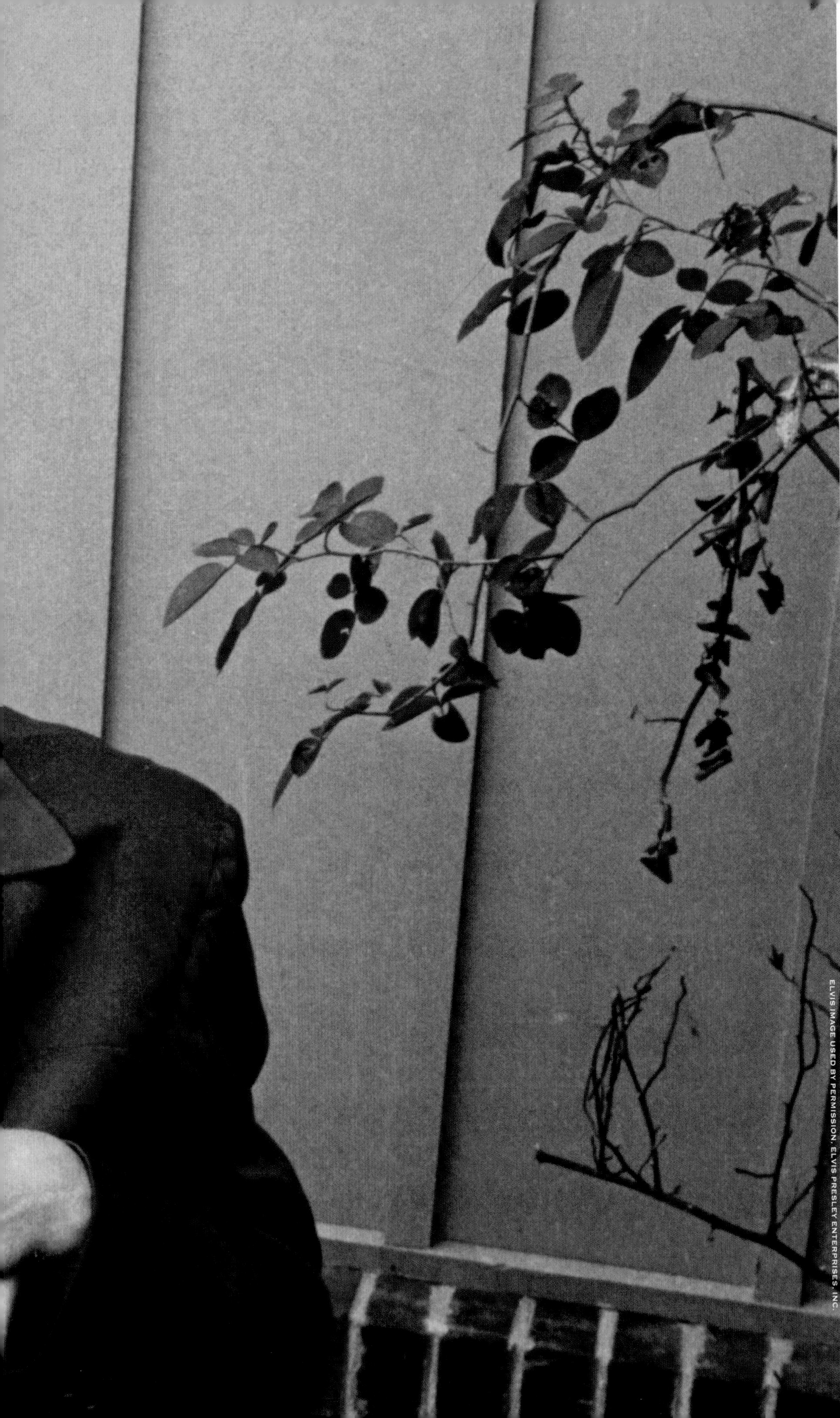

This photo, from Graceland's collection, was not taken at the mansion but on the patio of a house at 1034 Audubon Drive in Memphis—the very first house Elvis was able to purchase for his family. He bought it on March 12, 1956, for $29,500, and he, Vernon, Gladys and grandma Minnie Mae moved in a week later. For Elvis, the ranch-style home, built earlier in the '50s, was a dream come true. Having Elvis move in next door was not, however, a dream situation for some neighbors. The kids, of course, loved him, but as that cataclysmic year progressed and Elvis's celebrity grew by the day, the ruckus at 1034 grew apace. The Presleys tried to build bridges: Gladys gave out cookies and invited neighbors in to see her vegetable garden, while Elvis offered autographs and motorcycle rides. But, finally, it was clear that a larger, more private and altogether safer home was needed. One year after buying the house on Audubon Drive, Elvis traded it and cash ($102,000 purchase price in all) for Graceland. Today, the Audubon Drive house, too, is listed on the National Register of Historic Places.

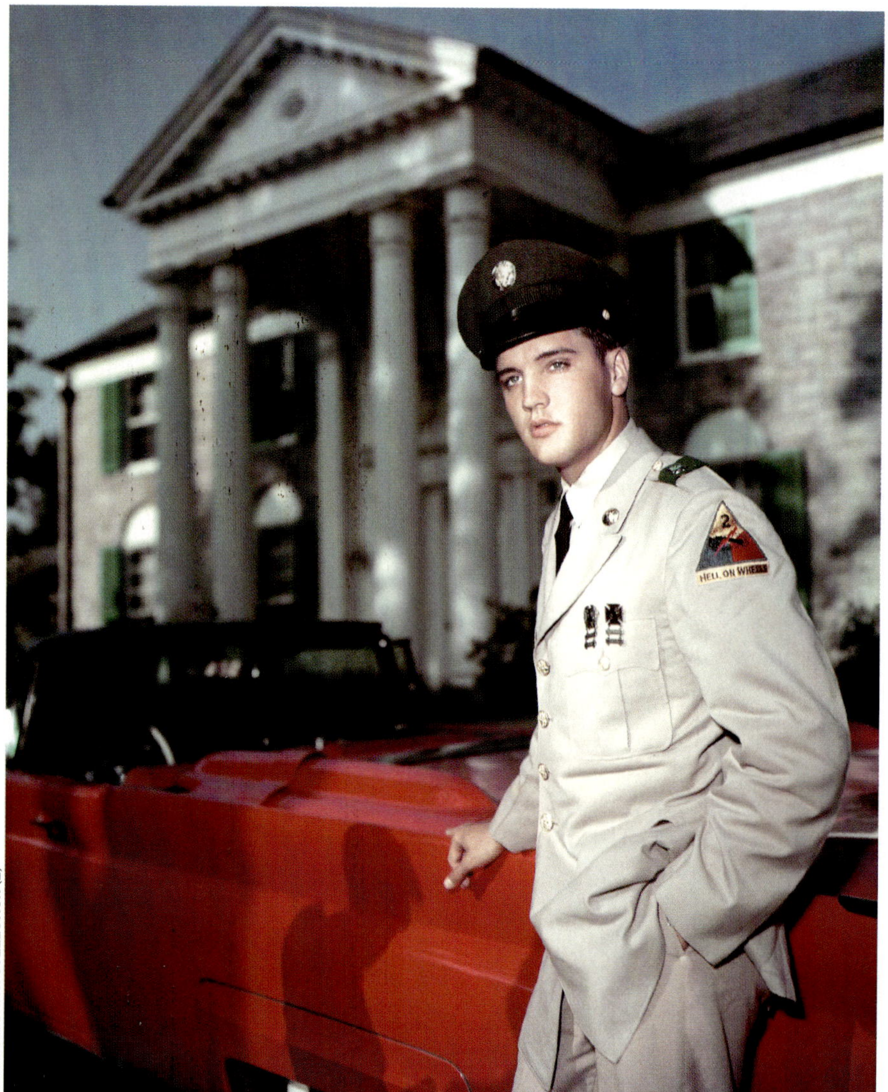

LYNN GOLDSMITH COLLECTION (2)

My heart broke when he went into the army," says Goldsmith, who obtained these shots during her searches. A man of many peculiarities, Elvis nevertheless did not have a hat fetish, but he liked them—particularly the sailor variety—and was happy to sign this chapeau for a fan at the gate of his Audubon Drive home. As for the Graceland shot, it's perhaps interesting that a famous subject of Goldsmith's, Bruce Springsteen, vaulted the wall there in 1976, hoping for a royal audience. Elvis wasn't home. Bruce told the guards who he was, and that *Born to Run* was a big hit, but still the Boss was booted from the grounds.

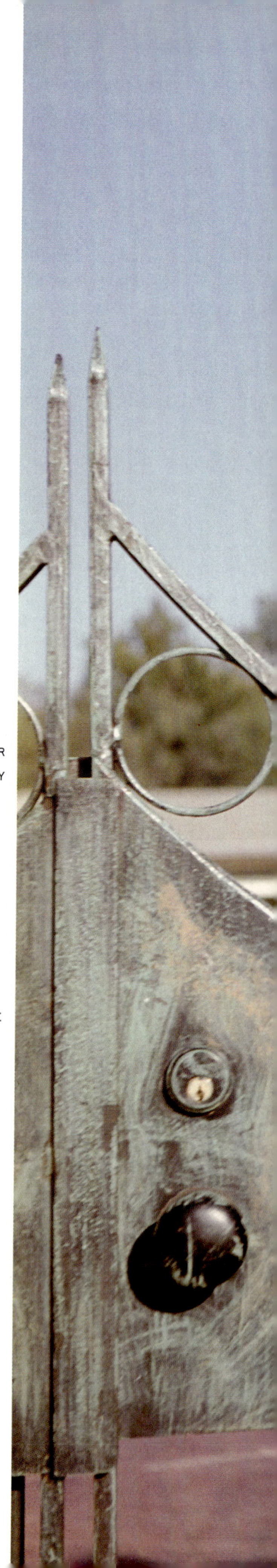

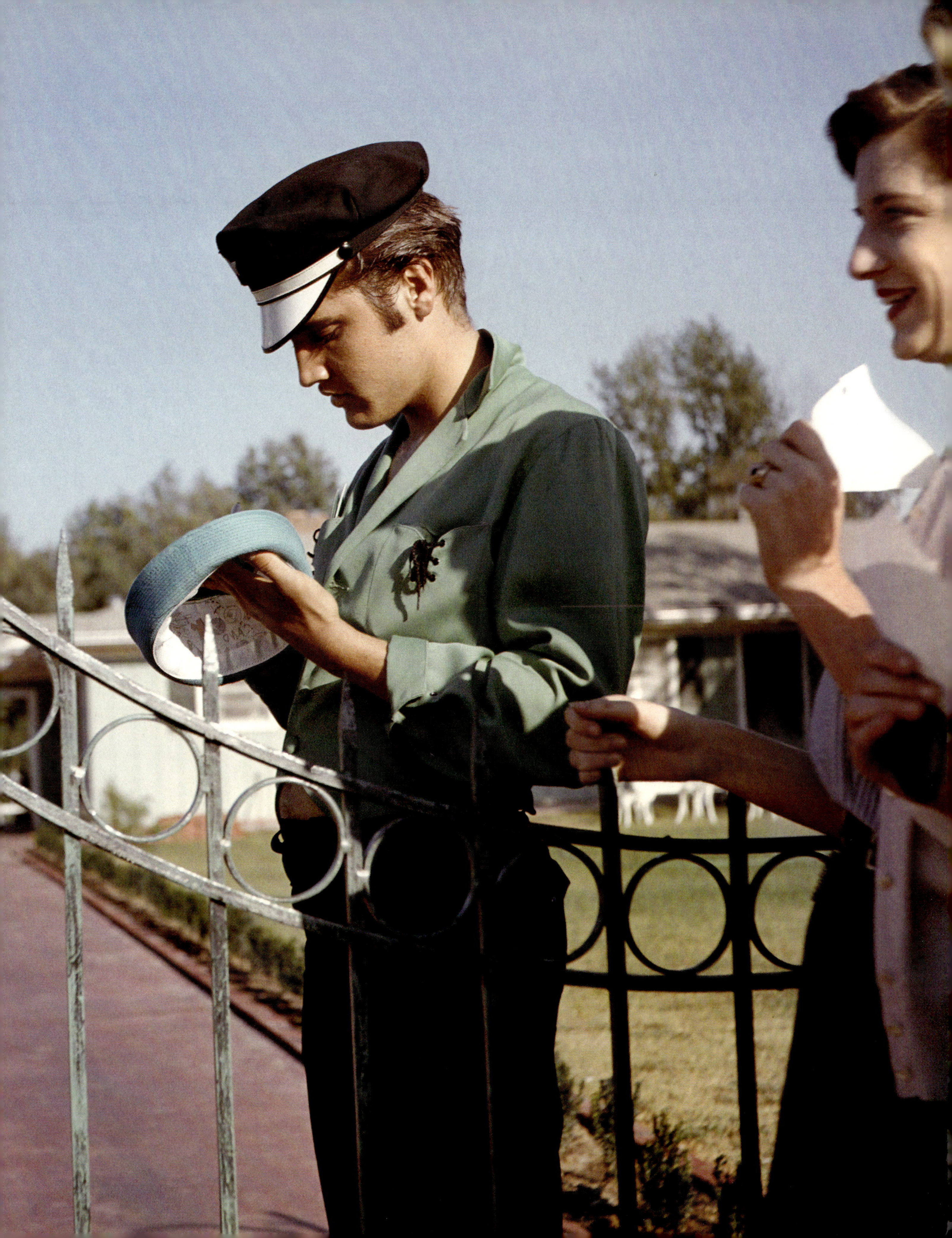

Captain Elvis was captured aboard a deep-sea fishing boat called the *Aunt Jennie* in July of 1956; the photo now resides in the vaults at Graceland. The girl in the picture is a fan about to take a snapshot of the rising rock and roll star as the boat pulls into a Biloxi, Miss., dock. However, the unseen girl behind the picture is June Juanico, a former beauty queen who met Elvis after a concert in Biloxi, her hometown, in 1955. She and Elvis dated seriously that year and the next; she was by his side as he started to ascend the showbiz heights. Some sources call her Elvis's first sweetheart, and others say she was the only girl Gladys ever approved of. Elvis's mom must indeed have liked Juanico, for Gladys, too, was on the *Aunt Jennie* that day, as was Vernon, for a fishing junket that June had arranged. Elvis and June also took the senior Presleys for a tour of nearby New Orleans. This summer vacation in 1956 can now be seen as a final idyll for Elvis before he was engulfed by the maelstrom.

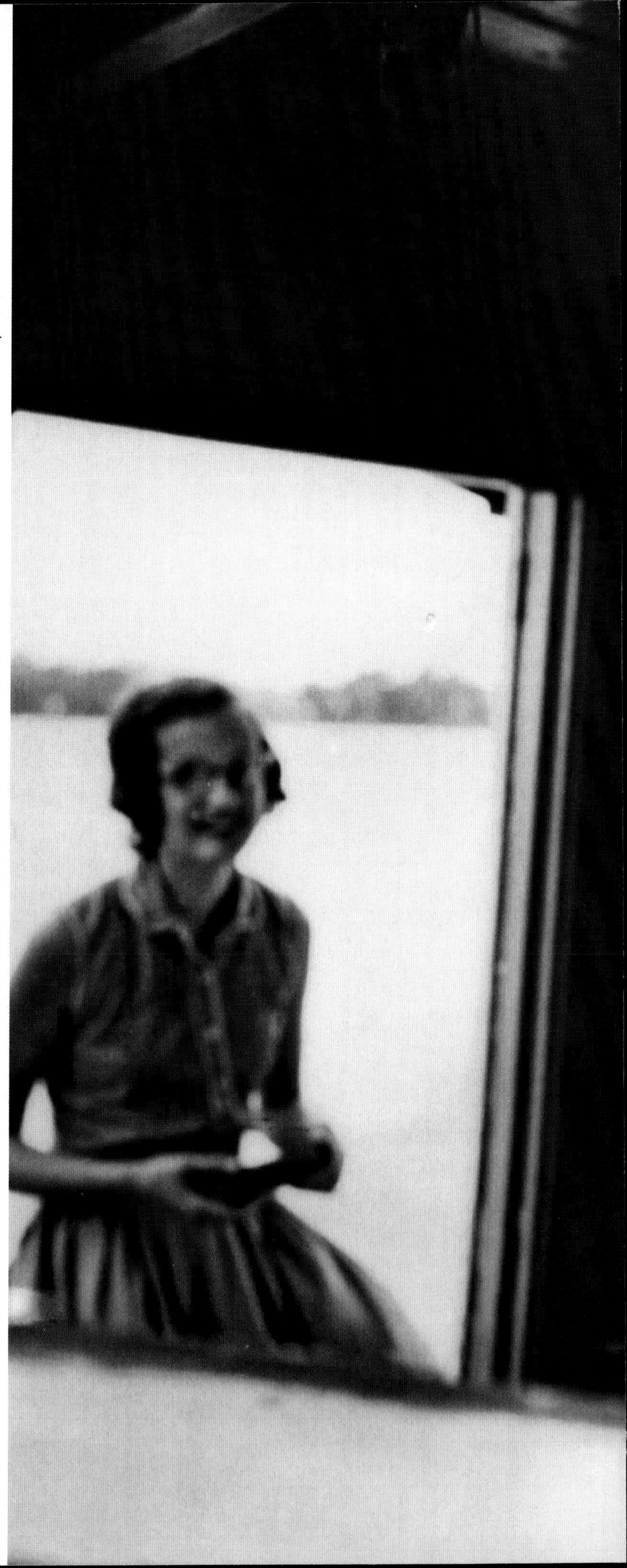

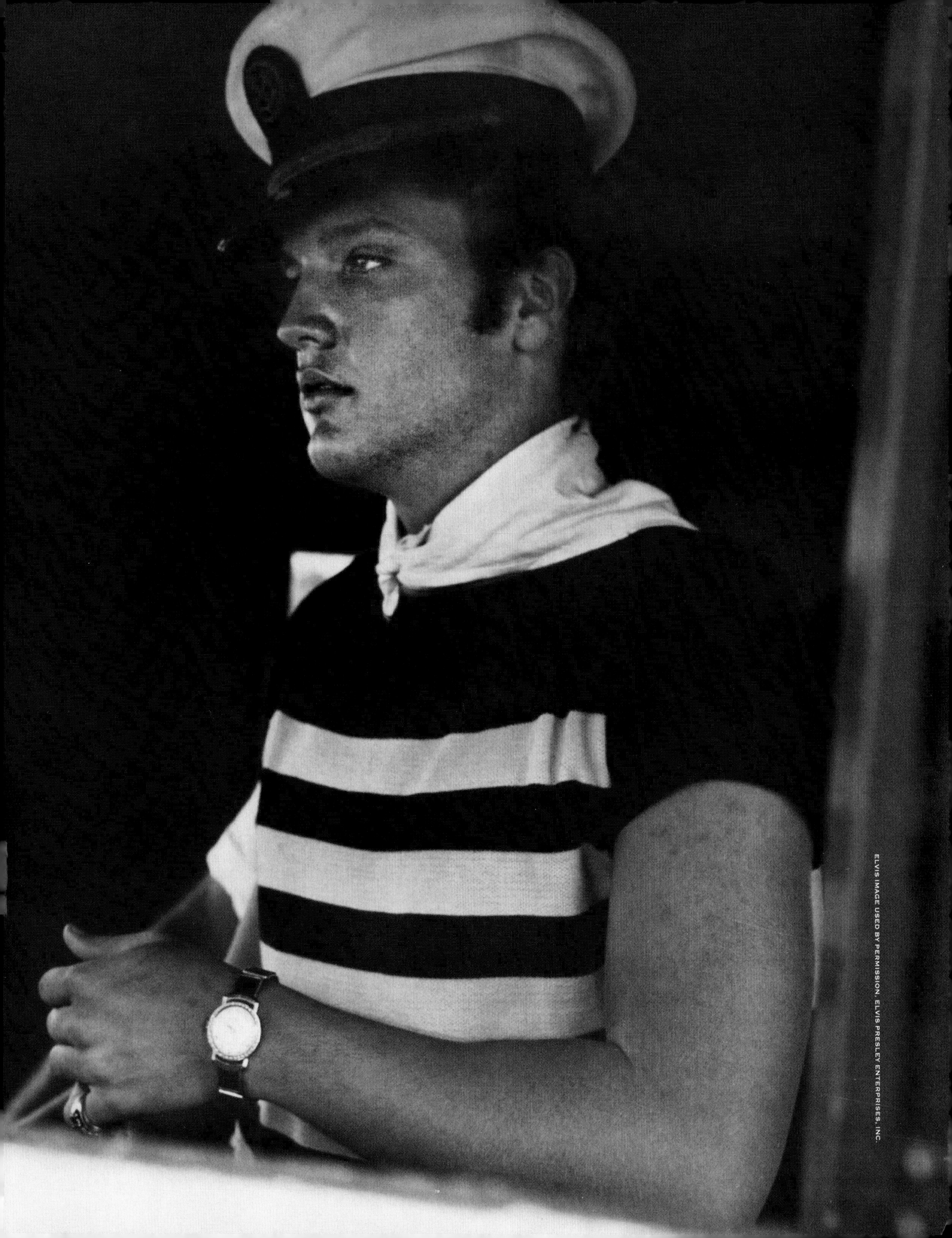

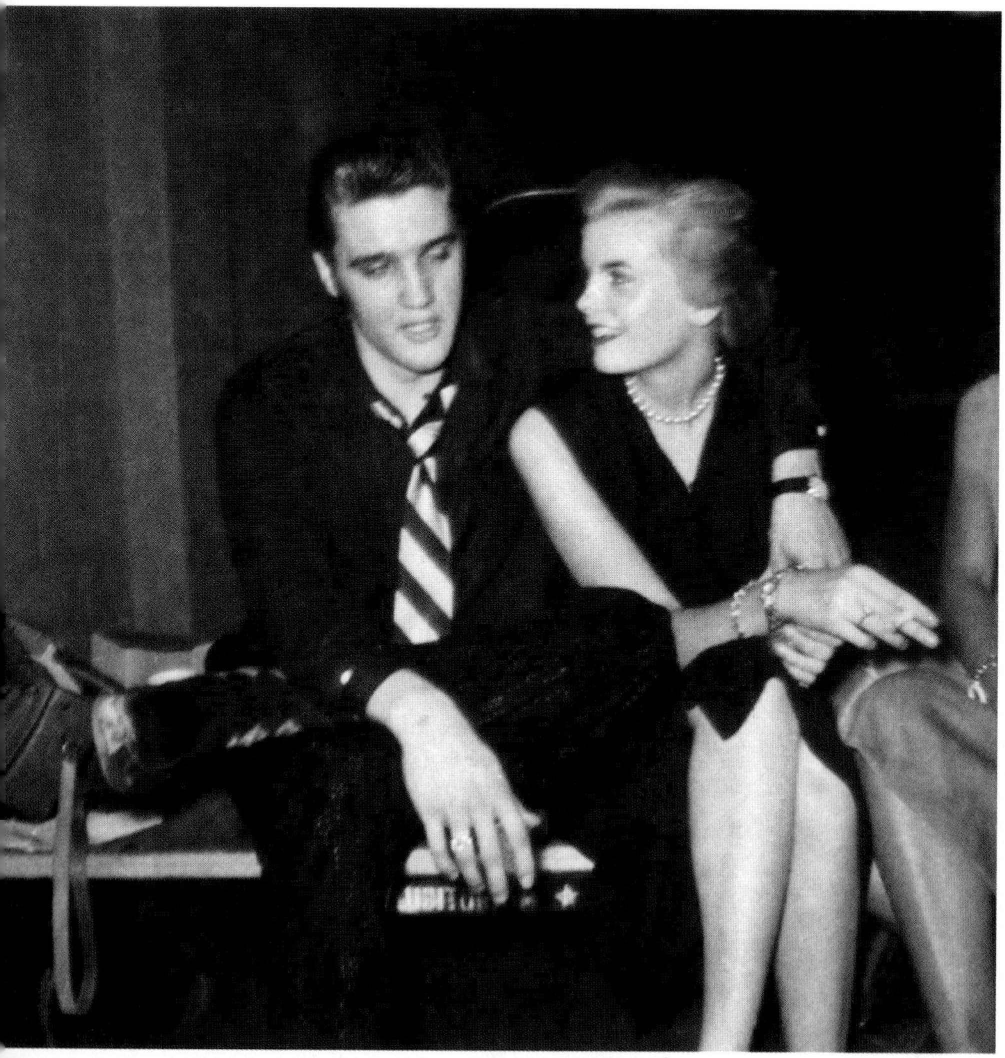

GRACELAND IS REPOSITORY FOR MANY WONDERFUL BITS OF PRESLEYANA THAT ENTERTAIN US EVEN AS THEY RETAIN THEIR AURA OF MYSTERY. ABOUT THE PICTURE AT LEFT, WHAT WE KNOW IS THIS: "ELVIS WITH UNKNOWN FAN, CIRCA 1955/56." WHAT WE WANT TO KNOW, OF COURSE, IS: WHAT KIND OF FAN? HOW BIG A FAN? WHO IS THIS WOMAN IN THE BLACK DRESS, ONE OF SO MANY AROUND WHOSE SHOULDERS ELVIS'S ARM WAS ONCE DRAPED? ABOUT THE SNARL AT RIGHT, WE KNOW A BIT MORE. ELVIS WAS NOT EXAGGERATING HIS HUNKA-HUNKA MANNERISMS, AS HE SOMETIMES DID IN HIS VEGAS ACT IN LATER YEARS. HE WAS, IN FACT, REACTING FOR THE CAMERA TO A TRAFFIC TICKET THAT HE HAD JUST BEEN ISSUED IN MEMPHIS IN 1956.

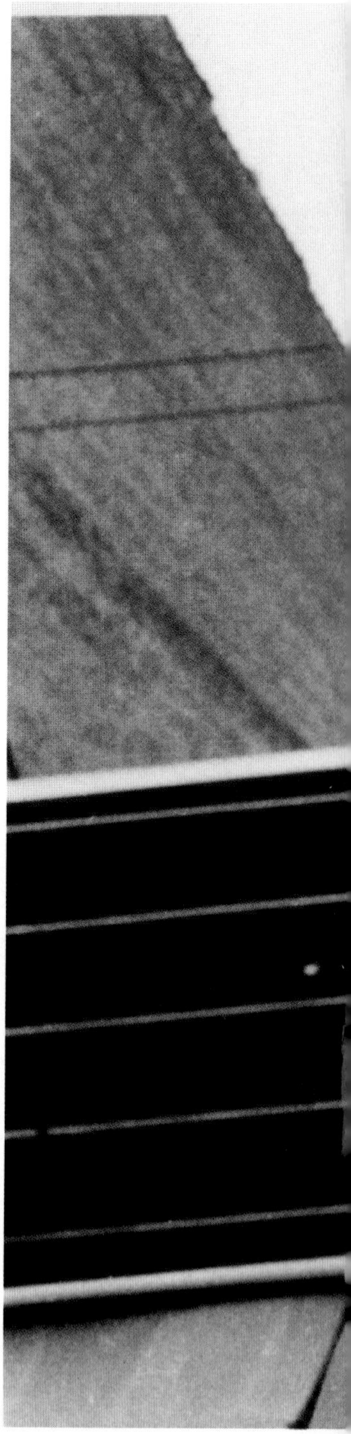

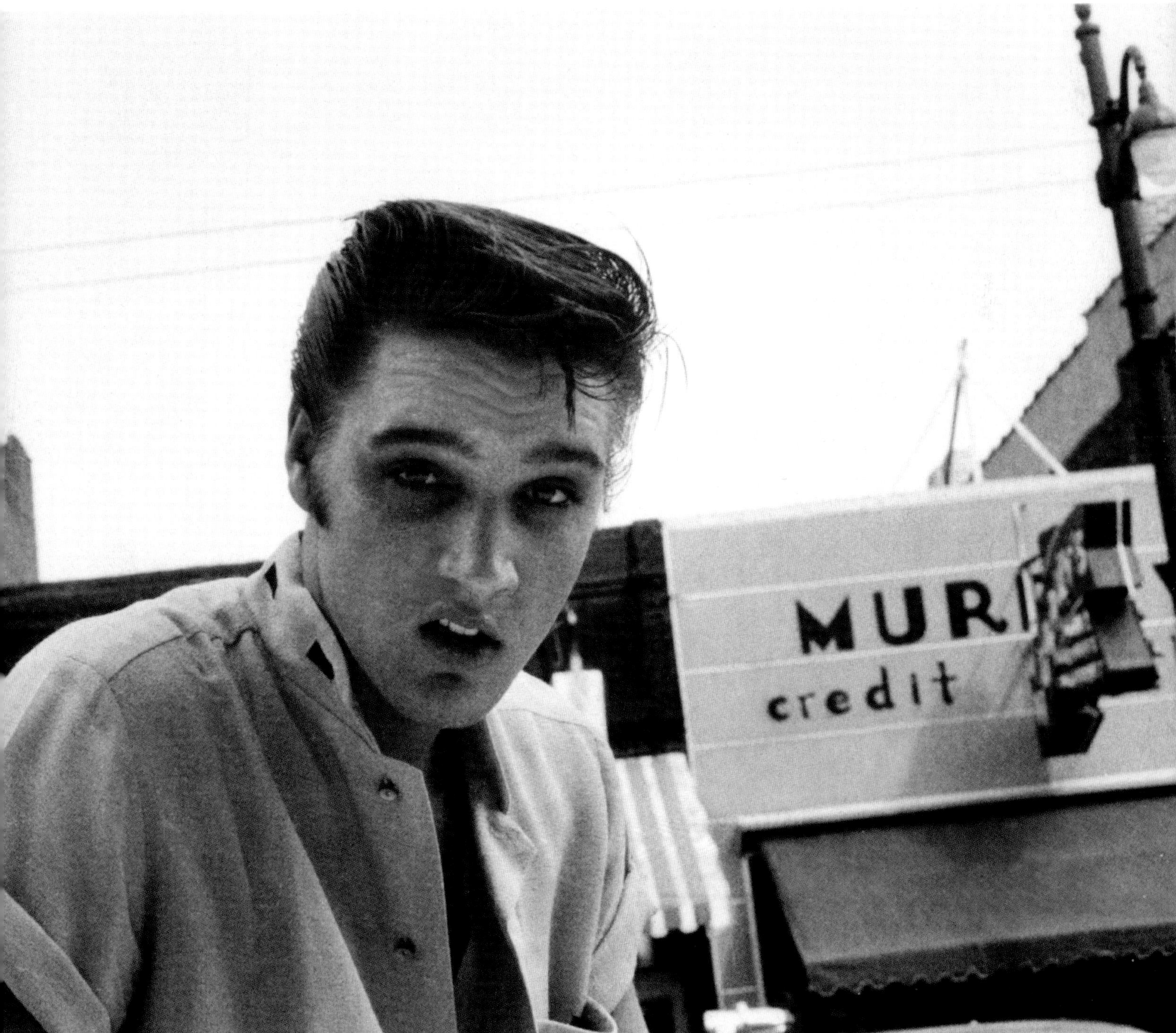
MUR
credit

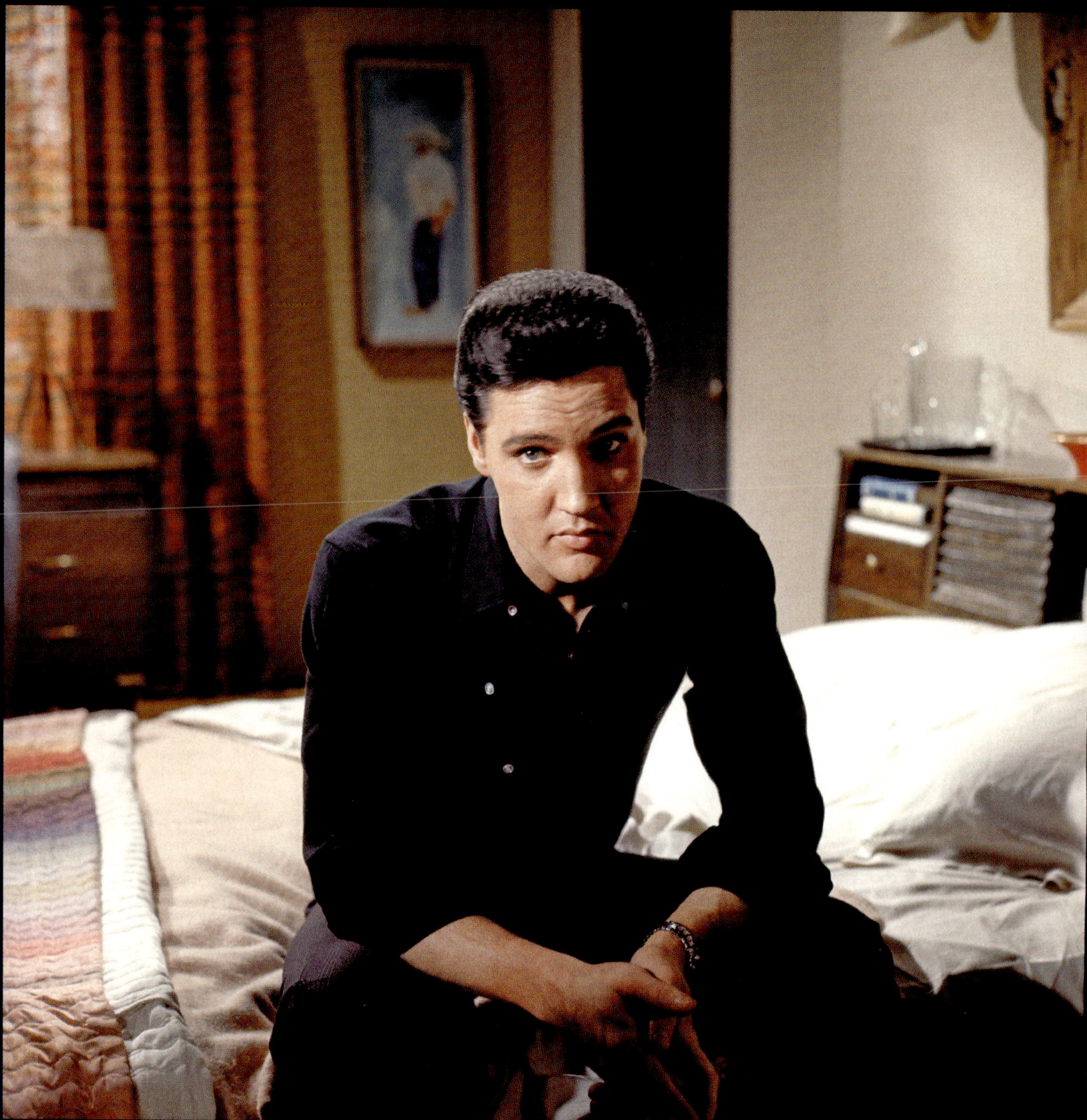

LYNN GOLDSMITH COLLECTION

LYNN GOLDSMITH, WHO FOUND THIS PHOTO, GETS THE LAST WORD, AND SPEAKS FOR MANY OF US WHEN SHE SAYS, "HE'S STILL THE KING TO ME."